CHINESE
LIVES

华夏人生

CHINESE LIVES

THE PEOPLE WHO MADE A CIVILIZATION

VICTOR H. MAIR
SANPING CHEN
FRANCES WOOD

83 illustrations, 52 in color

Thames & Hudson

Frontispiece Painting of the favourite concubine
of Emperor Xuanzong, Yang Guifei (Biography 41).

First published in 2013 in hardcover in the United States
of America by Thames & Hudson Inc., 500 Fifth Avenue,
New York, New York 10110

thamesandhudsonusa.com

Library of Congress Catalog Card Number 2012944890

ISBN 978-0-500-25192-8

Printed and bound in Singapore by
Tien Wah Press (Pte) Ltd

CONTENTS

INTRODUCTION
CHINA
AND
ITS
PEOPLE

VICTOR H. MAIR

C hina is the most populous nation on earth. It also has
the longest history among all existing nations. These
two facts alone make the task of choosing representative figures about whom to write short biographies a difficult
and challenging one; yet there are additional factors that
complicate the choice. One is the sheer multifariousness and
colourfulness of the different walks of life that have existed in
China: military men, political leaders, scholars, artists, musi-
cians, actors, craftsmen, scientists, physicians, literary figures
and so forth. The list is almost endless. Add to this the plethora
of outstanding personages within each category and one is
soon faced with many thousands of potential candidates from
whom to pick.

Take literary figures, for instance. Simply to cite the larger
categories, there are poets, essayists, novelists, short story
writers, dramatists and so on. Then, among poets, there are
many different types, depending upon the genres in which they
excelled: lyrics, rhapsodies, elegies, ballads and many others.

Beyond these variables, there are striking regional and
ethnic differences among the Chinese populace. Individuals
from various parts of the north and the south have diverse
physical characteristics, temperaments and customs, and they
speak different languages. Anyone who says that China is a
'nation of uniformity' is gravely mistaken.

AFGHANISTAN

NEPAL

INDIA

The modern provinces of China.

In composing these biographies, our first aim was to select at least one individual from as many different types as possible. We also wanted to make sure that a wide range of regions and ethnicities would be included, and that we had a good balance among different periods and between men and women (unfortunately, the proportion of distinguished male personages in the historical record vastly outweighs the known female figures).

So what, after a rigorous selection process, have we ended up with? We are pleased that the very first person in the collection, also the earliest, is a woman about whom we know a surprising amount. Her name is Fu Hao (Lady Hao), a royal consort who was also a female warrior. The reason we know so much about Fu Hao is that we have access to her unlooted tomb, an exceptionally rare occurrence in Chinese archaeology.

In contrast to this high-ranking noble, whose life is relatively well-documented, we also have the story of a deserted wife whose very name remains hidden from us – we know her only in relation to her husband Mang, 'a travelling man', and we have to piece her story together from bits and pieces recorded in the *Shi jing* (Poetry Classic). Still, the tale of the wife of Mang is highly evocative and tells us much about the status of women and their feelings in ancient times.

Among the most influential of early figures, it is perhaps the thinkers who stand out conspicuously. In particular, the philosophers of the Warring States period (475–221 BC) are well known for establishing the fundamental patterns of Chinese thought that have lasted until modern times. These include, of course, Confucius, the 'First Sage', who has had such an enormous impact on the ethics and etiquette of the Chinese people. Sharply dissimilar to Confucius, who set great store by hierarchical relations and emphasized the centrality of the family, was Mo Zi, who stressed impartial love towards all human beings. The foundations of legalistic thought were laid down by Shang Yang, and Sun Bin put forward the essentials of military strategy. Our favourite thinker, however, was Zhuang Zi, who was more of a playful, creative author than a systematic philosopher.

Greatly influenced by the Legalists, the First Emperor of the Qin dynasty (pronounced 'chin') gave China its name. He declared himself emperor of a united China in 221 BC, launching the nation on a course of bureaucratic empire that lasted for more than two millennia. Another larger-than-life ruler was Emperor Wu of the Han, the dynasty that was so impressive that the modern Chinese people have taken its name as that of their ethnicity. The opening of the celebrated Silk Road was the result of Emperor Wu's sending the great explorer, Zhang Qian, off to the Western Regions (approximately Central Asia) in search of allies to confront the Xiongnu (Huns), the perennial nemeses of the Han. The first great historian of

A 17th-century depiction of the Western Han dynasty Emperor Wu Di leaving his palace.

China, who wrote stirring narratives of the Western Han (roughly the first two centuries BC) and earlier periods, Sima Qian, also lived during this time.

The Han dynasty was broken into Western/Former and Eastern/Latter periods by the usurper, Wang Mang, who founded the short-lived interregnum ambitiously styled the New (Xin, pronounced 'shin') dynasty. It was during the Eastern Han that Buddhism began to filter into China, with monumental consequences for religion, thought, literature, language and practically all other realms of human endeavour. One of the most profound responses to the advent of Buddhism was the transformation of Daoism from a system of thought to an organized religion. Two of the early Daoist patriarchs active during the latter part of the Eastern Han were Zhang Daoling and Zhang Jiao; their heritage persists to the present day.

With the break-up of the Eastern Han dynasty in AD 220, there emerged three competing kingdoms – Shu, Wu and Wei. The lore about these Three Kingdoms has given rise to a rich outpouring of legend, drama and fiction that persists today in manga, anime and video games, not to mention providing the inspiration for countless restaurant names, proverbs, poems and paintings. One of the giants of the age was the great general, Cao Cao (pronounced Ts'ao Ts'ao), who was pitted against Zhuge Liang, a wizard who won battles through cunning ruses and clever strategy.

The empire remained divided for several centuries, but the division actually led to the flowering of literary criticism, abstruse philosophy, breakthroughs in painting and sculpture and great achievements in other arts and sciences. It was during this prolonged disunion between the north and the south that such geniuses as Wang Xizhi (China's most famous calligrapher), Kumarajiva (the renowned Kuchean-Indian translator of Buddhist texts) and Tao Yuanming/Qian (beloved poet and essayist of the rural life) flourished and provided the canons of later intellectual and aesthetic advances.

Finally, four centuries after it had split apart, the empire was reunited in AD 581 by Emperor Yang of the short-lived Sui (pronounced 'sway') dynasty. The Sui was soon followed by the glorious Tang, which is widely recognized as the zenith of Chinese civilization. The Tang period (618–907) was the most cosmopolitan of any in Chinese history, a time when even the imperial family carried in its veins a goodly proportion of non-Sinitic blood from the northern steppe peoples. The celebrated Emperor Taizong won many important battles and established the dynasty on a solid institutional and cultural footing. Another remarkable ruler of the Tang dynasty was the formidable Wu Zetian, who began as a consort but ended as the only female emperor in Chinese history. The ethnic complexity of the Tang is underscored by the fact that one of its most noted generals, Gao Xianzhi, was a Korean who lost the Battle of Talas River (751), one of the most consequential military engagements in world history, and the fact that the commander-turned-rebel who almost brought down the dynasty, An Lushan (Roxan Arsacid), was of Sogdo-Turkic stock.

Genghis Khan (also, more accurately, spelled 'Chinggis Khan') left an indelible mark on world history when he led his mounted Mongol warriors to conquer the better part of Eurasia, but it was his grandson, Khubilai Khan, who expanded the Chinese empire to its greatest extent ever and made Peking (now called Beijing) a capital beyond compare. The Mongols' Yuan dynasty lasted for just under a century before it was replaced in 1368 by the nativist Ming dynasty.

It was under the Ming that China witnessed its boldest naval forays, a series of armadas led by the Muslim eunuch admiral, Zheng He, which sailed all the way to the east coast of Africa. (Rumours that he sailed as far as the New World are completely unfounded.) However, a more inward-looking approach soon overtook the nation. This was manifested in a diminished military posture and thinkers like Wang Yangming who were attracted to philosophical positions akin to Zen (Chinese 'Chan').

The transition from the Ming to the Manchu-dominated Qing (pronounced 'ching') dynasty in the 17th century was a tumultuous era, with mass murderers such as Zhang Xianzhong running amok, grossly decadent eunuchs such as Wei Zhongxian amassing vast fortunes, and traitors such as Wu Sangui changing the course of history. Yet once the Qing dynasty was securely established, it became one of the most glorious and long-abiding of all houses – native or foreign – to rule over China. Like the Mongols, the Manchus were northerners who extended the borders of the empire to include Tibet, Xinjiang (eastern Central Asia) and Mongolia, plus enormous tracts in the south. Several Qing emperors, including Kangxi and Qianlong, enjoyed extraordinarily long reigns.

Painting and literature flourished during the Qing. To mention only two of the most outstanding authors of the time, this was the age of Pu Songling, who wrote hundreds of strange stories from his 'Make-do Studio' (*Liaozhai*), and Wang Duan, a woman poet who led an incredibly eventful life.

As with all previous dynasties, internal conflicts and external pressures eventually led to the unravelling of the Qing. Despite the best efforts of honest officials such as Lin Zexu, the Opium Wars brought China to its knees, and it was around the same time (the mid-19th century) that the nation was convulsed by the Taiping (Great Peace) rebellion, led by the messianic madman Hong Xiuquan, who fancied he was the younger brother of Jesus Christ. Matters were not helped when the reins of the empire were handed over to the jaded Empress-dowager Cixi,

毛泽东思想万岁！

'Long live the thoughts of Chairman Mao' (1969), showing workers, peasants and students holding aloft the *Little Red Book* of Mao Zedong.

who, among other eccentricities, used the naval budget to pay for her infamous marble boat.

When the Qing dynasty toppled in 1911, it did so in the most spectacular fashion, taking with it the institutions, such as the civil service examination system and the bureaucratic structures, that had governed China for more than 2,000 years. Sun Yat-sen's Republican revolution brought about a tidal wave of transformation in Chinese society and culture, with intellectuals such as Lu Xun and Hu Shi writing and saying things that would not have been dreamed of a century earlier. Ultimately this led to the founding of the People's Republic of China by Mao Zedong in 1949, after which China was closed up behind a Bamboo Curtain for decades. Yet who would have thought during the darkest days of the Great Proletarian Cultural Revolution that a leader like Deng Xiaoping would emerge to shift China's course from doctrinaire communism to mercantilist capitalism? The pace of change in China has accelerated at a rate that truly boggles the mind and is such that one hardly knows what to expect in the coming decades. One can be assured, however, that whatever China becomes during this century, it will depend upon the activities of personalities such as those briefly described above and presented in greater detail in the pages of this book.

THE
SHANG
TO HAN
DYNASTIES

C. 16TH CENTURY BC TO AD 220

CENTRAL ASIA

STATE OF
DAYUAN

WESTERN REG.

WEST
ASIA

Silk Road

Historical divisions in China are based upon written records, and the first ruling house to leave accurate records of rulers and dates was the Shang (*c.* 16th century BC–*c.* 1045 BC). The Shang ruled over a small part of the Yellow River area, with many other different settlements and cultures spread across the vast landmass of today's China. The Shang dynasty was overthrown by the Zhou, who came from further west. Towards the end of the Zhou, the main landmass was divided between seven 'Warring States', which were eventually vanquished by the state of Qin.

The ruler of Qin, whose domains stretched from Mongolia to Guangdong and westwards into Sichuan, covering almost all of today's 'China', proclaimed himself the First Emperor. Though he united the empire, introduced many measures to standardize the different practices of the various states and imposed an empire-wide bureaucracy governed by detailed sets of rules and regulations, his empire did not long outlive him. The Han dynasty overthrew the Qin, though it adopted many of its government systems. During the Han, Chinese influence stretched westwards towards Central Asia, with military garrisons manning the westernmost end of the Great Wall and a line of beacons out in what is now Gansu province.

Shang (c. *1600 BC–c. 1045 BC*)
Zhou: Western Zhou c. *1045–771 BC*
Eastern Zhou 770–256 BC
  Spring and Autumn period
  770–476 BC
  Warring States period 475–221 BC

Qin 221–206 BC
Han 206 BC–AD 220
  Western/Former Han 206 BC–AD 9
  Xin AD 9–23
  Eastern/Latter Han AD 25–220

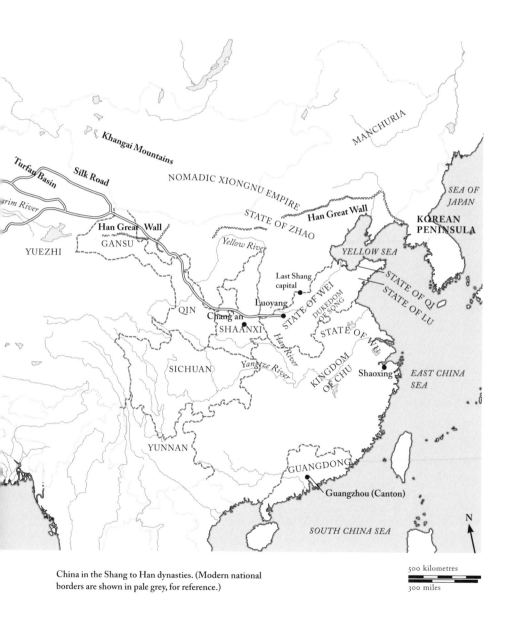

China in the Shang to Han dynasties. (Modern national
borders are shown in pale grey, for reference.)

500 kilometres

300 miles

1. FU HAO (LATE 13TH CENTURY BC)
Woman warrior of the Shang

One of several consorts of the 'Warrior King Ding' of the Shang dynasty, Fu (Lady) Hao is unique in that, despite her sex, she led troops into battle, acts recorded in China's earliest archival records and further attested by the ceremonial weapons found in her tomb.

The Shang (c. 1600–c. 1045 BC) was the first Chinese polity verifiable by its own records. Until a little over a century ago, such records consisted of inscriptions on a limited number of bronze objects of unverified provenance. This situation changed dramatically in 1899 when two Chinese scholars recognized the strange markings on the 'dragon bones' used in traditional medicine as the earliest known Chinese writings, records of divination. Well over 100,000 such 'oracle bones', usually turtle shells and ox scapulae, have since been discovered, many through archaeological excavation.

Hundreds of such oracle bones mention a royal lady named Fu Hao; in 1976 her undisturbed tomb was discovered in the last capital of the Shang, in the modern province of Henan. Together with the oracle bones bearing her name, the archaeological evidence from her tomb has permitted scholars to piece together information about this long-forgotten queen.

King Ding, known as 'Warrior King Ding', is thought to have reigned for fifty-nine years in the second half of the 13th century BC. Numerous oracle bone records refer to Fu Hao's participation in many of the campaigns and battles, leading thousands of soldiers. One such campaign mobilized the largest number of troops of the period. Among the many weapons accompanying her to the tomb were two bronze axes, one weighing 9 kg (20 lbs) and another 8.5 kg, both inscribed with the name Fu Hao. These may have been ceremonial and used to behead sacrificial victims. Her tomb is also important for the plentiful jades found there.

Surviving divination inscriptions describe her carrying out government functions, and the many records concerning her health, particularly as related to childbirth, suggest that she died after a long illness.

Though her existence was in oblivion for millennia, the very name of this remarkable queen – 'Hao' – nevertheless survived as the primordial Chinese word for 'good', a legacy of the royal Shang lady.

2. DUKE OF ZHOU (FL. 1042 BC)
The ideal statesman

Around 1045 BC, a date still hotly debated, the 'Martial King' of the Zhou tribes from the west defeated a major Shang army, sacked the Shang capital and killed the last Shang king. The Zhou dynasty thus established originated in a region west of the Shang realm and is consequently often referred to by Chinese historians as 'barbarian' (i.e. non-Chinese). Though the Zhou appropriated much of Shang high culture, especially a well-developed script for writing, and bronze metallurgy, they also brought many important changes and innovations. Their sky-god Tian became the universal supreme god, and the new Zhou king was described as a 'Son of Heaven' with a 'Mandate of Heaven' to rule the central states.

This founding King of Zhou died a few years after completing only the first part of the conquest. His son was too young to reign, so the boy's uncle, Zhou Gong, the Duke of Zhou, assumed the title, acting as regent but also likely as *de facto* and even *de jure* king. He effectively completed the military conquest after defeating a joint rebellion of Shang loyalists and the duke's own brothers. Through a combination of colonization and accommodation, he helped establish the longest-lasting dynasty of China, not only presiding over the construction of a new capital at Luoyang, but acting also as the principal architect of the Zhou feudal system. By strengthening the concept of a Mandate of Heaven dependent upon the ruler's behaviour (heaven could withdraw its mandate if a ruler proved to be immoral or incapable), the Duke of Zhou helped introduce an element of rationalism, in contrast to the Shang's reliance on superstition.

Bronze vessel of the Shang dynasty.

His continuing significance lies in the historical interpretation of his actions, principally in handing over power to the rightful heir, his nephew, the son of the 'Martial King', thus establishing the principle of lineal succession through primogeniture. Confucius (Biography 4) constantly praised the Duke of Zhou, and his name survives as the major exemplar of the 'good statesman'.

3. WIFE OF MANG (c. 7th century bc)
The story of a deserted wife

This figure appears in a folksong, dating back perhaps 2,500 or more years, from the state of Wei (roughly in the modern province of Henan). This region in ancient times was known for its tradition of 'free love'. The melancholy song rendered here shows that not all such love stories had happy endings, and that wife-desertion is an old and perennial theme of human society.

The *Shi jing* ('Poetry Classic'), sometimes rendered into English as the 'Book of Songs', is a collection of early folksongs from the 10th to 7th centuries bc, included as one of the Confucian Classics and thus one of the fundamental texts of the traditional Chinese educational system. It is traditionally (though wrongly) thought to have been compiled by Confucius (Biography 4) himself.

A travelling man, with such a silly smile on his face.
Carried cloth to trade for silk.
He did not really come to trade for silk –
It was me, [his childhood sweetheart,] who was the true objective of his trip.

I escorted you to wade across the Qi River.
All the way to Dun Hill.
It was not that I wanted to postpone the date of our union.
It was because you did not have a capable go-between.
And please, do not get angry with me –
Autumn would be such a good time for matrimony.

I climbed up what remained of our old village wall.
So I could see the narrow pass of your return route.
I did not see you come back to me through the pass
And my tears fell nonstop.

When I finally saw you show up again through the pass
I laughed, I talked, without end.

You divined with tortoiseshell, you divined with stalks.
The signs contained no bad omen.
Then you came with your cart
To carry me and my dowry.

Before the mulberry tree sheds [in fall].
Its leaves, [like the face of a young girl,] are so tender and shiny.
Oh, doves, [listen to my advice]:
Do not eat the mulberries.
[Lest you be intoxicated by the fermented fruits.]
Oh, young girls, listen to my advice:
Do not fall head over heels in love with men.
When a man falls in love
He can get out of it if he wants;
When a girl falls in love
She is hopelessly trapped.

[I am now aged,] like a shedding mulberry tree.
The leaves turning yellow and falling.
Since I came to your place.
For many years I have put up with poverty.
Now I am forced to cross the River Qi back home
Its rising water drenching the curtains of my carriage.
I have remained faithful as always.
But you have changed your behaviour.
You do not abide by morals.
Nor do you have integrity.

For many years I was your wife.
Assuming all the household chores [for which you did not lift a finger].
Early to rise and late to bed.
Day in and day out.
No sooner did you become well-off
Than you turned unbearably cruel and violent.

My brothers do not know [the real situation].

And laugh off [my heartbreaking return].

[Such pain and misery,] I can only quietly reflect upon.

Sustaining my grief all alone.

The two of us once swore to grow old together as one.

But now that I am old it fills me with regret.

[Wide as] the Qi River is, it still has its banks;

[Vast as] the marshland is, it still has its limits.

[So does my long forbearance for your betrayal and cruelty.]

Recalling our childhood together –

Such happy and innocent laughter and chitchat.

And then there were solemn vows of love and loyalty –

Who could have thought of the reversals today?

Reversals they are indeed and what's the use of dwelling on them?

The past is all over, [so is my love].

4. **CONFUCIUS** (551/2–479 BC)

Philosopher

Confucius (Kong Qiu or Kong fuzi) was born in 551 or 552 BC. His ancestors descended from the ruling house of the Dukedom of Song, a state established by the offspring of the royal kings of the Shang, but they took refuge in the state of Lu, which had been founded by the son of the Duke of Zhou (Biography 2). He was the only son of his mother but the second son of his father, who had some renown as a brave warrior but achieved little else. After the death of his father when Confucius was very young, his mother brought him back to her home town.

Confucius studied not only the skills deemed essential and practical for gentlemen, but also high culture and metaphysics. He became a well-known teacher and formed his basic political belief in the restoration of the (idealized) political order of the early Zhou dynasty, during which the benevolent Son of Heaven held all feudal lords in his sway.

At the age of about fifty, Confucius finally received his first important appointment in his home state, becoming a city mayor. He was then promoted to, in turn, junior Minister of Construction, Minister of Justice, and eventually even acting

Confucius, imagined in conversation with Lao Zi, a legendary founder of Daoism, and a Buddhist *arhat* (spiritual practitioner). Painting by Ding Yu.

Prime Minister. He was said to have scored a significant diplomatic victory at the bilateral summit between his home state of Lu and the much more powerful state of Qi.

However, Confucius's efforts to realize his political beliefs by shoring up the authority of the Duke of Lu, at the expense of the hereditary ministers and their dominant followers, brought him into direct conflict with these two groups, who in fact held the real power. He was forced into exile in 497 BC.

During his long years away from Lu, Confucius visited and stayed in several states, none of which found his anachronistic political theories particularly attractive. When one of his pupils rose to a prominent position in Lu, Confucius was finally invited back to his home state in 484 BC, when he was sixty-seven. At this advanced age, Confucius, while enjoying the status of a former statesman, spent his final years doing the only work at which he had truly excelled during his lifetime: teaching. According to legend, he edited the classic books that became the Confucian canon. After witnessing the deaths of his own son and his two favourite students, and failing to persuade any state to take up his political beliefs, Confucius died in 479 BC.

Confucius may have been unsuccessful in life, but the doctrines associated with him, based upon recollections assembled by his students in the 'Analects' (*Lun yu*), dominated Chinese government and society for over 2,000 years and had a profound effect on other East Asian societies. Rarely discussing the afterlife or spiritual matters, his pronouncements dealt with the management of society, preaching government based upon ethics. He looked back to an idealized historical period, when society was supposedly regulated by a 'good ruler' whose benevolent care for his subjects was rewarded with heavenly favour. When a ruler transgressed, heaven would withdraw its mandate. He believed in strict social hierarchies. 'Let the ruler be a ruler and the subject a subject, let the father be a father, and the son a son'; for, if everyone knew his place (with women naturally at the bottom of the social hierarchy), there would be peace and social harmony.

The extant Confucian writings consist of the Five Classics, all traditionally, though erroneously, attributed to Confucius himself. They are the 'Book of Songs' (a collection of some 305 odes dating back to the early Zhou), the 'Book of Documents' (relating to early Zhou and other archaic history), the *Yi Jing* or 'Book of Changes', the 'Spring and Autumn Annals' (a chronological description of events in the state of Lu 722–481 BC), and the 'Record of Rites', a miscellany of earlier works on the subject of ritual, supplemented by the 'Analects', or sayings of Confucius, compiled by his disciples. These texts and ideas became the basis of education in traditional China, which trained students to pass the entry examinations for the imperial bureaucracy. Thus 'Confucianism' came to underpin the entire system of government until the abolition of the examination system in 1905.

The extraordinary longevity and influence of Confucianism, which persists to this day, would seem to stem from the fact that both the rulers and the ruled found what they needed and liked in Confucius. For the rulers, it was the sage's emphasis on social order, particularly unwavering loyalty to the lord. Small wonder the current Chinese leaders have revived the sage's dream of a 'harmonious society'. For the ruled, it was the humanism, human love and rationalism preached by an untiring teacher, whose dedication to universal education was undeniably a major factor in the flourishing of East Asian civilization. Confucius is still honoured on 'Teacher's Day' (celebrated on 10 September), and his lineal descendant still lives on Taiwan.

5. MO ZI (FL. C. 480–390 BC)
Philosopher

Mo Zi ('Master Mo') was an egalitarian and anti-war philosopher who flourished *c.* 480–390 BC. Very little is known about his life, but his philosophy is contained in the book *Mo Zi*, which, like the works of Confucius, was compiled by his students and disciples over an extended period. His beliefs were extremely popular in the 4th and 3rd centuries BC, but had little influence thereafter.

Like Confucius (Biography 4), Mo Zi probably grew up in the state of Lu (in present-day Shandong province), but, unlike Confucius, he was a craftsman from the lower class. He was, however, educated, and he formed a well-organized group of disciples with whom he toured the country to spread his philosophy.

Mo Zi's main doctrines were the necessity of creating an egalitarian society based on devotion to the common good, his anti-war stance and his advocacy of universal love. From these derived his other doctrines, such as the need to reduce government expenditure, promote capable individuals and advocate frugal burial. He can be described as a utilitarian – he disapproved of music, which Confucius felt was a significant aspect of a gentleman's culture, because it contributed little to the material welfare of ordinary people, who suffered from three primary miseries: 'the hungry do not have food, the naked do not have clothes, and the toilers do not rest'.

It is traditionally believed that the majority of his disciples were craftsmen: carpenters, blacksmiths, mechanics and masons. Their social background seems to have contributed to Mo Zi's doctrine: things can be built and events can be made to happen through strenuous human effort. His pacifism was balanced by a strong element of active defence against unjustified invasion.

A story (which became current long after his death) described how in 442 BC a famous carpenter-craftsman, Lu Ban (the patron saint of carpenters and builders in the Chinese popular pantheon), built scaling ladders and other assault equipment for the kingdom of Chu to attack the Dukedom of Song. Mo Zi embarked on a long journey to prevent this war, walking nonstop for ten days and nights.

He first went to see Lu Ban and offered him 10 ounces of gold to kill a man, but Lu Ban refused this immoral request. Mo Zi then accused him of hypocrisy for helping plan an invasion that would kill thousands of innocent people. Cornered, Lu Ban replied that the Chu king was the decision-maker. Mo Zi then asked to see the king and offered to stage a war game with Lu Ban, despite the fact that the invasion was already under way.

In the game, Mo Zi put his belt on the table, to stand as the city wall, and used small pieces of wood as military equipment. He successfully thwarted nine different types of siege equipment used by Lu Ban, who commented that he still had one more strategy – to kill the pacifist.

Mo Zi then disclosed that 300 of his disciples had already marched to help the Song. This revelation finally persuaded the Chu king to cancel his expedition. The story illustrates the lengths to which Mo Zi would go to prevent war.

6. SHANG YANG (c. 390–338 BC)
Statesman and reformer

Shang Yang was born c. 390 BC in the small state of Wei, in the modern provinces of Henan and Shandong, during the early years of the Warring States period.

The Warring States period witnessed the irreversible decline of the 'classical' Zhou feudal system, the spread of iron tools, the growth of commerce and the gradual privatization of land ownership. With the old political order disintegrating, there was increasing competition among states for domination and supremacy.

One of the competing states was Qin, situated to the west and sometimes characterized as semi-barbarian. Perhaps encouraged by a call for 'foreign' talent by the Qin ruler, Shang Yang arrived in Qin in 361 BC and discussed with Duke Xiaogong the promotion of 'arts to enrich the state and strengthen it militarily'.

Modern statue of Shang Yang.

A debate was held at the Qin court during which Shang Yang and conservative Qin nobles exchanged polemics on the merits and necessity of reforms. The duke was persuaded to experiment with Legalist reforms recommended by Shang Yang, and, when initial results proved encouraging, Shang Yang was formally appointed as a court minister to launch full-fledged reforms.

The major points of Yang's reforms were: the organization of neighbourhood units with collective punishment and inducements to inform on others; a new system of nobility open to commoners who earned military honours, while royal clan members could not maintain their noble status without military accomplishments; the promotion of agricultural production and the downplaying of commerce.

Shang Yang's Legalist reforms contributed to the rapid rise of Qin power. In 354 BC Qin won a major military victory against Wei. Subsequently, Shang Yang was promoted to the position of Chancellor, with both civic and military powers.

In 350 BC, Shang Yang proposed further reforms: the enactment of a policy by which land could be bought and sold; administrative reorganization, which meant the establishment of counties and prefectures with salaried administrators to replace nobles; and the unification and standardization of measures. Shang Yang's reforms led to enormously improved efficiency in the Qin economy and administration, but they also generated deep resentment from vested interests, particularly the old noble class.

The Qin Duke Xiaogong died in 338 BC and was succeeded by the heir apparent, whose two tutors had been punished by Shang Yang for their opposition to his
reforms (one had his nose cut off and the other had his face tattooed). With this
change of regime, Shang Yang attempted to slip abroad, but because of his own
law forbidding hotels to shelter anyone without an official pass, he was thwarted.
He then led a futile insurgency but was captured and executed and his entire family
exterminated. However, his reforms survived him, eventually making a future ruler
of Qin the unifier of China.

7. SUN BIN (EARLY 4TH CENTURY BC)
Military strategist

According to Sima Qian (Biography 15), Sun Bin was born in the state of Qi,
in modern Shandong province, in the early years of the 4th century
BC. His exact dates and his real name are unknown, but he is said to be
a descendant of Sun Zi, the putative author of 'The Art of War'. It was long thought
that Sun Bin was joint author of the work, until 1972 when archaeologists unearthed
a separate treatise attributed to him. 'The Art of War' has a special place in Chinese
culture, as do stories about legendary martial figures, whether generals, cunning
military strategists, or bandits.

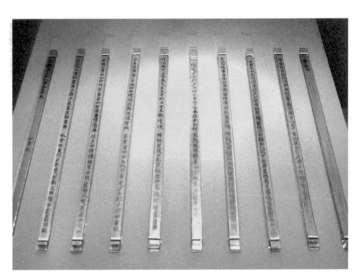

Inscribed bamboo slips from Sun Bin's treatise on military strategy.

Following in the footsteps of his alleged ancestor, Sun Bin studied military tactics and strategy with a classmate named Pang Juan. The incessant warfare during the Warring States period led to a demand for military talent. Pang Juan found employment in the state of Wei, the strongest power at the time, and rose to become a leading general.

Pang Juan was jealous of Sun Bin, but nevertheless sent for his former schoolmate to join him. However, no sooner had Sun Bin arrived than he was accused of conspiracy, convicted, and had his kneecaps removed and his face tattooed as punishment. From this point on, Sun would be known as Sun Bin, *bin* being the Chinese word for the punishment of removing a person's kneecaps.

Sun Bin managed to escape and was hired by Tian Ji, a general of the state of Qi. Sun Bin proved his cleverness by designing a simple yet ingenious scheme for his patron to win a big bet on a three-race equestrian game with the king. Sun Bin noted that the king's horses were all superior, so he proposed to race Tian Ji's third best horse against the king's best, his best horse against the king's second best, and his second best against the king's third best, securing a final score of 1:2 in Tian Ji's favour.

Sun Bin's first military triumph came in 354 BC, when the troops of Wei, under Pang Juan, laid siege to the capital of the state of Zhao. The King of Qi answered Zhao's appeal for help, and Sun Bin implemented the strategy of 'rescuing Zhao by laying siege to Wei', marching directly into Wei territories in 353 BC.

He then faked incompetence and small losses to mislead the Wei command, which continued its siege of the Zhao capital. News came that crack Qi troops were fast approaching the Wei capital. The Wei forces under Pang Juan rushed back and fell into the ambush set up by Sun Bin, suffering disastrous losses.

Several years later, in another confrontation with his old classmate Pang Juan, Sun Bin came up with a creative scheme to feign weakness: he had his expeditionary force turn around, heading home, and ordered the Qi soldiers to share their cooking fires progressively each night to reduce the number visible. Pang Juan counted the number of campfires to estimate the enemy strength and deduced that the Qi soldiers must be deserting en masse as the number of their campfires decreased from 100,000 to 30,000 in three days.

Thus, one winter night in 342–343 BC, a lightly armed Wei force was lured into a meticulously prepared trap in a narrow mountain passage at a place named Maling, where heavy carts were positioned to form barriers, and iron stakes were planted in the ground to impede the horses. With thousands of arrows falling like rain and all possibility of retreat cut off, Pang Juan committed suicide after acknowledging, 'Now I've made this scoundrel famous!'

8. ZHUANG ZI (4TH–3RD CENTURY BC)
Daoist philosopher

Zhuang Zi, one of the founding thinkers of Daoist philosophy, was from Song, a dukedom formed by the descendants of the Shang people who had been conquered by the Zhou. He lived around the 4th to the 3rd century BC and was said to have been the insignificant manager of a lacquer tree grove. Most stories about his life come from the book titled *Zhuang Zi* that is attributed to him, though the extant version appears to contain writings of later authors of varying philosophical bent.

Zhuang Zi never held an official position, and he is said to have refused an offer of a chancellorship by asking:

> Have you not seen the sacrificial ox? It is well fed for years and garbed in patterned
> embroidery, but when the time comes for it to be led into the great temple, though it wishes to
> be a solitary calf, how can it escape its fate? Be off with you, sir, and do not sully me! I'd rather
> be wallowing self-contentedly in a muddy creek than be controlled by the ruler of a kingdom.

He ridiculed sycophantic courtiers, saying to one of them:

> When the King of Qin is ill, he summons a physician. One who lances an abscess or drains
> a boil will receive one carriage. One who licks his haemorrhoids will receive five carriages.
> The lower the treatment, the greater the number of carriages received. Did you treat his
> haemorrhoids, sir? How did you get so many carriages? Begone!

The most remarkable aspect of the writings attributed to Zhuang Zi is their creative imagination, unmatched by any other early Chinese author. Here is one brief example, which reveals his rejection of absolute truth, paramount in the thought of Confucius and Mo Zi (Biographies 4 and 5):

> Once upon a time, Zhuang Zi dreamed that he was a butterfly, a butterfly flitting about
> happily enjoying himself. He didn't know that he was Zhuang Zi. Suddenly he awoke and
> was palpably Zhuang Zi. He didn't know whether he were Zhuang Zi who had dreamed
> of being a butterfly, or a butterfly who was dreaming that he was Zhuang Zi.

Zhuang Zi's principal influence comes from his philosophy of *ziran*, 'nature' or 'natural status' (literally, 'self-so'). Zhuang Zi is often juxtaposed with another great thinker, Lao Zi, another legendary founder of Daoism, due largely to their common

Eighteenth-century depiction of Zhuang Zi and the butterfly.

emphasis on the concept of *ziran*. Substantial differences exist, however. While Lao Zi's philosophy showed concern for the collective welfare of society, Zhuang Zi's thought was more individualistic, seeking unbounded personal freedom in the spiritual realm. He opposed all 'artificial' doctrines of human morality and social strictures, both of which are characteristic of Confucian thinking. The only reality was the principle of cosmic spontaneity embodied in the Dao ('way'), the underlying force of nature, the source of all being. The most suitable approach for an individual to adopt in response to cosmic spontaneity was *you*, 'play' or 'wandering'.

Terracotta statue of a mounted archer.

9. KING WULING OF THE ZHAO (D. 295 BC)

Famous warrior, and the man who brought trousers to China

When King Wuling started his reign over the state of Zhao in 325 BC, it was in a precarious situation, surrounded by powerful rivals and ferocious 'barbarian' enemies.

At the same time, a military revolution was being forced upon East Asia: the horse-drawn chariot, long a mainstay since its introduction from West and Central Asia in the late second millennium BC, was being upstaged by the horse-riding cavalry that was emerging among the northern barbarians. The lightly armoured barbarian bowmen proved superior in mobility and efficiency to the heavily armoured chariots used by the nobility and the slow-moving peasant infantry.

King Wuling decided to introduce cavalry, but he faced a cultural obstacle: the traditional loose dress worn by men, with its wide sleeves and skirt-like long gown, was ill suited for horse riding. Yet such clothing occupied a near-sacred place in Chinese culture. For example, when he was praising the Qi statesman Guanzhong for his successful resistance to the 'barbarians', Confucius (Biography 4) chose to do so through a metaphor drawn from the traditional dress code. So King Wuling's introduction of 'barbarian' trousers encountered strong upper-class opposition. In 307 BC, however, he convinced his noblemen of the dire necessity to strengthen the Zhao military and the need to adopt the narrow, short 'barbarian' dress, complete with trousers and boots.

Another estimable act was King Wuling's abdication in favour of his younger son in the summer of 299 BC. The retired king assumed the title of 'lord father' and concentrated on military affairs. This abdication had an unmistakable 'barbarian' flavour, reminiscent of the steppe tradition of maintaining a young, energetic khan, often via regicide, real or ritual.

Nonetheless, King Wuling came to disapprove of his successor's actions and brought forward his elder son, who had been passed over for succession. This led to a fratricidal battle in 295 BC. Not only was the elder brother mercilessly killed, but the followers of the young king also laid siege to Wuling's palace and he was reduced to searching out sparrow nests for chicks and eggs to eat, dying of slow starvation after more than three months under siege.

10. LÜ BUWEI (c. 284–235 BC)
Grand Councillor

The Grand Councillor Lü Buwei was born c. 284 BC to a rich merchant family in the state of Zhao in northern China. It is said that he decided upon a government career after a conversation with his father:

Son: What is the return of farming?
Father: Ten times.
Son: What is the return when dealing in jewels and jades?
Father: A hundred times.
Son: What is the return for setting up a monarch to rule a state?
Father: Incalculable.

His opportunity to move from the status of wealthy merchant to a position of 'incalculable' power came through his support for a young prince from the state of Qin who was being held hostage in the state of Zhao, a common practice during the Warring States period, that was intended to balance power between the states. Information about Lü Buwei's life, written by Confucian historians long after the events, is invariably coloured by the vilification of the state of Qin, begun in the succeeding Han dynasty. It was said that Lü Buwei passed on a pregnant concubine to the Qin prince, and her son, named Zheng, was born in 259 BC at Handan, ostensibly to the Qin prince. The boy was to become the formidable First Emperor of China (Biography 11).

Lü Buwei's support for this young prince during his exile in Zhao meant that, when the prince inherited the Qin throne in 250 BC, the merchant was appointed Grand Councillor and regent. The Grand Councillor worked hard not only to administer the kingdom efficiently, but also to expand it into an empire, a process accelerated when the twelve-year-old Zheng ascended to the Qin throne in 247 BC. Befitting Lü Buwei's status as regent, he was given the reverential title *Zhongfu* ('Second Uncle'). When a Chancellor or Prime Minister was called *Zhongfu*, the term traditionally was interpreted as signifying that he was respected as a fatherly figure.

With such an enormous return on his astute investment in a hostage prince, the former merchant became vastly wealthy, enfeoffed with an estate of 100,000 households and owning 10,000 house slaves. He also supported about 3,000 'dining guests', with assorted talents and skills. They assisted him in an intellectual undertaking: the compilation of *Lüshi chunqiu* ('The Spring and Autumn Annals of Mr Lü'), an impressive encyclopaedic collection of political theories and philosophies exposed through historical precedents.

In 236 BC, after a scandal involving his mother and a young man pretending to be a eunuch (supposedly introduced into her household by Lü Buwei), the king placed his mother, the queen-dowager, under house arrest, and his two stepbrothers were put to death together with the 'eunuch'. Though Lü Buwei was implicated, the young king moved against him slowly, initially only forcing him into retirement at his fiefdom. Having wielded immense power for a dozen years, Lü Buwei apparently continued to receive a never-ending stream of ambassadors and dignitaries. As a result, the king sent him a stern letter in 235 BC, condemning him and his family to exile in remote Sichuan, a region recently conquered by the Qin. Fearing worse punishment, the legendary investor committed suicide by taking poison.

11. QIN SHIHUANGDI (259–210 BC)
The First Emperor

The sensational archaeological discovery in 1974 of the army of terracotta soldiers guarding his tomb turned Prince Zheng, First Emperor of the Qin dynasty, into an international celebrity. The primary source on his life, however, remains the *Shiji* ('Records of the Grand Historian') of Sima Qian (Biography 15), written more than a century after the emperor's death and strongly influenced by the regime that overthrew his dynasty.

One of the half-life-size bronze chariots buried in the
First Emperor's magnificent tomb complex.

Zheng was born to a Qin prince serving as hostage in the capital of the neighbouring state of Zhao, in 259 BC. His early life was always precarious, because the
Zhao court, facing military attack by the Qin, repeatedly threatened to kill the
enemy hostage and his family. Zheng's father escaped back to Qin in 258 BC, leaving
his wife and son in captivity. It was not until 251 BC, when his grandfather succeeded
to the Qin throne and his father was formally appointed Crown Prince, that the
young Zheng first set foot in Qin.

Zheng's father succeeded to the Qin throne in 250 BC but ruled for only three
years. During this period, the powerful Qin army kept advancing against the other
states. On his father's death in 247 BC, the young Zheng inherited both the kingship
and a rapidly expanding kingdom.

Though Zheng himself never personally led any military expeditions, his role
in Qin expansion was vital. In addition to his enthusiasm for conquest, he supported a meritocracy (instead of the hereditary aristocracy) and was keen to recruit
talent from outside Qin. His major strategist and long-time Grand Chancellor,
Li Si, for instance, came from Chu, the kingdom that was Qin's arch-rival. With
an unmatched combination of capable ministers and generals, Qin destroyed and
annexed one state after another, concluding with the culturally advanced state of
Qi. In 221 BC he unified the whole of China under Qin rule.

He created a new title, *huangdi*, 'emperor', by combining two archaic and mythical monarchal terms, and thus he became Shihuangdi, 'First Emperor', intending
the imperial line to be continued by his descendants.

The successful and lasting creation of the entity we still know as China grew from his insistence on a highly centralized administrative system with an all-pervasive bureaucracy, with the court in direct control of all prefectures and counties; this largely spelled the end of feudalism in China. Equally significant was the standardization of weights, measures, currency and, most importantly, the written script. It can be argued that the establishment of this standard script has been the most powerful factor in keeping China together as a single nation.

In terms of ideology, the First Emperor largely followed the Legalist tradition (see Shang Yang, Biography 6), which tried to control the populace by an extensive web of laws, regulations and rules. Some of these laws and rules are explained and exemplified in detail in recently discovered Qin documents, which demonstrate a legal philosophy of great clarity and severe punishment. For instance, the theft of a pennyworth of mulberry leaves was punishable by thirty days of corvée labour. The punishment for organized burglary of even a small sum by a group of five or more persons was the cutting off of their left toes.

The unification and standardization campaign extended from the physical to the metaphysical world. The First Emperor tried to unify the behaviour, morality and thought of his subjects. The last proved a huge challenge after the pluralism experienced during several centuries of disunity. This, in conjunction with the Qin's long Legalist tradition, led to the First Emperor's increasing anti-Confucian, and later broad, anti-intellectual despotism. It culminated in 213–212 BC in decrees whereby he banned all books except those on medicine, divination and agriculture (though he retained copies of works on history and philosophy in the imperial library). The widespread belief that he buried hundreds of Confucian scholars alive is most likely a myth concocted by his detractors.

The emperor undertook gigantic construction projects, including linking up local walls into the Great Wall and building thousands of miles of state roads, canals, gigantic palaces and, of course, his own vast mausoleum complex. One estimate posits that 15 per cent of the entire Qin population was serving as corvée labourers and soldiers at any one time, a level of state service that placed an immense burden on ordinary people. It is little wonder that there were at least three assassination attempts made against him.

The First Emperor took a total of five grand tours of his vast new empire, setting up inscribed stelae glorifying his rule on mountaintops and seashores. He fell ill during his last such tour, in the summer of 210 BC, and, despite devoting much of his life to a search for physical immortality through alchemy, died not far from his birthplace in the former state of Zhao. His death on the road was kept secret by carrying rotten fish in his carriage to conceal the smell of his decaying body; this provided his younger son Huhai, who had accompanied him on the tour, the opportunity to conspire with a calculating eunuch to usurp the throne. This duo would see to the collapse of the mighty Qin dynasty in just four short years.

Vilified by the succeeding Han dynasty and by Confucians, whose philosophy and attachment to the past, often sanctified and sentimentalized, he sought to eradicate, his reign nevertheless defined China to a great extent for the next two millennia. Even the English name of China originated in the dynastic name of Qin (pronounced 'chin'). In their basic characteristics, the succeeding Han and later dynasties, while condemning the First Emperor as a tyrant, nevertheless continued the bureaucratic administration he pioneered and tried to maintain the broad unity he established. A void in his legacy is the lack of literary achievement during his reign, particularly in contrast to the two insurgent leaders (see Biography 12) who destroyed the Qin, who both left poignant poems.

12. XIANG YU (232–203 BC)
Rebel leader against the Qin

Xiang Yu (formal name Ji), who led a rebellion against the second emperor of the Qin, was born in 232 BC to a military family of Chu, a southern kingdom soon to be conquered by the Qin. Chu, with its unique southern culture and vast resources, maintained its resistance to the conquering Qin. In the autumn of the first year of the second emperor of the Qin (209 BC), an ordinary Chu peasant, Chen Sheng, launched the first uprising against the Qin, and named his regime *Zhang-Chu*, 'Expand the Chu'.

Xiang Yu was raised by his uncle, Xiang Liang, who became an outlaw living in what is now Shaoxing in the lower Yangtze delta. The uncle taught his nephew military strategy and tactics. After observing China's First Emperor (Biography 11) on his southern tour, Xiang Yu commented, 'This person can be taken out and replaced', and the uncle-nephew duo gradually amassed a small following. They joined the growing number of Chu notables who answered Chen Sheng's call to mount an anti-Qin insurgency, and it continued to spread.

Xiang Liang proclaimed a descendant of the earlier Chu royalty as the new king, establishing a loosely unified anti-Qin front that included another ambitious and popular commoner, Liu Bang, also from the former Chu realm. Xiang Liang was killed in a surprise counterattack by a Qin general, but Xiang Yu took his place as leader.

Portrait of Xiang Yu.

In the winter of 207–206 BC, Xiang Yu led a coalition of anti-Qin forces northward. After crossing the Zhang River (a branch of the Yellow River), Xiang Yu burned all his boats to show his soldiers that there was no retreat. While Xiang Yu, who had an alienating reputation for cruelty, was confronting the main Qin army, Liu Bang led a much smaller force into Qin territory, sacked the capital, and captured the last Qin emperor, a cousin of the murdered second emperor, during that same winter.

Xiang Yu then prepared his large force for an all-out assault on Liu Bang's army. Forewarned, Liu Bang offered his submission and apology. In early 206 BC, having burned the Qin palaces and killed the last emperor, Xiang Yu seized much of the territory for himself, giving Liu Bang the Han River valley and the remote Sichuan region. Liu Bang immediately started expanding his territories eastward and quickly occupied the central region. The war gradually turned in Liu Bang's favour, although Xiang Yu was able to win several important victories.

In 203 BC, Xiang Yu's demand for a personal duel with Liu Bang to settle their rivalry was rejected. Xiang Yu proposed a peace treaty, with the two sides dividing up the known world (*tianxia*) along the canal of Honggou. Liu Bang agreed to the treaty and won the safe return of his captured father and wife.

Almost immediately, however, Liu Bang breached the pact and resumed the war. In 202 BC he surrounded Xiang Yu's army at a place named Gaixia. One evening, Xiang Yu heard Liu Bang's troops encamped all around singing Chu folk-songs and was led to believe that Liu Bang had completely pacified his native Chu region. Disheartened, Xiang Yu sang this ballad to his concubine:

> My strength moves mountains, and my power covers the world.
> Yet the times are not propitious, and my piebald horse will run no more;
> What can I do, alas, now that my piebald horse will run no more?
> Lady Yu, O Lady Yu, what will happen to you?

Having bid goodbye to Lady Yu, Xiang Yu breached the siege with 800 cavalrymen before dawn. He crossed the Huai River, but the opposing forces caught up with them, and only a hundred men survived. Xiang Yu valiantly fought his way to the west bank of the Yangtze, from which position he could have fled to his former base, but, unwilling to survive the terrible loss of his troops, he committed suicide by the Yangtze. His body was torn to pieces by Liu Bang's soldiers, each seeking the reward offered for taking Xiang Yu, and the ensuing struggle resulted in the death of several dozen of the trophy-hunters.

Liu Bang, the winner in this struggle between two sons of Chu, was the founder of the Han dynasty.

13. EMPEROR WU OF THE HAN (156–87 BC)
China's expansionist emperor

Emperor Wu, or the 'Martial Emperor', celebrated for his expansion of the Chinese empire, succeeded to the throne as the fifth monarch of the Han dynasty in 140 BC at the age of sixteen. His father and grandfather were known for their laissez-faire policies marked by frugal government expenditures and low taxes, with the agricultural tax going down from the previous 6.7 per cent to 3.3 per cent, and frequently being waived. The result was rapid population growth and unprecedented prosperity. Naturally, such a domestic policy could only be maintained by peaceful foreign, or rather frontier, relations, especially vis-à-vis the great northern nomadic power Xiongnu. All this was to change under the energetic young emperor, especially after the death in 135 BC of his grandmother, Empress-dowager Dou, a Daoist.

The young emperor started promoting Confucianism in a process that would eventually establish it as the dominant ideology of East Asia for the next two millennia. He also led a militarist, expansionist 'foreign policy', most aggressively against the nomadic Xiongnu empire in the north.

From the very beginning, Emperor Wu actively sought and recruited military and diplomatic talents. With the abundant economic resources accumulated under the reigns of his father and grandfather, he launched repeated expeditions against the Xiongnu, most notably in 129 and 117 BC. The prolonged Han-Xiongnu war significantly weakened the once-dominant nomadic power, to such a degree that, in the words of an early history, 'there were no longer Xiongnu royal tents south of the Gobi Desert'. The Han built a vast military infrastructure in the north, including lengthening the Great Wall, adding beacon networks and scouting posts, and extending well into modern Mongolia.

Meanwhile, Emperor Wu opened military-diplomatic efforts to consolidate Han domination of Central Asia, greatly facilitating trade along the Silk Road. Aside from pushing north and northwest, Emperor Wu sent armies northeast to Manchuria and the Korean peninsula, establishing four commanderies there.

The expansion in the south was equally spectacular. The vast areas south of the Yangtze River at the time were mostly inhabited by non-Chinese. Emperor Wu sent generals and military colonists southward, conquering and absorbing these territories into the expanding empire, all the way to the modern city of Guangzhou (Canton) and northern Vietnam.

He established government control over iron-making and the salt trade to help finance the costly expansionist wars. He also completed the process, started by his father, of gradually asserting full administrative control over all hereditary princedoms and fiefdoms.

He is said to have abandoned the cousin to whom he was married, making a low-born singer his empress. Her brother and nephew were leading generals in the wars with the Xiongnu. The brother of another of his consorts was sent on costly expeditions to Central Asia to bring back the legendary 'heavenly horses' from Ferghana.

Emperor Wu ensured a peaceful succession (after an unsuccessful coup d'état launched by the Crown Prince in 91 BC) by the harsh expedient of killing a concubine (for fear of her potential control) and establishing her young son as the new heir. Like other rulers (including Qin Shihuangdi, Biography 11) who wished to further extend their worldly power, Emperor Wu was infatuated with immortality and the supernatural. In his search for elixirs and immortals, usually associated with Daoist mysticism, alchemy and astrology, he built elevated structures in the palace and travelled frequently to mountains and seashores. The emperor is still known by his posthumous title Wu ('martial'), demonstrating the importance of his conquests, and one of his legacies is the lasting, though sporadic, persistence of Chinese influence in Central Asia.

14. ZHANG QIAN (?–114 BC)
Explorer of Central Asia and beyond

From the 3rd century BC forward, the Xiongnu nomadic empire controlled the steppe and Central Asia, blocking westward expansion from China. This situation changed under the energetic Han Emperor Wu (Biography 13) and his explorer-diplomat Zhang Qian.

Zhang Qian was born in the mid-2nd century BC, a native of what is now modern Shaanxi province, at that time the centre of the Han empire, and entered government service as a low-ranking court attendant. Confronted by Xiongnu nomads to the northwest, the Han Emperor Wu sought an alliance with the Yuezhi (also pronounced Ruzhi, Rouzhi) tribes, who had formerly lived just to the north-west of the Chinese heartland. The tribes, believed to have spoken Tocharian, an ancient Indo-European language, had migrated westward several decades earlier to escape the Xiongnu. Zhang Qian volunteered to lead an embassy to the Yuezhi.

The diplomatic mission, consisting of more than a hundred people, left the Han capital Chang'an in 139 BC, guided by an ethnic Xiongnu, Tangyi Fu. The mission was intercepted by Xiongnu soldiers in the Gansu Corridor, and all members were made prisoners. Zhang Qian thus stayed in the Xiongnu domain for some ten years, married a Xiongnu wife, and had children.

In 129 BC, he managed to escape west with several members of his group, including the guide. They travelled through the Turfan Basin, along the Tarim River, reaching the state of Dayuan in the Ferghana Valley after crossing the Pamirs, an enormous distance across extremely difficult terrain. The king of Dayuan helped them travel further via Samarkand to their original destination, the new home of the Great Yuezhi in northern Afghanistan.

The formerly nomadic Yuezhi tribes, who had conquered Bactria and settled down to a prosperous sedentary life, refused to join an anti-Xiongnu alliance. Zhang Qian, however, gained useful knowledge about the 'Western Regions' of India, Central Asia and beyond. He was also intrigued to see products from Sichuan (in southwest China) offered in the local markets.

Cave mural showing Zhang Qian taking leave of Emperor Wu,
as he sets out on his journey to the Western Regions.

After a year or so in Bactria, he started home by the southernmost route possible, where he was once again intercepted by Xiongnu forces but managed to escape;
he succeeded in returning to the Han capital with his Xiongnu family.

Zhang Qian's mission encouraged Emperor Wu to undertake diplomatic and
military initiatives to push China's frontier westward, which in turn rapidly accelerated trade and cultural exchanges along the so-called Silk Road and also southwards.
Following Zhang Qian's report of Sichuanese goods in Bactria, unsuccessful attempts
were made to find a southern route through Sichuan to India. This ultimately failed,
but in the process Han territory was considerably expanded into Yunnan.

In 119 BC, Zhang Qian led a second, larger embassy to Central Asia through the
Gansu Corridor, which the Han had taken from the Xiongnu and now controlled.
Many of Zhang Qian's deputies were despatched from there to places as far away as
the Parthian empire in Iran.

Zhang Qian himself returned to the Han capital Chang'an in 115 BC, and died
a year later. His legacy lives on in everyday material items such as grapes, alfalfa,
sesame, cucumbers and walnuts, all first imported during the Han and now to be
found throughout China.

15. SIMA QIAN (c. 145/135–after 90 bc)
Historian

Sima Qian's father held the post of Grand Scribe under the Han Emperor Wu (Biography 13), when he began to write a general history of China. Sima Qian is said to have been born in 145 or 135 bc on the banks of the Yellow River, the cradle of Chinese civilization. He studied the 'Spring and Autumn Annals' with Dong Zhongshu, the scholar-philosopher most responsible for the eventual supremacy of Confucianism, and the 'Book of Documents' with a descendant of Confucius (Biography 4).

After completing his formal education, Sima Qian undertook a grand tour, covering large segments of the vast Han empire, especially the southern territories in the Yangtze River basin, which was still very much a frontier to northerners. Importantly for his future career, he visited many sites of actual or legendary historical events.

He started government service as a Gentleman of the Interior, the lowest rank of court attendant, and he travelled widely during Emperor Wu's frequent tours. In 110 bc, his father died, after entrusting his son with the completion of his historical treatise. Three years later, Sima Qian was given his father's post as Grand Scribe. After overseeing the production of a new calendar, formally adopted in 104 bc, he continued his father's historical work, making use of the imperial library as well as his father's manuscript.

In 99 bc, the Han launched a major attack on the Xiongnu. General Li Ling led 5,000 infantrymen deep into enemy territory and, after more than ten days of battle, surrendered. Sima Qian publicly defended Li Ling and was arrested, convicted and sentenced to death. At the time, it was possible to buy a pardon for such a crime, but the position of Grand Scribe was poorly paid, so the only way for Sima Qian to escape the death penalty was to request it be commuted to the humiliating punishment of castration. Sima Qian said, 'Death befalls all men alike. However, it may be weightier than Mount Tai or lighter than a feather', and that, with little to leave for posterity, his death would be like 'nine cattle losing a single hair'. Many chose suicide rather than face the imperial prosecutor, but Sima Qian chose to live and continue with his historical treatise.

After surviving the ignominious and degrading castration, Sima Qian devoted himself to the completion of the *Shiji*, or 'Records of the Grand Historian' (also known as 'The Grand Scribe's Records'), a general history of China from antiquity to his own period (he died some time after 90 bc). Through this work he came to be viewed as the father of historiography in China.

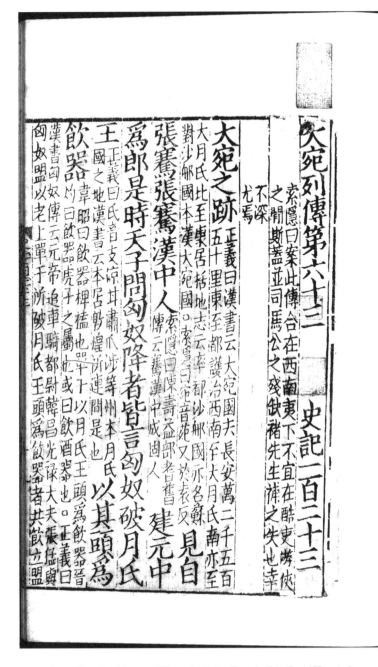

大宛列傳第六十三　　史記二百二十三

索隱曰案此傳合在西南夷下不宜在酷吏游俠之間蓋並司馬公之殘缺褚先生補之失也幸不深焉尤焉

大宛之跡　正義曰漢書云大宛國去長安萬二千五百五十里東至都護治西南至大月氏南亦至大月氏比至東居栘地志云率都沙郱國亦名蘇對少郱國本漢大宛國索隱曰宛音苑又於元反見自建元中

張騫張騫漢中人傳云張騫漢中成固人

爲郎是時天子問匈奴降者皆言匈奴破月氏王　正義曰氏音支凉甘肅瓜涉等州本月氏王國之地漢書云本居敦煌祁連間是也以其頭爲飲器　韋昭曰飲器椑榼也師古曰飲器虎子之屬也或曰飲酒器也　正義曰飲器晉灼的曰飲器飲酒器晉灼的曰飲器飲酒器飲器

漢書匈奴傳云元帝追車騎都尉韓昌光祿大夫張猛與匈奴盟以老上單于所破月氏王頭爲飲器者共飲盟

The *Shiji* set the model for the writing of chronicles and invented the biographical style that characterized all subsequent dynastic histories. It remains the primary source for China's early history. Though he is not always impartial or reliable, Sima Qian's records of the lineage of the Shang kings, for example, have been proven extraordinarily accurate when compared with oracle bone inscriptions unearthed thousands of years later. The work is also regarded as a literary masterpiece.

16. WANG MANG (45 BC–AD 23)
Usurper emperor

Wang Mang was born in 45 BC into a Han aristocratic family. One of his aunts was the chief consort of the Han Emperor Yuan and the mother of Emperor Cheng. Under her patronage, Wang Mang advanced rapidly and was appointed Grand Marshal in 8 BC. By spending his wealth to help the less fortunate, and by promoting many 'men of renown', Wang Mang became the most popular politician in the Han empire. His modesty is exemplified by an incident in which numerous aristocratic women who called on his ailing mother mistook his plainly dressed wife for a maid.

Emperor Cheng died in 7 BC without issue. The Wang family was then eclipsed by the two maternal clans of the succeeding Emperor Ai. Wang Mang bided his time, retiring to his fiefdom and keeping a low profile. His popularity, however, continued to grow after he forced his second son to commit suicide for killing a slave.

Wang Mang's aunt outlived both the grandmother and mother of Emperor Ai, who died in 1 BC, again without issue. Empress-dowager Wang immediately reasserted her power and recalled Wang Mang. Together they enthroned a boy emperor only eight years old, and Wang Mang became the *de facto* ruler. To conceal his ambitions and consolidate his power, he did not hesitate to have his eldest son killed. His popularity was enhanced by his donation of large amounts of money (which would normally have gone to official salaries and imperial rewards) as relief for the poor and his setting up of schools in every district.

For these actions, Wang Mang was praised as a saintly figure of the calibre of the Duke of Zhou (Biography 2). However, after poisoning the young emperor and enthroning an infant puppet in the winter of AD 5, Wang Mang assumed the position of 'Acting Emperor', and after numerous auspicious omens from heaven and little apparent opposition, he declared a 'New (Xin) Dynasty' in AD 9.

Wang Mang initiated extensive reforms according to his reading of the ancient Zhou political system. In addition to a reorganization of the government bureaucracy and the introduction of a new calendar, he proclaimed public ownership of all land and slaves, forbidding their private sale and purchase. He introduced strict government regulation and control of commerce and other economic activities, and made repeated monetary changes.

Wang Mang also imposed harsh legal penalties on anyone opposing his reforms, inevitably stirring up popular resentment. In less than a decade, the once popular ruler became a widely hated monarch, as more and more people grew nostalgic for Han rule.

Large-scale peasant uprisings started in AD 17. United in the aim of restoring the Han dynasty, the loosely organized insurgents grew progressively stronger. In the autumn of 23, after defeating Wang Mang's main force, the rebels finally broke into the capital, Chang'an. On 6 October, Wang Mang was killed in his palace. His severed head was painted and kept as a trophy by the 'restored' Eastern Han dynasty, until it was destroyed in a fire in 295 during the (Western) Jin dynasty. For his usurpation, he has been reviled throughout China's history.

Coins issued by Wang Mang.

17. THE BAN FAMILY (1ST CENTURY AD)
Historians

The family patriarch was Ban Biao (AD 3–54), who, despite his 'barbarian' Xiongnu ancestry, played a role in the Han restoration after the usurpation of Wang Mang (Biography 16). Also, more importantly, he started the long process for which the family is best remembered, the creation of the *Han shu* ('History of the Han'), China's very first dynastic history.

Sima Qian (Biography 15) wrote the *Shiji* ('Records of the Grand Historian'), a general treatise of history from antiquity down to his own lifetime. Ban Biao proposed to continue Sima Qian's work and record the full history of the entire Former Han dynasty. Unfortunately, Ban Biao died after drafting only several dozen chapters.

Ban Biao's eldest son, Ban Gu (32–92), showed exceptional literary talent while still a youth; he was described by Ban Biao's friend and pupil Wang Chong (Biography 18) as 'destined to record Han history'. On Ban Biao's death, Ban Gu cut short his study at the Imperial College and committed himself to completing his father's work.

Because his work was unauthorized, Ban Gu was arrested in 62, but his younger brother Ban Chao (33–102) rushed to the capital to appeal to Emperor Ming. Impressed by the confiscated manuscript, the emperor, who had a strong literary bent, assigned Ban Gu an official position in the imperial bureau of history records, where the resources and records of the imperial library greatly facilitated his work.

Ban Chao made a living as a scribe but declared, 'A true man ought to follow the example of Zhang Qian (Biography 14), and be enfeoffed for outstanding exploits in foreign lands'. After a short period as a lowly imperial secretary, Ban Chao joined an expedition against the Xiongnu and was despatched as an emissary to the Western Regions (Central Asia).

Han control over Central Asia had been lost during the Wang Mang interregnum, and the area

Ban Gu.

had been re-subjugated by the Xiongnu. Ban Chao managed gradually to restore Han domination in Central Asia. In 91, he was formally appointed the Protector-General, or Proconsul, of the Western Regions. Three years later, all the fifty or so city-states of the Western Regions accepted Han suzerainty and sent hostage-sons to the Han court. The next year (95), Chao was ennobled as a marquis. In 97, an envoy sent by Chao reached the coast of the 'Western Sea', possibly the Persian Gulf or even the Mediterranean, the westernmost point reached by a Han officer, or indeed any Chinese, during antiquity.

Meanwhile, Ban Gu had joined the staff of a prominent general in 89 and participated in expeditions against the Xiongnu. He reached the Khangai Mountains in modern Mongolia and drafted an inscription there to commemorate the Han military achievement. When the victorious general shortly after fell from imperial favour, Ban Gu was arrested and died in prison in 92.

At that time, the 'History of the Han' was not yet complete. The reigning emperor decreed that Ban Gu's youngest sister, Zhao, complete the monumental work.

Ban Zhao was a learned scholar and author in her own right, long widowed and known as Grand Dame Cao after her husband's surname. The 'History' was finally finished nearly eighty years after Ban Biao first started writing, and it has served as the model to be followed by all succeeding dynasties.

Ban Zhao became a highly respected tutor of princesses and imperial consorts; she played a significant political role during the long regency (105–21) of Empress-dowager Deng, one of her pupils. Ban Zhao's own writings are among the first works by a known female author in China. One of her most famous compositions is the 'Instructions for Women', which taught wives to be deferential to their husbands and to pay attention to housework – a model for female rectitude that lasted into the early years of the 20th century. In an age when illiteracy was the norm, particularly for women, Ban Zhao's literary achievements were remarkable.

After serving for more than thirty years in Central Asia, Ban Chao's request to return was not immediately granted, because the Han court could not find a successor of similar prestige. Zhao interceded on behalf of her brother, who was finally given a hero's welcome in the Han capital in the summer of 102. He died barely a month afterward at the age of 69. A few decades later, it would be his able son Yong's turn to pacify the Western Regions.

18. WANG CHONG (27–89/104)
Sceptical philosopher

Wang Chong was born in AD 27 near the modern city of Shaoxing in Zhejiang province, in the Yangtze River delta; he was one of the first prominent intellectuals to emerge from the south, then still 'semi-barbarian' territory.

His brilliance was such that he received a recommendation to travel to the capital, Luoyang, in his late teens, probably in the year 44, to study at the prestigious National University. His teacher was the famous scholar and historian Ban Biao (Biography 17).

Coming from a poor family, he could not afford many books, nor did he have access to the imperial library, but he was said to frequent the bookshops in the capital, memorizing the contents of a vast number of works. After his last government job as a staff member in the office of the Prefect of Yangzhou in 86–88, Wang Chong spent most of the rest of his life teaching and writing. He died sometime between 89 and 104. Only one of his many works, the 'Balanced Discussions' *(Lun heng)*, survives largely complete, and it reveals his position as an important thinker.

Critical and sceptical, Wang Chong questioned the stories about ancient sages, including Confucius (Biography 4), declaring that all Chinese books suffered from 'nine categories of falsehood and three types of exaggeration'. He used logic to attack the widespread and officially sanctioned belief in prophecy and other popular superstitions. Wang Chong dismissed the common belief in ghosts and spirits, saying that a man's clothing could not accompany him to the afterworld and, therefore, if ghosts existed, they could only appear naked, but that was not how people imagined them.

Jade and gold burial suit, typifying the superstition and extravagance attacked by Wang Chong.

In another of his works, the 'Satires Against Customs and Usages', since lost, he reportedly advocated the use of the vernacular as opposed to the literary language in writing – a revolutionary idea. It was not until the 20th century, nearly two thousand years later, that language reformers succeeded in gaining official status for the vernacular.

Wang Chong's works would have been forgotten had not Cai Yong, the father of the woman poet Cai Yan (Biography 22), rediscovered the 'Balanced Discussions' during his exile in the south. Regarded as heretical by the Confucian faithful, the work proved stimulating to many other non-mainstream pre-modern Chinese writers. Just as Zhuang Zi (Biography 8), the Daoist thinker, was uniquely playful (and inventive), so was Wang Chong without parallel for his rationality and opposition to superstition.

19 & 20. ZHANG DAOLING AND ZHANG JIAO
(2ND CENTURY AD)
Daoist patriarchs

The first Daoist sect to have a significant social impact was the 'Great Tranquillity Daoism' sect, founded by Zhang Jiao in the mid-2nd century. Daoism claimed its origins in the shadowy figure Lao Zi, to whom the *Dao De Jing* ('Classic of the Way and of Virtue') was attributed. It was an amalgam of traditional Chinese popular beliefs and mysticism allied to a search for immortality and transcendence.

Zhang Jiao was born in northern China and became a charismatic religious leader. His main appeal was an apparent ability to treat sickness via a combination of 'holy water' and personal repentance; he also called for egalitarianism and salvation. The idea of salvation was particularly attractive at the time, because the population was suffering from heavy tax burdens and natural disasters.

Zhang Jiao established a centralized organization consisting of thirty-six branches, each with a membership of between 6,000 and 10,000 believers. They planned an uprising to seize secular power in 184. Several hundred thousand insurgents wearing yellow headscarves (or turbans) simultaneously rose in eight regions, threatening the nearly four-century-old Han empire.

Zhang Jiao died of illness in the autumn of 184, depriving the Yellow Turban uprising of its charismatic leader. The uprising was put down, although centralized Han rule never recovered. The success of Cao Cao (Biography 21) in unifying

Drawing of Zhang Daoling (1923).

northern China started with his first suppressing, then taking over, a large Yellow
Turban force. Zhang Jiao thus can be said to have brought about the end of the
Han. He also started the Chinese tradition of employing popular religion or
'heterodox cults' to oppose the authorities, a pattern that would be repeated many
times throughout Chinese history.

The nearly contemporary Daoist sect founded by Zhang Daoling, another early
Daoist leader (also known as Zhang Ling), adopted a different course and encountered a completely different fate.

According to legend, Zhang Daoling was born in AD 34, lived for 122 years, and
'ascended live to heaven in broad daylight' in 156. He was originally from eastern
China but settled in Sichuan, where he founded his 'Five Pecks of Rice' sect. The
name came from the requirement that each adherent contribute five pecks of rice
to the church.

The doctrines of Five Pecks of Rice Daoism were similar to those of Great Tranquillity Daoism. The sect stressed personal honesty and the confession of sins, and it engaged in charity and relief work. Its growth occurred primarily during the leadership of Zhang Daoling's son and grandson. The latter established an independent Daoist theocracy in northern Sichuan and western Shaanxi during the late 2nd century that lasted until 215. He also opted to surrender to Cao Cao, the rebel general, and the Five Pecks of Rice sect gradually evolved into the mainstream of Daoist teaching in China. The lineal descendants of Zhang Daoling, the first 'celestial master', became the Daoist supreme patriarchs, a position sanctioned and honoured by the government. The sixty-third such 'celestial master' moved with the Nationalist government to Taiwan in 1949 and died there in 1969, passing the millennia-old patriarchship to his nephew.

It was during this period (late 2nd to early 3rd century) that the so-called Daoist religion gradually evolved out of an amalgam of the doctrines and practices of Zhang Daoling and Zhang Jiao, with selected aspects of the thought of Lao Zi and Zhuang Zi (Biography 8). Also playing an important role was the model of Buddhist institutions, scriptures and art, which arrived in China just before this period. The Daoist religious traditions that developed out of these roots are not to be confused with folk religious practices centred on countless local cults and deities.

21. CAO CAO (155–220)
Military tactician and literary hero

Cao Cao was born in 155. His father was the adopted son of a powerful palace eunuch, and Cao Cao had a privileged childhood and youth.

The Eastern Han dynasty at the time was in decay, with eunuchs and imperial relatives vying for control of the court. Cao Cao entered government service at the age of nineteen. In 184, in the wake of the Yellow Turban rebellion (Biography 20), he was appointed Commandant of Cavalry and assigned to help put down a series of similar uprisings. This was the start of his military career.

Cao Cao reorganized a band of Yellow Turban rebels into the Qingzhou Army and obtained control of a key region in central China and an appointment as Regional Governor, in effect a local warlord. His strategic masterstroke was to move the figurehead boy emperor to his own home base at Xuchang (in modern Henan province) in 196.

Cao Cao conquered several warlords with relative ease. However, in 200 he faced his greatest challenge in Yuan Shao, who came from a well-established family and opposed Cao Cao with ten times more soldiers at his command. With superb strategy and tactics, Cao managed first to destroy Shao's supplies and provisions, then to defeat the main force.

In 208, Cao Cao embarked on a campaign to conquer southern China, in which he made his only tactical error, losing to the numerically inferior coalition forces of Sun Quan and Liu Bei, advised by Zhuge Liang (Biography 23), at the celebrated Battle of the Red Cliff. This battle established the prolonged coexistence of three kingdoms: Sun and Liu would become the founders respectively of the Wu and Shu states, and Cao Cao's son would found the state of Wei.

Cao Cao was able to complete most of his military conquest of northern China, but he died in early 220, whereupon his son, Cao Pi, was formally enthroned as emperor of the new dynasty of Wei, terminating more than four centuries of Han rule. Cao Cao was posthumously named the Martial Emperor of the Wei.

In addition to his military exploits, Cao was known as a superb writer, his poetry representing the highest literary achievement of the era. Cao Cao's posthumous popular image was that of a successful general who used the cunning stratagems against his enemies that are seen in many folk stories and legends. His legend culminates in his characterization as the 'wicked champion' in the famous 14th-century novel, the 'Romance of Three Kingdoms'.

22. CAI YAN (CAI WENJI; C. 177–?)
Exiled woman poet

Cai Yan was the daughter of Cai Yong (132–92), a tragic literary talent. Cai Yan was born *c.* 177, just before her father was sentenced to death for offending powerful eunuch-courtiers. His sentence was commuted to exile to the north for a year. Cai Yong soon angered another powerful eunuch, however, and departed on self-imposed exile in the lower Yangtze delta until the reigning emperor died in 189.

Cai Yan became a poet. Like her father, who once rescued a burning piece of wood and turned it into a superb harp, Cai Yan was also musical. She could tell which harp string her father had broken when he played in the next room.

In 189, the warlord Dong Zhuo was appointed Minister of Works at the Han court. Before long, Dong Zhuo replaced the current boy emperor with the latter's half-brother, the last Han emperor. Long an admirer of Cai Yong's talent and fame, Dong Zhuo appointed Cai Yong to his administration. However, when Dong Zhuo was murdered in a coup d'état in 192, Cai Yong was arrested, and he died in prison.

Cai Yan was married around this time and widowed shortly afterwards. In 194–95 Dong Zhuo's generals staged an insurgency to avenge their leader's murder. Because Dong Zhuo's original power base was China's Western Regions (Central Asia), the revolt included a large number of Xiongnu and proto-Tibetan Qiang soldiers, who pillaged the Han metropolitan regions. In the chaos, Cai Yan was captured and carried off by Xiongnu troops. She became the consort of a Prince of the Xiongnu and bore him two sons.

When Cao Cao (Biography 21), an old friend of her father's, had gained control of northern China, he despatched Cai Yan's relatives to ransom her back from the 'barbarian' land, probably in 208.

She wrote of her exile:

The frontier wasteland is so different from China
The customs lack morality and reasoning.
So much frost and snow around my residence –
Even in spring and summer, the [cold] foreign wind keeps blowing…

But also of her sons by the Xiongnu prince:

While I myself can be ransomed
I must abandon my sons.
Endowed by heaven, they are stitched to my human heart.
Once departed, no chance to reunite –
Forever separated in this world.
How can I bear to bid goodbye?
My sons, clinging to my neck,
Ask, 'Mother, where are you going?
People say that you are leaving.
And will never return.
Mother, you've always been good to us.
Why are you now turning heartless?
We are still small children;
How could you turn your back on us?'
My insides completely torn apart by such a scene.

Painting of Cai Yan with her husband and sons.

As if I were losing my sanity.

Weeping and wailing, I caress them.

At the moment of departure, I am beset with doubt ...

On her return, she was married again to an officer named Dong Si, but he fell foul of the law and was sentenced to death.

Cai Yan rushed to court, barefoot and with her hair loose, on a cold winter day, to plead successfully for her new husband's life. Little else is known about her later life, though it is said that, at the request of Cao Cao, she transcribed from memory some 400 scrolls out of the more than 4,000 that had been bequeathed by her father.

THE PERIOD OF DISUNION TO THE SUI AND TANG DYNASTIES

220–907

A
t the fall of the Han, China was first divided between three 'warlords'. Then subsequent, often short-lived, dynasties rose and fell in different areas with, for example, six successive dynasties ruling from Nanjing between 222 and 589. During this period of uncertainty and disunion, Buddhism, which had come to China during the Han, flourished. In 581, the Sui reunified China but the dynasty was short-lived and succeeded by the Tang, often considered to be a 'golden age' of Chinese culture in which the cosmopolitan capital Chang'an (the largest city in the world at the time) saw traders from all over Central Asia bringing luxury goods and styles. It was during the period of disunion that religion, art, music and literature flourished as never before, and all of these aspects of culture were enriched by influences brought to China from near and far. It was at this time that canons of criticism and aesthetic standards were established that endured until the modern age.

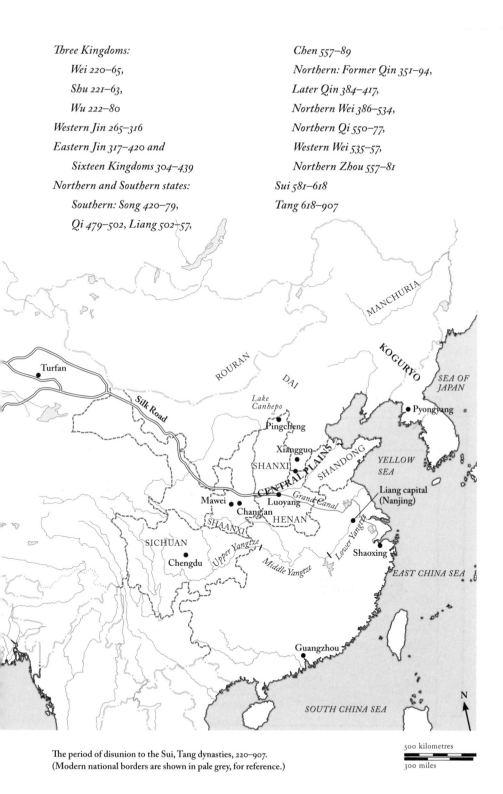

Three Kingdoms:
  Wei 220–65,
  Shu 221–63,
  Wu 222–80
Western Jin 265–316
Eastern Jin 317–420 and
  Sixteen Kingdoms 304–439
Northern and Southern states:
  Southern: Song 420–79,
  Qi 479–502, Liang 502–57,

Chen 557–89
Northern: Former Qin 351–94,
  Later Qin 384–417,
  Northern Wei 386–534,
  Northern Qi 550–77,
  Western Wei 535–57,
  Northern Zhou 557–81
Sui 581–618
Tang 618–907

Turfan

Silk Road

ROURAN

DAI

MANCHURIA

KOGURYO

SEA OF
JAPAN

Lake
Canhepo

Pingcheng

Pyongyang

Xiangguo

SHANXI

SHANDONG

YELLOW
SEA

CENTRAL PLAINS

Grand Canal

Liang capital
(Nanjing)

Maewi

Luoyang

Changʼan

HENAN

Lower Yangtze

SHAANXI

SICHUAN

Upper Yangtze

Middle Yangtze

Shaoxing

Chengdu

EAST CHINA SEA

Guangzhou

SOUTH CHINA SEA

N

The period of disunion to the Sui, Tang dynasties, 220–907.
(Modern national borders are shown in pale grey, for reference.)

500 kilometres

300 miles

23. ZHUGE LIANG (181–234)
Legendary statesman and strategist

Zhuge Liang was born in 181 into a northern gentry family and raised by an uncle. In 207, the warlord Liu Bei heard of his talent and made three attempts to call on him at his thatched house. Zhuge Liang finally agreed to join Liu Bei and designed for him a grand strategy. He advised Liu Bei to secure a base in the Middle and Upper Yangtze valley, ally with the warlord Sun Quan in the Lower Yangtze region against Cao Cao (Biography 21) in northern China, and then bide his time for a two-pronged conquest of the north.

This strategy foresaw the Three Kingdoms that would emerge a dozen years later, but its implementation was no easy matter. In 208, Cao Cao led an overwhelming expeditionary force southward with the intention of unifying China. Advised by Zhuge Liang, the Sun Quan–Liu Bei polity jointly defeated Cao Cao's army in the famous Battle of the Red Cliff on the Yangtze.

A sea battle in which enemies of China are routed.

In 214, Zhuge Liang helped Liu Bei take control of the Upper Yangtze valley and the large, rich region of Sichuan. In 219 Liu Bei's general Guan Yu, who had been guarding Liu's mid-Yangtze holdings, was killed by Sun Quan's forces.

After Cao Cao's son, Cao Pi, deposed the puppet Eastern Han emperor and declared the new dynasty of Wei in 220, Liu Bei enthroned himself with the justification that he was continuing Han legitimacy. His dynasty-state, however, was generally known as Shu, an ancient name for the Sichuan region. Zhuge Liang was appointed Grand Chancellor.

Liu Bei died in 223, shortly after losing a battle against Sun Quan, which Zhuge Liang had warned him against undertaking. Sun Quan declared a new dynasty-state of Wu. Liu Bei's son was ineffectual, and Zhuge Liang assumed power in the state of Shu. While Zhuge Liang ran the Shu state efficiently, he knew that it was no match for the larger state of Wei. Nevertheless he led expeditions against Wei, all of which were repelled. Zhuge Liang died of illness during the last campaign in 234 at the age of fifty-three.

Almost immediately after he died, Zhuge Liang began to acquire a significant reputation as a cunning strategist. Folklore said, for example, that he had once bluffed a huge enemy army by calmly playing a harp on the wall of a virtually undefended empty city. He was also credited with inventing the wheelbarrow and a device that enabled troops to cross lakes and rivers. Over the centuries, his image as preternatural military genius continued to grow. When popular vernacular literature started to spread in the Song dynasty, Zhuge Liang emerged as an all-knowing, daring military strategist, a deification largely completed by the time of his apotheosis in the 14th-century novel 'Romance of the Three Kingdoms'.

24. SHI CHONG (249–300)
Decadent aristocrat

Shi Chong was born in 249 to an aristocrat father, Shi Bao, who played an important role in the founding of the (Western) Jin dynasty, and who was richly rewarded by the founding emperor. He rose to become a Chief Justice.

As a privileged aristocratic son, Shi Chong was appointed Regional Inspector of Jingzhou, which by virtue of its central location (along the middle reaches of the Yangtze River in what is now Hubei province) controlled the vast north-south and east-west transitional commerce. Shi Chong accumulated enormous wealth by extortion from all the merchants who passed through the region.

Shi Chong's total holdings reportedly included more than 100 concubines, over thirty water mills, more than 800 slaves and servants, plus large quantities of jewels and precious stones, money, land and real estate.

He became famous for his competition with another rich aristocrat, Wang Kai, who, as the maternal uncle of the Jin emperor, received ample help from his emperor nephew. When Wang Kai created a 21-km-long (13-mile) screen corridor using expensive purple cloth, Shi Chong immediately topped it with one of hand-woven silk brocade over 27 km in length. When Wang Kai proudly showed off a 30-cm-high (2-ft) coral tree, a rare and exotic gift from the emperor, Shi Chong broke it into pieces and offered to replace it from his own collection of much bigger and more beautiful coral trees. Wang Kai had his kitchen utensils washed in (diluted) syrups, but Shi Chong matched his extravagance by using wax as cooking fuel.

Shi Chong's intellectual tastes were elegant. He built a suburban mountain retreat, the Golden Valley Garden. All guests were asked to compose a poem commemorating a gathering that took place in 296 in decorated pavilions, towers, stages and terraced halls nestled among springs, fountains and woods. Those who could not complete their compositions were punished by being forced to drink 3 litres (6 pints) of wine.

Of the hundred-plus concubines in Shi Chong's personal harem, his favourite was a very beautiful Vietnamese girl named Lüzhu ('Green Pearl'), who excelled in playing the bamboo flute. Shi Chong bought this rare beauty for 'three bushels of pearls'.

Shi Chong was on the losing side of political intrigues and was dismissed from court in 300. An upstart courtier, Sun Xiu, then wanted to acquire Green Pearl. Shi Chong refused.

Thereupon Sun Xiu manufactured a plot that implicated Shi Chong. Green Pearl committed suicide by jumping from a tower at Golden Valley when soldiers came to arrest her master. Shi Chong and a fellow aristocrat poet friend went to the execution ground together, as prophesied by his friend's poem in 'A Collection at the Golden Valley': 'white-haired, we head to the same destination'.

25. WANG YAN (256–311)
Metaphysicist and courtier

The early Western Jin dynasty (265–316) was, according to the established aristocracy, the best of times, an age of wisdom. For Confucianism, however, it was the worst of times, an age of foolishness. Confucian morality and a sense of social responsibility fell by the wayside, and Daoism grew popular.

Wang Yan, famous for his pursuit of Abstruse Learning (which focused on metaphysical notions of being and non-being), was born in 256 to a prominent aristocratic clan in today's coastal province of Shandong. During his childhood, a leading author was said to have remarked, 'What old woman could have given birth to such a handsome boy! But he may well turn out to be the person who shall cause misery for the entire population'.

As a rich aristocrat who never needed to worry about money, Wang Yan demonstrated his high-mindedness by eschewing the use of the word 'money' entirely. His avaricious wife, to challenge him, once had his bed barricaded by piles of money as he slept. In the morning, he ordered the chambermaids to get rid of it without using the vulgar word: 'Move this stuff away from me!' When the emperor asked his cousin, one of the Seven Sages of the Bamboo Grove (a group of painters and poets who gathered to drink and converse and escape the dangers and complexities of everyday life), what contemporary figure Wang Yan could be compared to, the reply was 'nobody of the day'.

The Jin court was dominated by like-minded aristocrats from prominent, endogamous clans. Wang Yan rose steadily in the government, from Gentleman Attendant at the Palace Gate to Minister of Works and Minister of Education, despite his express lack of interest in worldly affairs and his pronounced preference for metaphysics. The Western Jin, facing worsening political chaos, began to collapse. Wang Yan was most interested in preserving his own status, so much so that when his son-in-law, the Crown Prince, fell out with a scheming empress, Wang Yan immediately sued for his daughter's divorce, an opportunistic act that greatly augmented his haughty reputation.

The 'Anarchy of the Eight Princes' (a messy falling-out among members of the royal family after the death of the founding emperor in 290) and the ensuing insurgence soon caught up with him, however. Wang Yan tried to retire from government service, but was forced into taking military command as Defender-in-chief and Marshal. In early summer of 311, an entire Jin force of more than 100,000 troops was annihilated by the 'barbarian' leader Shi Le (Biography 26). A large group of royals and nobles, including Wang Yan, were taken prisoner.

'The Seven Sages of the Bamboo Grove', a painting from the Summer Palace in Beijing.

Interrogated by Shi Le, Wang Yan claimed never to have had any interest in politics, blamed the collapse of the Jin on others, and sycophantically encouraged Shi Le to ascend the throne. Shi Le ordered the disloyal opportunist to be crushed to death by a falling wall, fulfilling the prophecy that Wang Yan would 'doom the country' by engaging in 'pure conversation'.

26. SHI LE (274–333)
Slave who became the founding emperor of the (Later) Zhao

Shi Le was born in 274, during the early years of the Western Jin dynasty, to an ethnic Jie family in Wuxiang county (modern Shanxi province).

The Jie were said to be a Caucasoid group that once belonged to the nomadic northern Xiongnu confederacy. Though such peoples are often linked to migrants from Central Asia along the Silk Road during historic times, there is evidence indicating that prehistoric Indo-European populations lived side by side with early sinitic groups in northern China from the Bronze and Early Iron Ages. The Jie were probably a combination of native and migrant elements.

The Western Jin declined rapidly after the death of the founding emperor in 290 and the internecine struggle called the 'Anarchy of the Eight Princes' (291–306), and open civil war broke out in northern China in 300. While everyone suffered, the ethnic minorities undoubtedly fared even worse during this period of political chaos and economic distress.

During the period of 302–3, many from the Jie clans to which Shi Le belonged were captured by local warlords and sold as slaves. Shi Le was enslaved and sent as a prisoner, restrained with another in a cangue (wooden neckboard), as far as coastal Shandong province, where he was sold to a Han landlord.

Shi Le was subsequently freed, either willingly by his Han owner (as Chinese records state) or by his own efforts, and after further imprisonment by Jin soldiers, he escaped and formed a bandit group whose members clearly included other 'barbarians', which soon expanded to 'Eighteen Knights'. In 305, they joined a herdsman leader, Ji Sang, to form a militia group nominally serving one of the warring Jin princes. It was said that Ji Sang gave the former slave his Chinese name, Shi Le.

When Ji Sang was killed by a Jin general, Shi Le was forced to join Liu Yuan, the Southern Xiongnu leader who in 304 had founded the (Former) Zhao (one of the Sixteen Kingdoms, initially known as Han), the first ethnic dynasty in northern China.

Shi Le was a capable general who played a major role in destroying Jin forces by ingenious combinations of military campaigns, fake submission and divide-and-conquer schemes. He proved that he was a farseeing leader, not just a pillaging former 'barbarian slave', and rose rapidly. He soon recruited a capable Han councillor, Zhang Bin, and organized a 'camp of gentlemen' consisting of Han gentry.

In 311 Shi Le's long-lost mother was returned by a Jin general. Shi Le successfully annihilated a large Jin force, capturing and killing a group of Jin aristocrats headed by the quintessential 'gentleman of renown', Wang Yan (Biography 25), and joined the Southern Xiongnu forces in sacking the Jin capital Luoyang.

Shi Le gradually became independent, formally splitting with the Southern Xiongnu dynasty in 319. Proclaiming himself King of Zhao, he established his own court at Xiangguo (the modern city of Xingtai in Hebei province). In 330, Shi Le enthroned himself as Heavenly King and 'acting emperor'; he eventually cleared the Jin forces from the territory between the Yellow and Huai Rivers.

While elevating his own ethnic group to the highest status as a 'national people', Shi Le also set up schools at the capital and in the provinces for traditional (Confucian) learning and encouraged population growth by making special rewards for triplet and quadruplet births. Although illiterate, he enjoyed listening to the reading of Chinese histories.

A Central Asian Buddhist monk, Fotucheng, became his chief advisor. He advised Shi Le to confront his erstwhile overlord, the Southern Xiongnu king, Liu Yao (successor of Liu Yuan), whom he had defeated in a decisive battle in 329, thereby establishing himself as the undisputed sovereign of northern China.

Despite his success, Shi Le was modest. Responding to a Han courtier's flattery that he was the best emperor since the mythical demigod rulers of antiquity, Shi Le said:

> Doesn't a man know himself? Your comparisons are overblown. Had I been with [the founding emperor of the Former Han], I would have willingly submitted to him and competed with [his leading generals] for the top rewards. Had I met [the founding emperor of the Later Han], the two of us would have been rivals in conquering the Central Plains, with the eventual winner hard to tell. A true man should act openly and squarely under the sun and moon, and in no way behave like Cao Cao and Sima Yi [the actual founder of the Western Jin] who shamefully stole the throne from widows and orphans.

Shi Le died in 333 at the height of his power. He was buried in secret, a sign of his steppe heritage. The throne, which should have gone to his son, was then usurped by his nephew Shi Hu, whose continued patronage of the monk Fotucheng and the latter's faith offered a critical opportunity for proselytizing of this 'barbarian' (Buddhist) religion among the ordinary Chinese populace during a time of social unrest.

27. WANG XIZHI (c. 303–61)
China's greatest calligrapher

Wang Xizhi was born c. 303 into a prominent aristocratic family in what is now Shandong province, but the family fled the fighting in the north to settle in the Yangtze delta. The Wang clan played such a crucial role in establishing the new Eastern Jin dynasty (ostensibly a restoration of the imperial Sima house) that it was said that 'the Wangs and Simas are co-sovereigns'.

All Wang clansmen were therefore assured of good official posts. Advanced by such family connections and powerful patrons, Wang Xizhi's government career prospered, and he rose to such prominent positions as Regional Inspector of Jiangzhou and General of the Right Army. However, he did not have much political ambition and, after a conflict with a powerful Wang clansman, swore in front of his parents' tomb never again to serve in the Jin bureaucracy. He is also said to have employed Abstruse Learning and 'naturalness' to gain a wife. The powerful Defender-in-chief Xi Jian sent an emissary to find a husband for his daughter among the Wang clan. All the young men behaved pretentiously except Wang Xizhi, who lay, bare-bellied, on a couch eating a snack as if nothing was happening and was therefore chosen for his lack of pretention.

His eternal fame is due to his wonderful calligraphy. At the time, Chinese writing was undergoing an important transformation from the rigid 'scribal script' (*lishu*) to the less-restrained 'regular script' (*kaishu*) still in use today, plus the derived freestyle 'running script' (*xingshu*) and the even more cursive 'grass hand' (*caoshu*). Wang Xizhi proved to be a master of these new styles of writing. According to legend, he practised calligraphy so much that the pond in which he cleaned his writing-brush and inkstone turned completely black.

He wrote the preface to the 'Collected Poems from the Orchid Pavilion', on 22 April 353, to commemorate a springtime gathering of forty-one notable literati members at the scenic piedmont outside modern Shaoxing. As part of the entertainment, wine-cups were floated down a winding brook, and the guests were asked to write a poem before the cups passed their seats or else drink a forfeit. Twenty-six guests were able to comply, and Wang Xizhi wrote a rather melancholy introduction to the resulting volume. This has since become the single most celebrated calligraphic work in Chinese history. The Tang Emperor Taizong (Biography 34) was said to have fallen so deeply in love with this piece of art that he ordered the original copy be buried with him (the emperor also personally wrote Wang Xizhi's biography in the 'History of the Jin'). Today only copies survive, the earliest dating back to the early Tang dynasty. One was a favourite of the Qianlong emperor (Biography 83) and kept in his study in the Forbidden City.

Wang Xizhi's family was Daoist, and he is said to have composed a lengthy Daoist scripture in exchange for a flock of beautiful white geese that he coveted. His youngest son also became a celebrated calligrapher.

Wang Xizhi, who died at the age of fifty-eight, is still known as China's great calligrapher-sage.

Wang Xizhi in a pavilion watching geese, painted by the Yuan dynasty artist Qian Xuan.

28. KUMARAJIVA (c. 344–413)
Translator of Buddhist sutras

Kumarajiva was born c. 344 to a father said to be descended from a hereditary Chief Minister's family in India, hence the name Kumara or 'prince'. His father abandoned the palace to become a Buddhist monk and travel to Central Asia. The king of Qiuci (present-day Kuche in Xinjiang) invited him to serve as the 'national preceptor'. The king's younger sister fell in love with him, so he abandoned monkhood and married her; Kumarajiva was their first-born son. Both his parents remained devout Buddhists, his mother eventually divorcing her husband to become a nun and taking Kumarajiva to Kashmir to study Buddhism for some thirteen years.

Kumarajiva returned to Qiuci at the age of about nineteen, and his fame as a Buddhist teacher soon spread. When Emperor Fu Jian of the proto-Tibetan Former Qin dynasty in northern China despatched an expeditionary force to Central Asia in 382, one of the ostensible objectives was to bring Kumarajiva to court, which was accomplished. When the Former Qin dynasty collapsed,

Statue of Kumarajiva.

Kumarajiva was retained by the ruler of the proto-Tibetan Later Liang when he studied Chinese. In 401, the Later Liang was defeated by another proto-Tibetan power, the Later Qin, whose Buddhist ruler welcomed Kumarajiva to the capital, Chang'an.

Kumarajiva headed the first ever court-sponsored project to translate Buddhist sutras into Chinese. With his mixed Indo-Central Asian parentage, command of Chinese and mastery of Buddhist scriptures and doctrines, Kumarajiva was uniquely fitted to improve on the existing translations.

The texts were first translated orally, then transcribed and compared with the Sanskrit original; then they underwent further checks to produce a faithful yet elegant Chinese version. Nonetheless, Kumarajiva described translation as the thankless task of 'chewing rice to feed another person'.

Within about a dozen years, Kumarajiva's team translated thirty-five sutras totalling 294 scrolls, an achievement exceeded only by the Tang dynasty master Xuanzang (Biography 35). Kumarajiva's versions of the sutras continue to be used today, and they represent the first effort systematically to introduce a large body of

Indo-Buddhist theology, doctrine and culture into medieval China. An advocate of Mahāyāna Buddhism, Kumarajiva nevertheless did not exclude the Hinayana (Theravada) school; he also introduced Mādhyamika ('middle school') philosophy.

Kumarajiva died on 28 May 413.

29. TAO YUANMING (365–427)
Hermit poet

Tao Yuanming, also known as Tao Qian, was, according to his official biography, born in 365 in the Lower Yangtze region under the Eastern Jin dynasty. He was the great-grandson of a famous Grand Marshal from a sinicized southern minority group, though the family's fortunes had since declined. Tao Yuanming entered government service, always serving in low-level positions. He served, at different times, on the staffs of two opposing and powerful Jin warlords.

Painting of Tao Yuanming carried in a sedan chair, by Chen Hongshou.

The first temporarily usurped the Jin throne, and the second, after defeating and killing the first, founded the new dynasty of Song (420–79).

In the year 405, Tao Yuanming retired from government service for good, saying, 'I cannot bow and stoop to some worthless local superior for the sake of a few bushels of grain for a government salary!' Until his death in 427, he lived the life of a reclusive farmer. In a short essay widely regarded as autobiographical, he described a 'Mr Five Willows':

It is not known where this gentleman is from, and his surname, first name, and courtesy name are not clear either. Because there are five willow trees by the side of his residence, he is nicknamed Mr Five Willows. He is easygoing and taciturn, and does not crave glory and wealth. He loves to read books, yet does not aim for elaborate analysis. Nevertheless, when he resonates with what he reads, he would be so happy as to be oblivious of eating. Wine is his soft spot, but is often wanting due to poverty. Knowing this, his relatives and friends would at times invite him to drink. He would always come and finish the wine, with the intention of becoming inebriated, after which he would bid adieu to the host and leave without lingering. His residence is dilapidated and can hardly shelter him from the elements. He is dressed in rags and is often short of food. But he is content with such a life. He frequently writes essays to amuse himself and to show his aspirations. He neglects (what are normally regarded as) gains and losses, and intends to live out his life this way.

His many poems, especially the pastoral ones, became enormously influential posthumously. For instance, one of his 'Poems after Drinking Wine' (No. 5) was highly praised by the Song politician-literatus Wang Anshi (Biography 49):

I built my hut beside a travelled road
Yet hear no noise of passing carts and horses.
You would like to know how it is done?
With the mind detached, one's place becomes remote.
Picking chrysanthemums by the eastern hedge
I catch sight of the distant southern hills:
The mountain air is lovely as the sun sets
And flocks of flying birds return together.
In these things is a fundamental truth
I would like to tell, but lack the words.

Key expressions in the two concluding verses come from *Zhuang Zi*, the source of the idea of 'naturalness' to which Tao Yuanming and other Chinese intellectuals aspired in an effort to escape from constricting Confucianism. Characteristic was his essay 'The Peach Blossom Spring', which described a community of ordinary people, descendants of refugees who escaped from the tyranny and chaos of the Qin dynasty, to live a simple and peaceful life without any government in a remote and hidden mountain valley. This utopia was found and described by a fisherman, but nobody was able to rediscover it. The story shows his deep longing for an ideal society before the 'Three Sage Emperors', a reflection of the nostalgia for an idealized past without lords and kings.

30. TUOBA GUI (DAOWU DI; 371–409)
Tribal chief and China's khan

Tuoba Gui was born on 4 August 371, to the chief family of the nomadic Tuoba (Tabghach) group, near Canhepo, a lake in eastern Inner Mongolia. A recent archaeological discovery suggests that the Tuoba originated in western Manchuria, and their leaders, including Gui, were called *kehan* or *khan*. By the time of Gui's birth, the group had migrated to northern China as one of many tribal groups loosely ascribed to the Xianbei conglomerate that had earlier displaced the Xiongnu as the dominant power in North Asia.

Tuoba Gui was born a posthumous son. When he was only five years old, the Tuoba state of Dai, headed by his grandfather, disintegrated, and he and his mother were forced to seek refuge among the clans of his maternal uncles. In early 386, he formally proclaimed himself as the chief or 'king' of the Tuoba, a hereditary position. He soon faced a challenger and sought the help of the Later Yan, a polity set up by another Xianbei branch – the Murong, the first tribal group ever to use the steppe regal title *khan* or *qaghan*.

After re-establishing a coherent Tuoba tribal state, Gui gradually expanded his domain and came into confrontation with his erstwhile ally: the leading Murong power of the Later Yan. In spring 395, the Later Yan despatched a large expeditionary force of nearly 100,000 soldiers under the command of the heir apparent Murong Bao against the Tuoba. Facing the superior Yan army, Tuoba Gui led his followers into a long retreat by crossing to the west bank of the Yellow River. The evasive manoeuvres of the Tuoba deprived the stronger Murong forces of an opportunity for a decisive battle in the summer and autumn months.

The leader of the Murong eventually decided to withdraw on the night of 23 November, after burning all the boats intended for crossing the Yellow River.

The caves at Yungang, a famous Buddhist site. Buddhism flourished under Tuoba Gui's rule.

The Yellow River unexpectedly froze solid barely a week after the departure of the Murong army, and Tuoba Gui led a cavalry force of 20,000 men across the frozen river in hot pursuit. They arrived after six days at the western shore of Lake Canhepo, his birthplace, while the Murong troops camped on the eastern shore by a river, completely unaware of their pursuers. At sunrise the next morning (8 December), the Tuoba cavalry launched their attack from a hilltop, with another unit blocking the escape route.

The Yan army was caught utterly by surprise. Tens of thousands were trampled to death or drowned in the pandemonium. About 40,000 to 50,000 troops simply dropped their weapons and were captured. Only a few thousand cavalrymen escaped with Murong Bao. All Murong prisoners were massacred.

Eight months after the decisive battle at Canhepo, Tuoba Gui adopted Chinese imperial protocol, leading the way for successive dynasties, namely the Sui and the Tang, to unify the entire empire.

In 398, the Tuoba renamed their dynasty (originally founded in 386) Wei, known later in history as the Later or Northern Wei. Tuoba Gui ordered the construction of a new, permanent capital at Pingcheng, near Datong in Shanxi province, and in the spring of 400 personally carried out the Chinese imperial rite in which the emperor ploughs the land. A 'Tuoba characteristic' of his regime can be seen in the 'equal land' system (distribution of arable land according to household size), which greatly increased agricultural production.

Tuoba Gui died a violent death on the night of 6 November 409, in a patricide committed by his rebellious son, Tuoba Shao, then fifteen, when Tuoba Gui was preparing to execute the boy's mother.

31. CUI HAO (?–450)
Han courtier who served the khans

Cui Hao was from a prominent aristocratic clan in northern China. His great-grandfather fought the Xiongnu and the Jie 'barbarians' as a loyal Jin subject. His father failed to move south to serve the Eastern Jin court and submitted to the rising Tuoba power in the north.

Cui Hao and his father were northern literati, well versed in traditional Chinese culture and the established political system. Cui Hao was recruited by Tuoba Gui (Biography 30) as a tutor of the succeeding Tuoba Emperor Mingyuan, and he became a trusted advisor at the Tuoba court.

The overall military and diplomatic strategy Cui Hao designed for Emperor Mingyuan and his son, the ambitious Emperor Taiwu, was the pacification of competing 'barbarian' powers in northern China and coexistence with the Chinese regime in the south. Following his 'north first' strategy, the Tuoba soon became the undisputed masters of northern China.

Cui Hao offered support in 429, over nearly universal opposition from the Tuoba nobles, to the attack on the Rouran in Mongolia, which resulted in a great military victory and the surrender of more than 300,000 families of nomads. The emperor praised him to the nomads:

> You fellows look at this feeble and bookish person, whose hands cannot even draw a bow
> or hold a spear. But what he has in his chest is more powerful than troops and armours! I earlier
> hesitated to launch this expedition. All the military successes are thus the result of his advice.

Cui Hao abhorred Buddhism (he called the Buddha 'a foreign god') and promoted native Daoism, possibly for strategic reasons. At his instigation, Emperor Taiwu proscribed the 'foreign' faith of Buddhism in 446.

For his loyal service, Cui Hao was rewarded with the noble rank of duke and top appointments, such as Minister of Education. At the court's request, he compiled the Tuoba's 'national history', which was 'published' in the form of stone inscriptions. However, his descriptions of the acts of Tuoba forefathers were regarded as racially insulting, and Emperor Taiwu ordered the execution of Cui Hao and his entire extended clan in the summer of 450.

32. EMPEROR WU (464–549)
Founder of the Liang dynasty

Xiao Yan, the founding emperor of the Liang dynasty (502–57) in southern China during the division between the north and the south, was born in 464 to an aristocratic family that belonged to the same imperial clan as that of the ruling Southern Qi dynasty. Yan therefore enjoyed a comfortable early life and an easy entrance into government service. Despite his posthumous epithet Wu ('Martial Emperor'), he was a talented writer and deeply religious.

During the Yongming reign period (484–93) of the Qi, Xiao Yan was known as one of the 'Eight Friends of Prince Jingling', all accomplished poets. Yet from 493 to 494 he showed his political acumen by helping the Qi prince, Xiao Luan, assume the imperial throne. Xiao Yan was rewarded with the important post of Gentleman Attendant at the Palace Gate, thus starting his political rise. After he frustrated a Tuoba Wei (see Biography 30) invasion in 495, his military prowess was also recognized, and in 498 he was appointed Regional Inspector of Yongzhou, a region in modern Hubei province, which became his power base.

In 500, he launched a successful revolt against Xiao Luan's successor, and in 502, at the age of thirty-eight, Xiao Yan ascended the imperial throne himself and declared the new dynasty of Liang. He was a diligent monarch, getting up early every morning to administer his southern empire, and working so hard that his hands chapped during winter. He lived a frugal personal life, wearing the same hat for three years.

He continued to promote literature, personally collecting southern folksongs and helping develop the new genre of heptasyllabic verse. The 'Literary Selections' (*Wen xuan*) compiled by his eldest son, Xiao Tong, remains an important anthology.

The most significant aspect of Emperor Wu's life was his devotion to Buddhism. This new foreign faith was popular among the southern intelligentsia, while in the north it spread among the uneducated general population. Emperor Wu, originally heavily influenced by Daoism, became more and more attached to Buddhism, and he is frequently depicted among monks, nuns and bodhisattvas in the frontispiece to woodblock editions of the Buddhist sutras.

Between 527 and 547, Emperor Wu made four attempts to become a monk but each time the court and government officials paid the Buddhist monastery huge amounts of money to 'ransom' the emperor back to civilian life.

In early 547, against the advice of many courtiers, he accepted the surrender of Hou Jing, a talented but treacherous northern general of Caucasian ethnicity, who led a revolt the very next year. After a long siege, Hou Jing finally breached the Liang capital (the modern city of Nanjing) on 24 April 549. Emperor Wu was imprisoned in his own palace and died on 12 June of slow starvation.

33. EMPEROR YANG (569–618)
Second emperor of the Sui dynasty

The second emperor of the Sui was born in 569 in today's Shaanxi province to the Yang family, a prominent northern military clan. His mother, née Dugu, was from a Xianbei-Xiongnu family. His father, regent of the Northern Zhou dynasty, the post-Tuoba 'barbarian' power that unified northern China in 575, seized power in 581 and declared the new dynasty of Sui.

As the new emperor's second son, the future Emperor Yang was made the Prince of Jin and appointed Area Commander-in-chief of the Bingzhou region (northern Shanxi), then the frontier facing the Eastern Turk empire. In 584, he married a southern princess née Xiao, the daughter of a puppet emperor of the Later Liang court in the mid-Yangtze region, and a descendant of the Buddhist Emperor Wu (Biography 32).

He was recalled to the capital Chang'an in 586 and put in charge of the metropolitan region. When in 588 the Sui finally decided to conquer the southern Chen dynasty and reunify China, he was chosen as commander-in-chief of the expedition that would succeed in taking the last Chen ruler prisoner early the next year.

The Sui nominally adopted the Chinese primogenitary principle of succession and appointed his elder brother Yong as the Crown Prince, but in late 600 Crown Prince Yong was deposed and imprisoned as a madman. The future Emperor Yang was declared the new heir apparent on 13 December and, to eliminate further competition, he managed to have his younger brother Xiu imprisoned as well. When his father died in 605, the new emperor was said to have appropriated his father's

Portrait of Emperor Yang.

concubines overnight, and also to have put to death his elder brother and the latter's eight sons. Considering the circumstances, there is a strong suspicion of patricide, which even Buddhist sources acknowledge.

Emperor Yang soon initiated numerous grand engineering projects. The first was the construction of an 'Eastern Capital' at Luoyang, mobilizing as many as 2 million labourers. A more costly undertaking, building a Grand Canal linking the Yangtze delta to the new Eastern Capital, was born of the need to link the capital with southern China, 'rice-basket' of the empire. It was also of greater historical significance: the long-operating and still extant Beijing-Hangzhou Grand Canal was originally part of the system built by Emperor Yang.

These exploits and military expansions propelled the Sui empire to unprecedented greatness. Yet the grand achievements came at the cost of enormous suffering for the overburdened populace. For example, digging the Grand Canal was an operation of such vast scope that it required women to join the corvée labour force, there being not enough men to do the work.

The largest share of misery, however, was caused by the emperor's wars of expansion. Under the founding emperor, the Sui had already succeeded in weakening the once mighty Turks, forcing several Turk khans to acknowledge Sui suzerainty, and the emperor tried repeatedly to conquer the small yet powerful kingdom of Koguryo.

The first Sui expedition in 612 was defeated at Pyongyang. Undeterred, and despite growing peasant insurgency across the empire, Emperor Yang led a second expedition in 613. Just when the Sui troops were finally about to breach the Koguryo defence, news came that a prominent Sui general had revolted in the rear and was marching on the capital. The expedition was abandoned and though the revolt was quickly suppressed, it signified that members of the ruling aristocracy were starting to desert the emperor. In 614, a third expedition was sent against Koguryo but troops began to desert to join insurgent groups. The Koguryo king sued for peace and the expedition was abandoned.

A frequent traveller, the emperor started on his third and last southern tour in 616 as peasant uprisings multiplied and the aristocracy became increasingly disaffected. He settled in Jiangdu (modern Yangzhou) in the Lower Yangtze delta, according to legend floating through lavish parks in flower boats with feather-stuffed cushions. On 10 April 618 the imperial bodyguards mutinied, murdering the emperor and his many sons and grandsons the next day. Two months later, on 12 June, the new Tang dynasty was formally proclaimed in Chang'an.

Emperor Yang is one of the figures traditionally vilified, along with the First Emperor of the Qin (Biography 11) and Empress Wu Zetian (Biography 36). Traditional historiography, whereby the history of the last dynasty was written by its victorious successor, involves the justification for the overthrow, which is frequently couched in terms of personal vilification.

34. EMPEROR TAIZONG (599–649)
Consolidator of the Tang dynasty

If Emperor Yang of the Sui (Biography 33) is caricatured as one of China's worst monarchs, then Emperor Taizong of the Tang, born in 599 with the name Li Shimin, is traditionally held up as one of the best. However, the two had many things in common, in addition to being second sons and then second emperors of a new dynasty.

They were, in fact, close relatives. Li Shimin's father, Li Yuan, the founding emperor of the Tang, was a cousin of Emperor Yang. In early 617, sensing that the

Sui was in terminal decline, Li Yuan, then a regent at Taiyuan on the northern frontier, began his own insurgency.

With the critical help of the Eastern Turks, Li Yuan marched his troops towards the Sui capital Chang'an, taking it on 12 December. The next year, the new dynasty of Tang was proclaimed. The founding emperor, posthumously known as Emperor Gaozu, duly appointed his eldest son Li Jiancheng the heir apparent and Li Shimin the Prince of Qin, as both had played important roles in establishing the rule of the dynasty.

By 624, the Tang had largely reunified the old Sui realm and successfully fended off the Turks' encroachments. Conflicts arose between the heir apparent, selected according to the Chinese tradition of primogeniture, and his younger brother, a distinguished military leader who also established as early as 621 an academy to patronize classical literature and scholarship, winning a large Confucian following.

On 2 July 626, Li Shimin launched the coup of Xuanwu Gate, ambushing and killing both his elder brother, the Crown Prince, and a younger brother at the palace entrance. All male offspring of the two murdered brothers were consequently executed also. The Tang founding emperor was forced to abdicate and 'retire' on 3 September. Though standard histories tried to conceal the near-patricidal atmosphere of this succession, a popular Buddhist literary work accused Li Shimin of fratricide and incarcerating his father, revealing that the last years of the 'retired' emperor may not have been happy. While shocking by Confucian standards of filial piety, the violent means by which Li Shimin came to power were in keeping with the principle of tanistry, whereby the most capable of eligible heirs should lead the tribe. This principle was exercised not only in the early stages of the Tang, but also later in the dynasty, as well as by many other dynasties founded by the steppe peoples who ruled over part or all of what is now China.

Li Shimin, posthumously known as Emperor Taizong, began the consolidation and expansion of the new Tang empire. He enlarged the newly established civil service examinations, tapping into a source of Confucian talent and loosening the aristocracy's strong hold on political power. He learned his lessons from Emperor Yang's negative example, adopted a frugal fiscal policy, and encouraged criticism and dissent, exhibiting a tolerance almost unique among China's emperors. These measures, together with the implementation of the Tang's 'equal land' policy of joint state-private land ownership (taken over and adapted from the Tuoba), led to rapid economic recovery and prosperity.

The Tang completely destroyed the Eastern Turk power in 629–30 and captured its most powerful ruler, Jieli Khan, subsequently adopting an enlightened ethnic policy of 'equal treatment of Chinese and "barbarians"', leading to half of

Taizong, surrounded by court ladies,
receives an envoy from Tibet.

the court positions being taken up by Turks who had submitted and other ethnic leaders. The emperor assumed the title 'Heavenly Khan' in spring 630, asserting his sovereignty over the vast steppeland and the nomadic tribes who inhabited it. It was during his reign that Nestorian Christians were allowed to settle in the capital, and the Byzantine Emperor Theodosius sent a mission to his court in 643.

In his mid to late forties, Taizong grew less tolerant and more extravagant. He commanded an expedition against Koguryo in 645, which was no more successful than the attempts of Emperor Yang. Undaunted, he turned his attention westward and initiated hostilities against the Western Turks. Moderating his earlier preference for Daoism, Taizong also became more receptive to Buddhism, likely motivated by the faith's important role in the Tang's 'foreign policy'.

Chronically ill, Taizong frequently withdrew from his court duties and appointed his heir apparent as acting regent for long periods. Yet he clearly felt that maintaining his standing among the steppe peoples was of great importance, because in the summer of 646 he decided to make a journey to the frontier prefecture of Lingzhou to meet nomadic chieftains and have them reassert their allegiance. Taizong died on 10 July 649, at the age of fifty.

Tang dynasty depiction of a pilgrim monk travelling with a tiger,
later conventionally (but mistakenly) identified as Xuanzang.

35. XUANZANG (600–64)
Buddhist pilgrim and translator

Xuanzang is the religious name of Chen Yi, who was born in Henan in 600. At the age of twelve, he followed the example of his elder brother and became a Buddhist monk. Xuanzang established himself as a learned Buddhist master, but he was dissatisfied with the available Chinese versions of Buddhist sutras, often translated from Central Asian versions and by people whose knowledge of either Chinese or the original language was inadequate.

Emperor Taizong (Biography 34) did not favour Buddhism at that time, and Xuanzang's request to leave on a pilgrimage to India was repeatedly refused. He set off without permission in 629 and only managed to leave because of the help of several border officials who were Buddhists. After nearly dying of thirst in the desert, he was detained by the King of Gaochang in Turfan, who wanted to keep him as a teacher. Xuanzang persuaded the king to let him go, and he proceeded through Central Asia to Kashmir, crossing the Pamirs and the Hindu Kush. Xuanzang saw and recorded the two great Bamiyan Buddha statues, in what is now Afghanistan, and after three years he finally reached northern India.

Xuanzang stayed in India for about a dozen years, visiting many monasteries and Buddhist holy places across the subcontinent, including five years of study at the famous Nalanda University, then the greatest centre of Buddhist learning. After collecting a large number of Buddhist documents and relics, he returned to his homeland, arriving in the Tang capital Chang'an at the beginning of 645.

Emperor Taizong now provided ample support for a massive translation enterprise, to which Xuanzang devoted most of his remaining life. The output eventually totalled 1,335 chapters and more than 13 million characters. Xuanzang was also said to have rendered some Chinese texts into Sanskrit, but they have never been found. He died in Chang'an in 664.

Xuanzong described his journey in the 'Records of the Western Regions of the Great Tang'. It describes in detail 110 states Xuanzang visited in Central Asia and India, and another twenty-eight states he heard about. The great importance of Xuanzang's 'Records' is that ancient India lacked a tradition of historical writing, although it produced countless outstanding philosophers, linguists, mathematicians, logicians and other thinkers. Xuanzang's meticulous report is therefore an indispensable source on medieval Indian history.

Xuanzang's travels through Central Asia and South Asia formed the basis of the famous Ming vernacular novel, 'Journey to the West' (*Xiyou Ji*), in which the pilgrim Xuanzang (called Tripitaka, meaning 'Three Baskets [of Scripture]') is accompanied by three companions – Monkey, Pigsy and Sandy – on his long journey to India.

36. WU ZETIAN (624–705)
Empress of China

W u Zetian, also known as Zhao, was, for nearly half a century, China's *de facto* sovereign, and for fifteen years the *de jure* emperor, the only woman formally to be emperor in China's long history.

She was born in 624. Her father, a former lumber merchant on China's northern frontier in modern Shanxi province, joined the cause of the Tang's founding emperor early on and rose to prominent positions. His second wife, from the former Sui imperial family, enhanced his social status. Wu Zetian was the second daughter of the marriage.

Wu Zetian spent her childhood in Sichuan, where her father was Commander-in-chief. In 637 she entered the harem of Emperor Taizong (Biography 34). Upon the death of Taizong twelve years later, Wu Zetian briefly became a Buddhist nun, as was the practice for imperial widows. The succeeding Emperor Gaozong fell in love with her, however, and summoned her back to the palace. Chinese sources, critical of this powerful woman, suggested that this was the resumption of an illicit relationship that had begun when Emperor Taizong was still alive. In the context of the 'barbarian' roots of both Wu Zetian and the Tang ruling house, such a levirate marriage (by which a man took over his dead father's or brother's widow) was not unacceptable; it was, however, considered highly improper in the Confucian context. The relationship may also have been promoted by the jealous intrigue of Emperor Gaozong's first empress, Wang, who needed help in gaining the upper hand over a rival consort.

Wu Zetian bore the emperor four sons. To bring about the downfall of her erstwhile collaborator Empress Wang, she smothered her own newborn daughter and accused the empress, her rival, of murder. Empress Wang was consequently deposed in favour of Wu Zetian, who had herself declared empress in 655. From her new position of power, she forced all her opponents into exile.

Emperor Gaozong was weak and troubled by chronic poor health. In 674 Wu Zetian and her husband were given equal status as 'dual-emperors'. The next year, she was officially declared regent of the empire, with the sickly emperor completely withdrawing from politics. From 678 on, she would receive in the palace, alone, courtiers and foreign dignitaries.

Her eldest son Hong, the Crown Prince, died unexpectedly in 675, widely believed to have been poisoned by his own mother. The next Crown Prince, Xian, was banished to Sichuan, where he was eventually forced by his mother to commit suicide in 684.

Emperor Gaozong finally died in 683, to be succeeded nominally by Wu Zetian's third son, Emperor Zhongzong, who was dethroned after only fifty-five days and replaced by her fourth son, Emperor Ruizong. Before long Emperor Ruizong 'voluntarily' abdicated to become an 'emperor-in-waiting', and, in 690, Wu Zetian formally ascended the imperial throne and changed the name of the dynasty from Tang to Zhou.

In order to consolidate her power she imposed a reign of terror, recruiting informants and merciless officials. She has also been accused of building up a harem of gigolos, including monks. Even the most prejudiced of Chinese historians nevertheless acknowledge her ability to discover outstanding, talented individuals to serve her loyally and effectively.

With these able statesmen in her service, the Tang (or Zhou) empire fared well during her reign. The economy boomed and frontier expansion continued. Measured by the number of households, the population grew by 60 per cent in half a century. In almost all respects, Wu Zetian's long reign was successful.

Wall painting from the tomb of Wu Zetian's granddaughter, Princess Yongtai.
She was killed at the age of seventeen for gossiping about the empress.

When the manifesto of an armed rebellion penned by a gifted poet was read out to her, Wu Zetian was so impressed by the venomous, yet elegantly written, personal attacks against herself that she coolly commented that it was due to the negligence of the Chief Ministers that this young talent had not been discovered and recruited for the court.

She moved the court from Chang'an to the Eastern Capital Luoyang and initiated several grand construction projects. She favoured Buddhism and promoted copying projects that may have involved some of the earliest printing in the world, in particular the printing of a short sutra that foresaw a future female ruler.

On 20 February 705, a palace coup occurred in which several of Wu Zetian's reputed lovers and loyalists were killed and she was forced to abdicate, dying on 16 December of that year under virtual house arrest. Because her offspring continued to rule the Tang for two more centuries, the 'Celestial Empress' received the full honour of being buried together with Emperor Gaozong in a massive tumulus outside modern Xi'an. Intriguingly, her tombstone has no inscription.

37. GAO XIANZHI (?–756)
Korean general of the Tang dynasty

Gao Xianzhi was an ethnic Korean who started his military career in Central Asia and gradually won the high regard of Fumeng Lingcha (an ethnic Qiang from a proto-Tibetan group), the Tang Proconsul of its vast territories in Central Asia.

Many states in Central Asia, especially in the Kashmir region, had switched their allegiance to the rising Tibetan power. In 747, Gao Xianzhi led an expeditionary force of about 10,000 troops to attack Bolor Minor, a leading Kashmir state whose king had married a Tibetan princess. Gao Xianzhi marched from the Tang Central Asian headquarters at Kucha (modern Kuche in Xinjiang) across the Pamirs and the Murghab River, successfully capturing Bolor Minor's capital and its king and queen before the arrival of Tibetan reinforcements.

Gao reported his victory directly to the Tang court, without going through the Proconsul's office at Kucha. His direct superior reprimanded him, but the Tang court was impressed, recalled Fumeng Lingcha, and appointed Gao as his successor.

In 750, Gao led an expedition against the city-state of Shi (around the modern city of Tashkent), whose king was brought to the Tang capital and publicly executed.

The Buddha statue at Bamiyan. Buddhism declined in Central Asia
after Gao Xianzhi's defeat at the Battle of Talas River.

Gao Xianzhi also pillaged a large quantity of jewelry and gold as his personal spoils. The betrayal of the king of Tashkent and Gao's greed caused resentment, and the son of the executed king sought help from the Arabs who had conquered Sassanid Iran not long before. This led to the Battle of Talas River.

In 751, Gao Xianzhi commanded a coalition force of 30,000 soldiers to meet the Arab army on the banks of the Talas River in today's Kazakhstan. After five days the Turkic Karluk soldiers in the Tang coalition suddenly reversed their allegiance and went over to the side of the Arabs, resulting in a crushing defeat of the Tang army. Gao Xianzhi escaped with several thousand troops; the rest were either killed or captured.

The Battle of Talas River was a watershed event. According to an unfounded tradition, it led to the westward spread of the Chinese technology of papermaking (although paper had in fact been widely used along the Silk Road for centuries). It was, however, the beginning of the end of Tang dominance in Central Asia. The result was the disappearance of Buddhist, Confucian and pre-Islamic Iranian heritages in Central Asia, and the eventual Islamicization of the entire region.

Gao Xianzhi's career swiftly declined. In the winter of 755, he was asked to command a hastily recruited and poorly organized defence force against the rapidly advancing rebel army of An Lushan (Biography 38), and he suffered an ignominious defeat. He was executed, probably at the beginning of 756.

38. AN LUSHAN (c. 703–57)
Rebel

An Lushan was born c. 703 to a Sogdian father and a Turkic shaman mother on the northeast frontier of Tang China in modern Manchuria. He grew up among the Turks with his mother, who later married another Sogdian, surnamed An. The presence of a large Iranic-speaking Central Asian community as far east as Manchuria testifies to the long-prevailing pre-Islamic Iranic influence among the Altaic people in northern Asia.

In Chinese records, the surname An was mostly given to Central Asians from Bukhara in modern Uzbekistan. An Lushan thus took his surname from his stepfather. He was able to speak at least half a dozen languages and worked as a semi-official middleman in the booming border trade. Implicated in a sheep theft, he was about to be executed, but Zhang Shougui, the Tang military commissioner of the region, recognized his talents, pardoned him and offered him a military post.

An Lushan excelled in fighting the Khitan and related proto-Mongolian-speaking tribes, then the Tang's principal threat in the northeast. He rose quickly and was adopted by Zhang Shougui as a foster son, a custom popular among frontier generals for building up a trusted force.

By 736, An Lushan was already a general of the Guards. He suffered a disastrous loss in suppressing a Khitan 'rebellion' that year and should have faced death by court-martial. But when the case was reported to the throne, Emperor Xuanzong overruled the Prime Minister and pardoned him.

An Lushan advanced steadily to the position of military commissioner in 744. He won the trust of Emperor Xuanzong, who enjoyed the immensely fat general's performances of the 'Sogdian Whirling Dance'. In addition to other imperial favours, An Lushan was enfeoffed in 750 with the rank of Commandery Prince.

An Lushan painstakingly built up a power base. His command eventually covered all three military regions in the northeast, stretching from Shanxi to Manchuria, with headquarters at Fanyang, near modern Beijing. On 16 December 755, he launched a long-planned rebellion. His troops, numbering more than 100,000, swept, almost unopposed, through the Central Plains to Luoyang, the Tang's Eastern Capital, which fell in only thirty-four days.

At Chinese New Year (5 February) in 756, An Lushan formally enthroned himself as the emperor of a new dynasty called Great Yan at Luoyang. A large number of former Tang courtiers and officials swore allegiance. Several months later, the rebel troops routed the Tang force guarding the pass that led to the main capital, Chang'an. This defeat forced the Tang imperial house to flee Chang'an for

Emperor Xuanzong flees the capital during An Lushan's rebellion.

Song dynasty portrait of Li Bai.

the distant southwest and led to the death of the emperor's favourite, plump concubine Yang Guifei (ostensibly at the hands of mutinous troops; see Biography 41).

In January 757, An Lushan was murdered in a patricidal plot. It took six more years for the Tang government finally to suppress the rebellion, with the help of the Uyghurs, but the dynasty never fully recovered.

39 & 40. LI BAI (li po; 701–62) AND DU FU (712–70)
China's greatest poets

L i Bai (also traditionally known as Li Po), the elder of the two great poets, was born in 701, apparently a descendant of exiles in or natives of Central Asia.

Du Fu was born eleven years later (712) into a well-known Confucian literati family in present-day Henan province. His grandfather was a celebrated early Tang poet and bureaucrat, and his father was a District Magistrate.

Both poets showed their exceptional gifts early on, but their paths started somewhat differently. Li Bai never attempted the civil service examinations, seeking entry to prestigious posts through direct patronage instead. However, he failed to succeed at court and expressed his frustration in several outstanding poems, including 'The Difficulty of Travelling' and 'Hard is the Way to Sichuan'.

In the autumn of 742, just when Li Bai was about to give up his political ambition, Emperor Xuanzong finally summoned him to the capital. Aside from his growing poetic renown, the imperial attention was partly due to Li Bai's life-long interest in Daoism, of which Emperor Xuanzong was a follower. Li Bai was appointed to the prestigious Hanlin Academy, and the following two years were his most glorious period. Upon his arrival at court, an elderly statesman and Daoist poet praised Li Bai as 'a transcendant banished from heaven'. The emperor received him in 'the golden palace' and even personally served the poet a bowl of soup.

Li Bai is famous for versifying while drunk, composing three lyrical poems about the extraordinary beauty of the emperor's favourite concubine, Yang Guifei (Biography 41). Despite his celebrity, however, life as a court poet proved restrictive. In 744, he returned to his mountain residence.

Du Fu's mother died shortly after his birth, and he was raised by his aunt. Like Li Bai, Du Fu travelled extensively during his youth and married the daughter of a high court official (Deputy Minister of the Court of National Granaries). Du Fu failed the civil service examinations and was forced into seeking social connections for employment.

The poets met when Li Bai had left the court and Du Fu was still waiting for patronage in Luoyang. Despite the differences in their family background, age, personal traits, literary style and beliefs, their friendship was described by Du Fu as 'like brotherhood'.

The An Lushan rebellion (Biography 38) changed the lives of both poets. Du Fu was captured by the rebel troops but managed to escape to join the new Tang Emperor Suzong. He was rewarded with a post, not of high rank, but very close to the emperor. Before long, however, he was demoted for speaking on behalf of a disgraced Chief Minister. Du Fu wrote poems on the misery and suffering caused by the rebellion. He soon abandoned his government career and moved his family to Sichuan, where he built a thatched cottage in Chengdu.

Meanwhile, Li Bai unwisely joined with a Tang imperial prince who coveted the throne, and who was soon to be defeated by his emperor brother. Li Bai was arrested and convicted of treason. His death sentence was later commuted to permanent exile in the far southwest, and he was eventually pardoned.

Du Fu wrote several poems praising his old friend's literary achievement and praying for Li Bai's survival. Li Bai reportedly died in 762 on the banks of the Yangtze in modern Anhui province. According to legend, he drowned trying to catch the image of the moon in the water after getting drunk, based no doubt on one of his most famous poems, in which he invites the moon to drink with him.

Du Fu remained dependent upon patronage. Soon after the sudden death in 765 of his patron Yan Wu, the all-powerful Military Commissioner of Sichuan, Du Fu left the province. In the winter of 770, he died on a boat somewhere between the River Xiang and Lake Dongting in the modern province of Hunan.

Li Bai and Du Fu are recognized as the two greatest poets in Chinese history, and their poems are still learned by all schoolchildren. Li Bai was the more romantic and imaginative, while Du Fu's descriptive verse was more realistic, providing a vivid poetic history of his eventful era.

Here are brief examples of their poetry:

'To Send to Du Fu as a Joke' by Li Bai (Li Po)

I ran into Du Fu by a Rice Grain Mountain,
In a bamboo hat with the sun at high noon.
Hasn't he got awfully thin since our parting?
It must be the struggle of writing his poems.

North and south of my cottage, spring waters everywhere –
All I can see are a flock of terns that come day after day;
The flowery path has not been swept for any guests,
Only today do I finally open my gate for you.

The market is far, so our supper platter lacks variety,
Our family is poor, so the wine flask holds but old home-brew;
If you're willing to sing with the gaffer next door,
I'll call across the fence for him to finish the last cup.

41. YANG GUIFEI (719–56)
Imperial concubine

Lady Yang, also called Yuhuan ('Jade Ring'), was born in 719 to an old aristo-cratic family. In 734 she was selected as the wife of Prince Shou, son of the reigning Emperor Xuanzong by the emperor's favourite consort nèe Wu (from the clan of Empress Wu Zetian, Biography 36).

Xuanzong came to power through a palace coup in 710 and was formally enthroned in 712. The Tang reached its zenith during the first half of his long reign, when he ruled an empire stretching from the Oxus River in Central Asia to the Sea of Japan. However, as he aged, the once militant and enterprising young monarch gradually turned into an old sovereign more interested in enjoying a good life than in national affairs.

In late 737, Xuanzong's favourite consort Wu died, after court intrigues that led to the execution of three of Xuanzong's sons, including the Crown Prince. The emperor fell into a melancholy state.

In about 740, perhaps encouraged by a trusted eunuch, Xuanzong fell in love with Lady Yang. After a fig-leaf legitimization of the union, the former daughter-in-law became the inseparable newfound love of the emperor. This happened during the short sojourn of the great poet Li Bai (Biography 39) in the Tang capital, and he wrote three lyrical poems celebrating her beauty. They were soon set to music and sung to the couple by the leading tenor of the day.

Both the emperor and Lady Yang were fond of Central Asian music and the 'Sogdian Whirling Dance' introduced from Samarkand. These reflected the

Yang Guifei mounts a horse to flee during the An Lushan rebellion.

contemporary popularity of Central Asian styles, from loose clothing to dance and music. Lady Yang was said to be plump and to prefer loose Central Asian robes to the tight bodices and narrow sleeves of Chinese women's dress. The change in fashion, regarding both plump women and loose robes, can be seen in ceramic tomb figures of the period.

In the spring of 745, Lady Yang was officially named Guifei or Honoured Consort. The emperor expanded the imperial villa at the Mount Li hot springs, near the capital, for her and mobilized the government postal service to deliver her favourite lychees, brought fresh from the tropical south to the capital in days.

The ambitious Turkic general An Lushan (Biography 38) also made use of Lady Yang, who had no children, by asking to become her adopted son. An Lushan finally launched his rebellion in the early winter of 755. He conquered much of northern China in half a year. On 14 July 756, the emperor fled the capital, arriving next day at a postal station named Mawei. There, mutinous soldiers began killing the once powerful relatives of Lady Yang and insisted that Guifei herself must be executed. The emperor was forced to consent to her hanging.

Soon after, the Crown Prince declared himself emperor. After a year and half, the 'retired emperor' returned from Sichuan to the capital, a heartbroken old man, and was soon put under virtual house arrest by his son, the reigning emperor. Both in exile in Sichuan and during his remaining years as a prisoner in the palace, Emperor Xuanzong mourned his lost love.

Half a century after the incident at Mawei, the poet Bai Juyi (Biography 42) commemorated the story in the 'Song of Everlasting Regret', probably the most famous account of doomed love in Chinese literature. The poem includes an alleged séance staged by a Daoist priest who helped the Emperor Xuanzong communicate with the dead Lady Yang. The allusion was likely prompted by contemporary folk legends that Lady Yang was not really killed but smuggled to some remote island. Even today, there are Japanese families who claim to be her descendants, showing the power of eternal love.

42. BAI JUYI (772–846)
Popular poet

Bai (or Bo) Juyi was born in 772 in Taiyuan in today's Henan province to a self-proclaimed 'Confucian' family that in all likelihood originated centuries earlier in Central Asia.

In 799, he succeeded in the civil service examination, becoming a Presented Scholar and beginning his government career in 800. He became a member of the Hanlin Academy in 807, and was appointed Censor of the Left the following year, a position with direct access to the emperor. He took the mandatory 'mourning

Portrait of Bai Juyi.

leave' after his mother's death in 811, but in 815, shortly after resuming his career as a senior staff member of the Crown Prince, he encountered serious political trouble. The original dispute over whether he violated Confucian ethics in connection with some family scandal involving his mother escalated with the threat of public exposure of skeletons in the Bai family closet.

Bai Juyi was demoted to a provincial post. After several assignments in southeast China, he finally obtained prestigious yet largely ceremonial appointments in the Tang Eastern Capital of Luoyang, eventually becoming a Junior Mentor of the Heir Apparent with the noble rank of marquis in 835.

Throughout his life he was a prolific poet, leaving behind over 3,000 poems, more than any of his contemporaries. His style was simple, and it was said that he would not consider a poem finished if it could not be understood when read aloud to a washerwoman. He was also musical, composing the 'Ballad of the Lute' and coining the term 'New Ballad' for an innovative poetic genre, closely related to folk music, that he pioneered. An example of Bai Juyi's poetry follows. The 'Precious Consort' refers to Yang Guifei (Biography 41).

From 'Iranian Whirling Girls'

The Precious Consort stole the ruler's heart with her Iranian Whirl,
And when she was murdered by mutinous troops at Mawei, he thought of her all the more.
From then on, heaven and earth have been out of kilter,
And for fifty years it has been impossible to suppress the dissolution.

Iranian Whirling girl, don't dance to no purpose;
Sing this song several times to enlighten our illustrious sovereign.

Bai Juyi married late, but enjoyed the companionship of several beautiful 'sing-song' girls. Among his children, only one daughter grew to maturity. His younger brother Xingjian, also a Presented Scholar, was one of the first authors of popular romance and reportedly was responsible for a pornographic rhapsody that has recently been rediscovered among the Dunhuang Buddhist cave manuscripts.

Bai Juyi had strong reactions to the Tang's loss of Central Asia to the Tibetans, perhaps reflecting a lingering attachment to his ancestral homeland. In 842, he retired with the honorary post of Minister of Justice. It is said that the reigning emperor wanted to make him a Chief Minister, but that this was vetoed by the powerful Chancellor, Li Deyu (Biography 44) who, as the last standard-bearer of the old Confucian aristocracy, detested upstarts like Bai Juyi who bore questionable

Confucian credentials. One of Bai's remote cousins, Bai Minzhong, however, though still regarded as a 'barbarian', later did achieve the position of Chief Minister.

Later in his life Bai Juyi had a nomadic tent set up at his residence and spent eighteen winters in it, writing thirteen poems in all about his cherished tent. He died in Luoyang on 8 September 846. An elegy attributed to Emperor Xuanzong (reigned 846–59) summarized his legacy:

> Even children know how to recite 'The Song of Everlasting Regret',
> And 'barbarian' lads are able to sing the 'Ballad of the Lute'...

43. XUE TAO (770s–832)
Poet and courtesan

Modern statue of Xue Tao.

The date of Xue Tao's birth is uncertain; she was probably born in Sichuan, where her father held a low-level official post at a safe distance from a northern China devastated by the An Lushan rebellion (Biography 38). Her father died when she was young, and Xue Tao eventually entered the service of the Military Commissioner of Sichuan, Wei Gao, as a 'registered entertainer', or courtesan. Despite his protection, she was accused of taking bribes and exiled to the western border of Sichuan. She was eventually pardoned and returned to Chengdu, the capital of Sichuan. She took up residence by the pretty Washing-Flower Brook, surrounded by flowers, and apparently was supported by a series of patrons who included at least five of the ten successive Military Commissioners who succeeded General Wei Gao.

The best indication of Xue Tao's literary fame was this story: Commissioner Wu Yuanheng, arriving in Sichuan in 807 with the concurrent rank of Chief Minister, assigned her to the post of Editing Clerk. It is not known if the appointment was sanctioned by the Tang court, but Xue Tao was often referred to by her contemporaries as a Lady Clerk, a most unusual position for a woman at the time.

It is also widely reported that Yuan Zhen, celebrated poet, future Chief Minister and best friend of Bai Juyi (Biography 42), fell in love with her when he was despatched by the court to Sichuan as an Investigating Censor in 809. The affection was apparently returned, but Yuan Zhen sought prestige and connections through marriage, and Xue Tao's past was against her.

Xue Tao composed mostly short poems. Since she favoured the colour red, her name came to be associated with the fine, small, reddish sheets of paper that she got the local paper mills to make for her and that she used for writing such poems.

Many sophisticated Tang women who failed to find husbands ended up as Daoist nuns (fewer choosing the Buddhist alternative). Xue Tao became a Daoist nun and died in the summer of 832, leaving behind her emotion-filled verses:

> The days of romantic flower are in decline.
> The good times fade into the distance;
> Not finding a same-heart person to know with.
> Vainly I knot same-heart grass.

44. LI DEYU (787–850)
Late Tang Prime Minister

L i Deyu came from an old aristocratic clan of the Zhao prefecture in the modern province of Hebei, and was himself the son of a Tang Prime Minister. Well educated, he could have entered the bureaucracy through the examination system, but with the contemptuous remark that, 'good mules and horses do not pass through post stations', he opted for the hereditary *yin* privilege.

Li Deyu's government career extended more than four decades under six emperors. During this long period factional infighting at the Tang court intensified, mostly between Li Deyu's 'Li clique', representing old northern aristocratic clans, and a 'Niu clique' headed by the long-time Prime Minister Niu Sengru, representing 'upstarts' rising via civil service examinations. As a result, Deyu's first term as Prime Minister lasted barely twenty months (833–34). But after

Scholars take the civil service examinations, which Li Deyu refused to enter.

demonstrating outstanding results in the provinces, he was again appointed Prime Minister in 840.

Under his administration, military campaigns eliminated a remnant Uyghur component harassing Tang borderlands, after the Kirghiz's destruction of the centralized Uyghur power in Mongolia, and reasserted of central authority in areas such as Hebei, An Lushan's old base (Biography 38). In 845, the court proscribed all 'foreign' religions. Buddhism, though weakened, was not destroyed, but faiths like Zoroastrianism and Nestorian Christianity did not survive this persecution in China.

Headed by Bai Minzhong, second cousin of Bai Juyi (Biography 42), the Niu clique returned to power after the death of Emperor Wuzong in 846. Li Deyu was demoted and exiled, ending his career in 848 as a local revenue manager on remote Hainan Island. He died there two years later. An irony for this last representative par excellence of the northern Han aristocracy is that reportedly some of Li's descendants were stranded on Hainan Island, where they were gradually 'barbarianized' into members of the non-sinitic local minority group.

45. HUANG CHAO (?–884)
Bandit and rebel leader

Huang Chao was born in what is today's coastal Shandong; he became rich through illegally trading in salt, which had been a government monopoly since the Han dynasty. He is said to have repeatedly failed the civil service examination and thereby developed a strong sense of injustice.

In the spring of 875, Huang Chao raised a bandit army in response to an uprising started the previous year by Wang Xianzhi, another illegal salt trader. Wang Xianzhi was killed by government troops in 878, and Huang Chao absorbed Wang's remnant followers, becoming the leader of the uprising with the grandiose title of 'Heaven-Towering Generalissimo'. As the main capital was well guarded, Huang Chao led his peasant army south, crossed the Yangtze, and took large parts of the modern provinces of Zhejiang, Jiangxi and Fujian. In these areas, he exterminated Tang officials and loyalists in the name of egalitarianism, but he rarely set up permanent bases, moving on after each conquest.

The southward march culminated in 879 in the sack of the southern port city of Guangzhou (Canton), then the greatest East Asian centre of international trade. Here Huang Chao's troops massacred the non-Chinese population, primarily Muslims but also Christians and Jews. The massacre was reported in Arab sources but is unrecorded in the Chinese official records. Estimates of the number of foreign residents killed in Canton range from 120,000 to 200,000, demonstrating the scale of Chinese-Middle Eastern trade, which took many years to re-establish.

In mid-880, Huang Chao marched north, crossed the Yangtze, and captured the Tang Eastern Capital of Luoyang on 22 December. The main capital, Chang'an, fell on 8 January 881, forcing the reigning Tang Emperor Xizong into exile in Sichuan. On 16 January Huang Chao proclaimed himself the emperor of a new dynasty called Qi.

While recruiting many low-level Tang officials into service, he demonstrated his hatred of the old order by executing prominent courtiers and killing all imperial clan members trapped in the capital. His peasant army also ransacked royal and private properties. A young poet witness summarized the pandemonium in 'The Song of a Metropolitan Woman':

> The brocades and satins in the royal warehouses burned to ashes;
> Spread all over the Celestial Boulevard were the bones of nobles and ministers.

Huang Chao's success was short-lived. With no economic resources, his regime could not resist government counterattacks. He fled Chang'an in early 883 and was finally cornered in 884, near the coast not far from his birthplace, and killed on 13 July. However, the Tang dynasty never recovered; it was finally overthrown in 907 by Zhu Wen, who had previously served with Huang Chao.

THE PERIOD OF DISUNION TO THE YUAN DYNASTY

907–1368

Population growth and natural disasters (and a declining administrative capacity to deal with them), together with the rising power of regional commanders, led to a series of revolts which ended the Tang and saw yet another period of disunion in which China was divided between many separate kingdoms. The empire was once again unified under the Song in 960, when many of the characteristics of modern city life, with streets lined with restaurants, shops and bookstalls, began to flourish. However, the dynasty was unable to hold the north and the court fled south to Hangzhou, leaving the north of China in the hands of a series of non-sinitic empires, culminating in the reconquest of the whole of China by the Mongols, who proclaimed the Yuan dynasty in 1279. As in previous periods of division, this was a time when intellectual and artistic endeavours were vibrant. The glory of the Song was above all the establishment of Neo-Confucian thought, an impressive synthesis of Confucianism and Buddhism that during the Ming and Qing periods stultified and became an inflexible orthodoxy.

Tianshan Mou

Five Dynasties and Ten Kingdoms

Five Dynasties 907–60:

    Later Liang 907–23,

    Later Tang 923–36,

    Later Jin 936–46,

    Later Han 947–50,

    Later Zhou 951–60

Ten Kingdoms 902–79

Song:

    Northern Song 960–1127

    Southern Song 1127–1279

Liao 907–1125

Xi Xia 1032–1227

Jin 1115–1234

Yuan 1279–1368

The period of disunion to the Yuan dynasty, 907–1386.
(Modern national borders are shown in pale grey, for reference.)

500 kilometres

300 miles

46. ABAOJI (872–962)
Khitan chieftain

Abaoji was born in 872 in the Yila tribe of the Khitan, a nomadic group most likely speaking a proto-Mongolian language. Abaoji's rise was not unlike that of the first Tuoba emperor Tuoba Gui (Biography 30) or Genghis Khan. At the time, his tribe, though increasingly powerful, was not the leading clan of the Khitan. Abaoji spent the first part of his life winning support and defeating enemies within the loosely organized Khitan confederacy, rising to become the commander of the khan's royal guard before the age of thirty.

In 901, Abaoji was elected chieftain of his tribe. Not long afterwards he assumed the title of *yuyue*, the khan's second-in-command. In 907, at the triennial assembly or council of Khitan nobles (similar to the *khuriltai* of the Mongols), Abaoji was elected the new khan of the Khitan.

Traditions die hard, and Abaoji faced numerous internal rebellions by Khitan nobles including his own uncle and younger brothers, especially when the khanship was due for re-election. He managed to thwart all these attempts through a combination of brutal suppression, clever scheming, use of external force and false retreats. Abaoji, already versed in the Chinese language, adopted a Chinese-style political system to maintain permanent power and to establish the lineal succession of the khanship.

He declared himself emperor, probably as early as 916, and adopted a reign title on the Chinese model, becoming Emperor Taizu (of the Liao). He also proclaimed his eldest son as heir apparent, following the Chinese primogeniture rule and ending the claims to succession of other members of the Khitan nobility. In addition to building the first Confucian temple among the Khitan, he ordered the construction of a permanent capital city in today's Inner Mongolia in 918.

Abaoji ordered the creation of a 'large script' for the Khitan language, which was promulgated in 920. This siniform script was cumbersome to use, so he had his younger brother create the 'small script', which was syllabic and adapted from the Turkic Uyghur alphabet. Abaoji developed a dual system of government for ruling his nomadic followers and the increasing number of Han Chinese (ethnic Chinese) subjects under his sovereignty.

In spite of several major and minor skirmishes, Abaoji maintained an uneasy coexistence with the warlords in northern China. After he had thoroughly consolidated his power, he expanded his territory, largely at the expense of his nomadic neighbours to the north and west. Before he could turn his conquering army southward, however, Abaoji died on 6 September 962.

Abaoji's eldest son riding with his entourage.

The khanship then passed, not to Abaoji's designated heir, but to his more militaristic second son, who turned the Khitan state into the fully fledged Liao dynasty, with Beijing as one of its capitals. One of the names by which China was known in the West is Kitai or Cathay, a variant of the old ethnic name Khitan.

47. LI CUNXU (885–926)
Turkic prince and emperor of China

Li Cunxu was born in 885 in what is today Shanxi province, the eldest son of the Shatuo chief Li Keyong, who was later enfeoffed as Prince of Jin as a reward for suppressing the Huang Chao rebellion (see Biography 45). The Shatuo Turks are generally identified as having once been part of the Western Turk confederation, later subjugated by the rising Tibetan power that expanded into Central Asia and northwest China after the An Lushan rebellion (see Biography 38). Before the end of the 8th century, the Shatuo tribes moved from today's Xinjiang into Gansu province. Then, around 807–8, they migrated into northern China, losing more than two-thirds of their original population of 30,000 households to the onslaught of the Tibetan army. They played an important role in fighting the Tang's domestic and foreign enemies, and the Shatuo cavalry was the deciding factor in the final defeat of the peasant army of Huang Chao. As a reward for his loyalty, the Tang house bestowed the imperial surname Li on the Shatuo chieftain clan.

The regional conflicts of the era gradually evolved into a rivalry between the Shatuo Li clan and Zhu Wen, once a member of the Huang Chao army, who eventually overthrew the Tang dynasty in 907.

Shortly after his father's death in 908, Li Cunxu won a major victory against the Liang forces in the daring Battle of Sanchui Mound on 3 June. He spent the next fifteen years gradually conquering the economically stronger Liang polity, and, in 913, he drove the Liang from today's Beijing area. In 917, his forces defeated a large Khitan army.

In 923, Li Cunxu declared himself the succeeding emperor of the Tang, founding the Later Tang dynasty. He took the Liang capital Kaifeng later that year and moved his court to the old Tang Eastern Capital of Luoyang the next spring.

Li Cunxu shared with many earlier Tang emperors a strong love for the performing arts. He not only promoted many of his favourite actors to important political positions, but also personally participated in stage performances. However, he failed to form an effective civil government and conditions rapidly deteriorated, with severe internal strife in the originally united Shatuo group. In early 926, one general after another rebelled. On 5 May, the Imperial Guards mutinied and attacked the palace. Li Cunxu, Emperor Zhuangzong, was struck by an arrow and died soon afterwards. A loyal court musician piled musical instruments over the body to provide the fuel to cremate him.

48. EMPEROR TAIZU (927–76)
Founding emperor of the Song dynasty

Zhao Kuangyin, the first Song emperor, was born on 21 March 927, at Luoyang. The Zhao clan came from Youzhou, in the vicinity of modern Beijing, the home base of An Lushan (Biography 38), under whom his great-great-grandfather, Zhao Tiao, had served as a general. Zhao Kuangyin's great-grandfather and grandfather were both officials under the independent warlords of the region.

Zhao Kuangyin's father was a low-ranking military officer under a warlord of Uyghur lineage, and he subsequently served two successor Turkic dynasties, the Later Tang (923–36) and the Later Jin (936–46). Seeking his own fortune, Zhao Kuangyin joined the army of the charismatic military leader Guo Wei and then became a low-level Imperial Guard in the Later Zhou dynasty (951–60) founded by Guo. He befriended the heir apparent, Chai Rong, who would soon succeed to the throne. Zhao Kuangyin was rewarded with a high-level military appointment

Song dynasty scroll painting of Li Cunxu.

Portrait of Song Taizu.

after showing exceptional bravery in a crucial battle against the Turkic Northern Han in 954.

The talented young Emperor Chai Rong died in 959, leaving a six-year-old son to succeed him. As the Later Zhou court was celebrating its first Chinese New Year under the boy emperor, the news came that the Khitan Liao state and the Northern Han (951–79) had launched a joint invasion. Zhao Kuangyin led a defence force north. Shortly after the army left the capital, a large group of its officers and soldiers called for their popular commander to be enthroned as the new emperor.

The reported invading force mysteriously retreated and, in an almost bloodless coup (only one high courtier and his family were killed), Zhao Kuangyin proclaimed a new dynasty, the Song, but spared the lives of the previous imperial family.

Despite the fact that their support had given him the throne, the new Emperor Taizu was wary of the military. In the summer of 961, he gathered all his former comrades, most of them involved in his coup, to drink a glass of wine. He then stated that an emperor's position was precarious, for a similar military coup could happen again. In an event that came to be known as 'relieving military command after a glass of wine', all the generals present 'voluntarily' requested to be relieved of their military commands the next day 'due to poor health', in exchange for monetary rewards and a life of semi-retirement.

For similar reasons, despite coming from a military background himself and being suspicious of educated men, Emperor Taizu actively promoted the status of civilian intellectuals over the military. As a result, the Chinese intelligentsia flourished in the Song, producing some of the greatest cultural achievements in China's history. However, the policy of promoting culture at the expense of the military, as well as measures to strengthen the central government's overall control of military and financial affairs, had serious side effects, the most prominent being a weak national defence against external threats. The Song not only lost opportunities to subjugate the Khitan Liao, but were also threatened by the independent Tangut Xia state. The most significant legacy of this policy, however, was the permanent loss of (northern) Vietnam, which had been ruled by China for over a thousand years.

For the Song's founding emperor, the early cultural success of his new dynasty came to a sudden end on the night of 14 November 976, when he died after a drinking party with his younger brother, who immediately succeeded to the throne. A Song Buddhist monk, Wenying, described the event as 'the sound of an axe under the shadow of candles', and the circumspect Song historian, Sima Guang, hinted at a coup.

49. WANG ANSHI (1021–86)
Statesman and reformer

Wang Anshi, born in 1021, was from a gentry family in the southern province of Jiangxi. Although at the time China's economic centre had long since moved to the Yangtze valley, the intellectual and political fields were still heavily dominated by northerners. The south was rapidly catching up, however, thanks to the expansion of civil service examinations under the Song and, even more importantly, the flourishing education system, product of the equally flourishing local economy. Wang Anshi spent most of his adolescence in Nanjing on the Yangtze; he placed fourth in the national civil service exam of 1042, becoming a Presented Scholar. He spent much of the next twenty-five years working as a provincial official or magistrate, gaining first-hand experience of the rural economy.

A serious government deficit at the time was made worse by numbers of large estates buying political influence to reduce their taxes and to evade their corvée labour obligations, increasing the burden on small farmers. The Song maintained a regular army of more than one million soldiers, chiefly to fend off the independent Khitan Liao state and the Xi Xia (the Tangut empire) in the north, which constituted a serious drain on government revenue. In 1059, Wang Anshi submitted a ten-thousand-character memorial to the throne, detailing some of the challenges and the need for reform, particularly of the inefficient bureaucracy.

In 1067, a proactive monarch, posthumously known as Emperor Shenzong, succeeded to the Song throne. Eager to revitalize the dynasty, he called Wang Anshi to the capital and appointed him, in 1069, to the powerful post of Vice Grand Councillor, soon promoting him to full Grand Councillorship. Wang Anshi implemented his reforms through a series of 'New Policies', economic, military and bureaucratic.

The economic measures Wang Anshi advocated included government loans to farmers, the replacement of corvée obligation by hired labour paid for by taxes, more equitable taxation through new land surveys, and state regulation of markets and commerce to foil speculation and break up monopolies. In the military domain, rural households were organized into units of ten, and a militia was creayed and trained to partly replace regular army soldiers. The radical reforms met strong resistance from vested interests and conservatives such as Su Dongpo (Biography 51) and Sima Guang (who retired from court politics to write a major history).

In 1074, there was a severe drought in northern China, and resulting political pressure forced the temporary resignation of Wang Anshi and the suspension of the New Policies. Emperor Shenzong recalled him to court the next year. However, the opposition to his reforms grew so strong that Wang Anshi retired from politics for good in the spring of 1076, and he died in 1086.

Wang Anshi was personally frugal and also known for his obstinacy. He attempted to reform the examination system in order to stress wide knowledge of practical subjects rather than elegant literary style. He was also very widely read, noting that he had read all sorts of books including botanical works and had 'dipped into treatises on agriculture and on needlework, all of which I have found very profitable'. He left behind a body of powerful essays and memorable verse.

'Bald Mountain'

My duties took me to a spot by the sea –
there to gaze upon a mountain isle I stopped my boat
as I wondered who had denuded it so;
a villager explained it to me and I quote:

'One monkey on the mountain did chatter,
another followed in playful pursuit;
they mated and gave birth to a son –
a host of sons – and still more grandsons to boot.

Lush vegetation covered the mountain,
roots and berries, at first, they easily took;
they clambered up to the highest places
and, crouching, ferreted out every nook.

Each in this host of monkeys made himself sleek and fat,
while the mountain was utterly ravished;
wrangling with each other to fill their stomachs,
on talk of conversation no leisure was lavished.

The big monkeys found the going tough,
the small monkeys were, of course, all the more constrained;
little by little, they nipped and they nibbled,
till not a single blade of grass remained.'

Though the monkey possesses superhuman craft,
he isn't adept at wielding hoe and plough himself;
the craving he has for fruit and grain
is invariably satisfied through pelf.

Alas for this mountain encircled by sea!
On all four sides they spy, but there's nowhere to flee;
while the progression of life goes on without cease
and the year draws to a close, what plan will there be?

50. SHEN GUA (1032–c. 1096)
Historian of science

S hen Gua (or Kuo) was born in 1032, in today's Hangzhou. His family epito-
mized the expanding class of the well-educated southern gentry, and both his
paternal and maternal clans produced a number of prominent civil service
examination graduates.

Shen Gua was a late child, born when his father, a mid-level government official, was already fifty-four, and his mother forty-six. He was initially educated by
his mother and lived in numerous places, mostly in southern China where his father
was posted, so as a young boy he was exposed to varied environments and customs.

Modern bust of Shen Gua from the Beijing Observatory.

In 1051, while Shen Gua was studying and staying with his maternal clan in Suzhou, his septuagenarian father died in Hangzhou. After the burial the following year, Shen Gua and his elder brother Shen Pi went to request that Wang Anshi, a rising southern literary and political star (Biography 49) and a distant relation, write an epitaph.

Shen Gua entered government service through hereditary privilege devolving from his father's official position. Though he soon rose to acting District Magistrate and successfully oversaw substantive irrigation work, hereditary privilege was a dead-end career route. So he resigned and concentrated on studying for the civil service examination. While staying with his elder brother, who was a District Magistrate in Anhui, Shen Gua witnessed and recorded a major water conservancy project.

In 1063, Shen Gua passed the highest civil service exam and became a respected Presented Scholar. His talents were soon recognized by an influential provincial governor, Zhang Chu, who later married his third daughter to Shen Gua, probably in 1068, after Shen Gua's first wife died. Though this second wife turned out to be an untamable, tyrannical shrew, pulling out his beard with skin and blood attached and driving his son by his first wife out of the home, the political connection proved rewarding. Shen Gua was first appointed Editorial Assistant at the Palace Library (1065), then promoted to Proofreader in the Academy (1068), posts that afforded him access to the vast imperial holding of books and served as a stepping-stone to future ministerial appointments.

Shen Gua enthusiastically joined in the major reforms initiated by Wang Anshi. In addition to his other court responsibilities, he headed the Directorate of Astronomy, hiring a mathematical genius, Wei Pu, to compile a much-improved national calendar.

In 1075, Shen Gua led a vital embassy to the Khitan Liao court on territorial disputes. Though it is claimed that he won a diplomatic victory by arguing the Song case based on his vast historical and geographic knowledge, in fact the Song made major concessions to the Liao. The same year, he was named Provisional State Finance Commissioner, the highest authority in national finance.

Though he is today widely considered a visionary scientist, Shen Gua's encyclopaedic knowledge was not highly regarded by the contemporary elite, who believed that literature was the noblest pursuit. In that respect, Shen Gua was certainly eclipsed by Wang Anshi and Su Shi (Su Dongpo, Biography 51). Shen Gua informed the emperor that Su Shi's many poems contained criticism of the throne, which earned Shen Gua considerable enmity, especially from northern conservatives.

However, Emperor Shenzong still had full confidence in Shen Gua, and in 1080 he entrusted him with the defence against the Tangut Xixia state in the northwest. Taking advantage of the Tanguts' internal strife, Shen Gua secured several initial victories that won him the prestigious honorary appointment of Auxiliary Academician of the Dragon Chart Pavilion and the rank of viscount. But the situation quickly deteriorated when the court despatched another military strategist to the front. On 14 October 1082, Xixia troops overcame a newly built Song fortress, resulting in the loss of more than 12,000 defenders and the collapse of the Song front line.

Shen Gua's responsibility for this disaster spelled the end of his career. He was internally banished, and not until around 1090, after finishing an important national atlas, did he regain his freedom. He settled in present-day Zhenjiang, on the Yangtze, in a villa near a stream he named Dream Brook. In his remaining years, Shen Gua completed his most significant work, 'Brush Talks from Dream Brook'.

The book covered a wide range of subjects, from astronomy, mathematics, geology and medicine to myths and UFOs. He discussed the use of magnets as compasses and was the first to discover that they do not point to the true north. He coined the Chinese term 'rock oil' (*shiyou*) for petroleum, virtually identical in construction to the Latin word, and asserted that it was 'produced inexhaustibly within the earth'. He recognized geological and climate changes by observing fossil seashells on high mountains and fossilized subtropical plants in northern China. He also recorded and described in detail the world's first movable-type printing system. These discoveries and observations led the noted British scholar Joseph Needham to describe Shen Gua as 'one of the greatest scientific minds in Chinese history'. A planetoid discovered in 1964 was named after him.

51. SU DONGPO (SU SHI; 1037–1101)
Literary genius

Su Shi, later popularly known as Su Dongpo, one of China's most famous poet-essayists, was born on 8 January 1037 in a small town in Sichuan. He, his father and a younger brother, Su Zhe, are acclaimed as three of the 'Eight Great Prose Writers' of the Tang and Song dynasties.

In 1056, the father took his sons to the Song capital, Bianjing (today's Kaifeng), on the Yellow River. Su Dongpo and Su Zhe easily passed several levels of civil service exams and obtained the highest Presented Scholar degree the next spring. Su Dongpo's mother died before hearing of the brothers' successes, and they went home to observe the mandatory mourning period, returning in early 1060 to start their official careers. Within a few years, Su Dongpo's father and wife both died. Su Dongpo remarried and left Sichuan for good in late 1068.

The Song court had completely changed, with a new emperor and a reform-minded Chief Minister, Wang Anshi (Biography 49). The Su brothers were conservative and sought provincial appointments away from the politics of the capital as long as the reformists were in power. As Su Dongpo's fame as a poet and essayist spread, in 1079, reformists at court accused him of attacking the throne in his poems. He was arrested and escorted to prison in the capital.

Given the severity of the accusations, Su Dongpo faced execution, but the reigning Emperor Shenzong appreciated his literary gifts, and he was sent on internal exile to the city of Huangzhou on the Middle Yangtze. To feed his family and make ends meet, he cultivated a small farm on the hillside east of the town, built a house there, and called himself 'Hermit of the Eastern Slope' (*dongpo* means 'eastern slope'), a name by which he was subsequently known. He wrote some of his greatest works during these four years in exile, and he took a young, clever concubine named 'Morning Cloud'.

Coming back late from drinking one night, Su found himself locked out by his servant, who was already soundly asleep. He sang a new lyric poem expressing lamentation over never being the master of his own life, concluding: 'I would disappear on a small boat, to live out my remaining years in a faraway wilderness'. Next morning, the poem was the talk of the town, and the local magistrate rushed to his home, fearing that his celebrated prisoner had escaped, but he found the poet still snoring in his bed.

Emperor Shenzong died in 1085, and his mother, Empress-dowager Gao, assumed the regency. The conservatives made a comeback, with their leader, Sima Guang (1019–86), holding the Grand Chancellorship. Su Dongpo was recalled and

Su Dongpo's causeway across the West Lake.

promoted to the prestigious post of Hanlin Academician. As a moderate conservative, however, he was soon forced into the provinces again. In 1089, Su was appointed the Prefect of Hangzhou where he made the major contribution of dredging the West Lake, using the earth to build a causeway across the lake, a landmark that still carries his name.

Su Dongpo was a celebrity whose popularity came largely from his sense of humour and lack of snobbery. He famously boasted that he could happily converse with any being, from the supreme heavenly god to a beggar boy.

Empress-dowager Gao died in 1093 and the political pendulum swung back to the reformist 'New Party' under the young emperor. The following year, the aging Su Dongpo was exiled to the far south, accompanied by his loyal concubine Morning Cloud, who died shortly afterward, at the age of thirty-three.

While in exile at Huizhou in today's Guangdong (Canton) province, he wrote a poem that ended: 'Not to disturb my sweet spring sleep, the monks ring their morning bells softly'. The reformist Chancellor took it as an indication that he was comfortable in Huizhou and ordered that he be exiled still further south to the remote Hainan Island.

The young emperor died in 1100, to be succeeded by his brother, Huizong (Biography 53). In accordance with the standard general amnesty occasioned upon the enthronement, Su Dongpo was allowed to move north once again. He fell gravely ill while stopping at what is now the city of Changzhou in Jiangsu, and he died on 24 August 1101.

Su Dongpo left a legacy of both prose and poetry; he was also a celebrated calligrapher and painter, as well as a fine cook. Dongpo-style pork remains a delicacy.

'Tune: "Immortal by the River"'

I drank at night on East Slope, sobered up, got drunk again.
When I came home it was some time past midnight,
The houseboy was already snoring like thunder.
I pounded on the gate and got no response,
Then leaned on my staff and listened to the river noises.

I have long deplored that this body is not one's own.
When can I forget the restless striving?
The night is late, the wind still, the ripples smooth.
In a little boat I shall put out from here,
Entrusting my remaining days to river and sea.

52. FANG LA (?–1121)
Manichaean rebel leader

Fang La was the leader of a Manichaean sect in the late Song (Manichaeism was an Iranian gnostic religion that spread into China along the Silk Road). The 'Water Margin', a famous pre-modern Chinese novel, describes how 108 mostly northern 'good fellows' were forced by fate to become outlaws, then amnestied and enlisted by the Song court to help pacify a major rebellion in southern China. The tale of these outlaws-turned-government-soldiers was imaginary, but the southern rebellion, led by Chinese Manichaeans, was a real event that deeply shook the Song dynasty.

Of the many religions that came to China via the Silk Road, Manichaeism occupied a special place. It survived in various forms and variations for centuries in vast areas in southeast China, far away from its West Asian homeland, against all odds, not least the joint efforts by governments, Confucian literati and 'orthodox' Buddhists to eradicate it, before its final disappearance after the Yuan-Ming transition.

Fifteenth-century woodcut of a scene from the 'Water Margin'.

Manichaeism was propagated largely outside the Chinese intellectual and political mainstream. The faith created tightly knit and highly cohesive secret assemblies among the rural populace. Playing on a pun between the first syllable of the name Mani and the Chinese word *mo*, 'demon, devil', Confucian literati called these clandestine believers 'vegetarians who worship the demon'. Chinese Manichaeans were noted for their strong egalitarianism, their refusal of idolatry, including ancestor worship, and an Abrahamic monotheistic legacy that Manichaeism inherited from Christianity.

Under the aesthete Emperor Huizong (Biography 53), the Song court imposed heavy taxes. The most hated of all was the so-called 'flower and stone requisition', an ad hoc tribute of rare plants and exotically formed rocks demanded to satisfy Emperor Huizong's obsessive construction and expansion of imperial gardens and villas. Most of the exotic rocks came from southern lakes and southwestern mountain regions, and the subtropical south was a major source of rare plants. Ever since the mid-Tang, China's key economic regions had undergone a southward migration, and the Yangtze River basin thus assumed an increasingly heavy tax burden for sustaining a dynasty still dominated by northerners.

Fang La played upon southern popular resentment of the Song court's excesses. He even claimed that the southeasterners' 'blood and fat' were turned by the Song court into rich 'annual gifts' to placate the two northern ethnic regimes, the Khitan Liao and the Xi Xia.

In winter 1120 the local Manichaean sects risked exposure and persecution by the authorities. Fang La formally launched his uprising on 11 November, initially with only a few thousand co-religionists. After annihilating a government force, Fang La's new regime quickly expanded. On 21 December, the rebels took their first county seat, then their first prefectural seat, then the next prefecture. On 19 January 1121, Fang La's forces took Hangzhou.

The expansion of peasant power threatened the Northern Song court. In addition to its own advances, the rebellion also touched off numerous copycat uprisings in other parts of the southeast, from which the Song drew most of its tax revenue. Emperor Huizong was forced to fire a corrupt tax minister and suspend the widely hated 'flower and stone requisition'. The court also called off military skirmishes with the Khitan in order to organize and despatch a large force to put down the rebellions in the south.

Meanwhile, Fang La's rebellion destroyed Buddhist monasteries and images, burned down Confucian schools and killed many Confucian literati. Such acts alienated local Chinese gentry and many others.

In early 1121, a large Song army arrived in southern China and started a two-pronged offensive against Fang La's Manichaean regime, whose lack of both military experience and broad-based social support was immediately exposed. In a few short months, Fang La was reduced to his hidden home base – a remote and secluded mountain valley. The location of this secret hideout was betrayed by the son of a local landlord killed by Fang La. On 12 May, the valley was breached by government troops. After killing more than 70,000 diehard religionists, the government soldiers captured Fang La, his family and his close associates. These Manichaean leaders were publicly executed at the Song capital on 7 October. An unofficial source (*Qing Xi kougui*) reveals that more than 2 million southern souls fell victim to the major pacification campaign.

53. EMPEROR HUIZONG (1082–1135)
Cultivated emperor of the Song

Zhao Ji, born in 1082, was the eleventh son of Emperor Shenzong (who reigned 1067–85). His chances of succeeding to the throne seemed extremely slim, but his elder brother Emperor Zhezong died without issue in 1100 at the age of twenty-four and Zhao Ji's only surviving elder brother was blind in one eye. While his brothers indulged in their luxuries, Zhao Ji enjoyed books and painting and collected the finest brushes, paper, ink and other articles for the scholar's desk. The influential Empress-dowager Xiang, chief consort of Emperor Shenzong, chose him to inherit the Song throne, and he was known posthumously as Emperor Huizong.

Empress-dowager Xiang died within the year, and the young emperor assumed full power in 1100. He recalled Cai Jing (1047–1126) to court. Cai Jing, a brother of the son-in-law of the late 'reformist sage' Wang Anshi (Biography 49), was a corrupt politician. During Huizong's reign of twenty-six years, he served intermittently as Chancellor for a total of twenty-four years. Other courtiers employed by the emperor were similarly corrupt.

Huizong undertook a number of major construction projects at the capital. He preferred elegant and natural-looking villas, gardens and parks rather than grand palaces. To fill his elaborate gardens, a special and onerous tribute tax of rare plants and exotically formed rocks was imposed on southern China (see Fang La, Biography 52).

The emperor was said to have been a talented painter, particularly of birds and flowers, although it is unlikely that he was personally responsible for all the paintings ascribed to him. He was an innovative calligrapher. The 'slim-gold brush-style' he created was adopted by the emerging Song book-publishing industry as a standard printing font.

Huizong was also an insatiable art collector, accumulating famous paintings, calligraphy and other cultural treasures. He built a special palace with seventy-five rooms to house the more than 10,000 ancient bronzes in his collection, and he acquired a vast personal library of rare books.

Although his harem was filled with beautiful women, Huizong maintained a secret relationship with an artistically talented courtesan at the capital, a private liaison that seems to have afforded him great satisfaction.

Huizong was a fervent Daoist. His construction of Daoist temples across the country further worsened the Song finances and unbearably increased the tax burden on the population. This caused the widespread appearance of Robin Hood-type outlaws and 'bandits', a phenomenon that eventually inspired the popular

Painting of a pigeon on a branch, attributed to Emperor Huizong.

novel 'Water Margin'. One notable uprising, of Chinese Manichaeans in the south, shook the court, resulting in a short-lived restraint of Huizong's excesses.

Limited military successes against the Xi Xia state in the northwest prompted Huizong to entertain the dream of recovering the Song imperial family's original home region around today's Beijing, which had long been under the control of the Khitan Liao dynasty. He concluded an alliance with the emerging Jurchen power in Manchuria to jointly destroy the Liao, who had peacefully coexisted with the Song for more than a century. The alliance exposed the crumbling condition of the Song military forces to the Jurchens, who turned against the Song almost immediately after destroying the Liao. Huizong abdicated in favour of his Crown Prince but was lured back to the capital by a temporary retreat of the invading army, and together with his successor he was taken prisoner by the Jurchens.

After a long and humiliating trip, during which one of Huizong's young sons starved to death, the captured reigning emperor and 'retired emperor' were sent to a remote place in today's Heilongjiang, China's northernmost province, and left to support themselves on a small farm. In a poem he lamented:

> How could I not think of the whereabouts of my old palaces
> That I can now visit only in my dreams from time to time?
> Alas, with nothing to rely upon, even such dreams are becoming rare.

Half-hearted efforts by another son Gou, enthroned as Emperor Gaozong (reigned 1127–62) of the Southern Song in the south, were never successful in winning the release of Huizong, who died in 1135.

54. LI QINGZHAO (1084–?)
Woman poet of the Song

Born in 1084 in Shandong, the poet Li Qingzhao was a quintessential daughter of Song literati: her father, a Presented Scholar of 1076, was described by a Southern Song critic as 'the best prose writer since Sima Qian' (Biography 15). Her mother, who died while she was still an infant, was the eldest daughter of a famous Prime Minister. Her stepmother was the granddaughter of another famous courtier who became the national first-place Presented Scholar in 1030, at the age of eighteen. Li Qingzhao herself married Zhao Mingcheng, then a student at the Imperial Academy and the youngest son of a Prime Minister-in-waiting.

Even before her marriage at the age of seventeen, Li Qingzhao's poems were already a sensation in the Song capital. Her particular genius was to turn daily, commonplace expressions into unexpected yet beautiful verses.

'Tune: "Spring at Wu Ling"; Spring Ends'

The wind has subsided,
Faded all the flowers:
In the muddy earth
A lingering fragrance of petals.
Dusk falls. I'm in no mood to comb my hair.
Things remain, but all is lost
Now he's no more.
Tears choke my words.

I hear Twin Brooks is still sweet
With the breath of spring.
How I'd, too, love to go for a row,
On a light skiff.
I only fear at Twin Brooks my grasshopper of a boat
Wouldn't be able to bear
Such a load of grief.

The first few years of her marriage were happy for Li Qingzhao, who shared her husband's interest in ancient inscriptions and art objects. Her father, a close literary associate of Su Shi (or Su Dongpo, Biography 51), was labelled a member of the out-of-power 'Old Party', and banished from the capital, whereas her father-in-law, a sworn enemy of Su Shi, became a rising star in the 'New Party'. The young couple experienced long periods of physical separation driven by court politics and then worsened by Zhao Mingcheng's frequenting of 'sing-song girls'.

In 1107, her father-in-law died after losing an intra-New Party struggle and the Prime Ministership. This, ironically, brought the couple closer together, living as they did a quiet civilian life in Zhao Mingcheng's home town for over ten years. Li Qingzhao described their life together:

I have a power for memory, and sometimes after supper, sitting quietly in the Homecoming Hall, we would boil a pot of tea and, pointing to the piles of books on the shelves, make a guess as to which line of which page in which volume of a book contained a certain passage and see who was right, the one making the correct guess having the privilege of drinking his cup of tea first. When a guess was correct, we would lift up the cup and break out into loud laughter, so much so that sometimes the tea was spilled on our clothing and we were not able to drink at all. We were content to live and grow old in the world.

This tranquil period lasted until Zhao Mingcheng was appointed a magistrate of two districts in their home region. Then the Jurchen conquest of northern China began (see Biography 53) forcing the couple to flee to southern China. In the chaos, they lost almost all of their priceless collection of inscriptions, bronzes, rare books, paintings and other artefacts. Then Zhao Mingcheng died, in the summer of 1129.

Li Qingzhao quickly remarried, but she then exposed her new husband's fraudulent curriculum vitae, which he had used to obtain his government appointment. She demanded a separation and then paid the price: a two-year prison sentence, because she had violated the Confucian code forbidding a wife to inform against her husband. She was released from prison after nine days, thanks to the intervention of a highly placed cousin of her first husband.

After the divorce, Li lived a lonely life for more than twenty years.

55. YUE FEI (1103–42)
Patriot and national hero

Yue Fei was born on 24 March 1103. He received martial arts training and a rudimentary education. He enlisted in the government army as a foot soldier and may have participated in a failed expedition to reclaim the Khitan Liao's 'Southern Capital' (modern Beijing), during the Northern Song's strategic folly of an alliance with the Jurchen Jin.

The full-scale Jurchen invasion, which began in 1125, destroyed the Song in the north . However, it also provided opportunities for talents such as Yue Fei, who rose through the military under the first emperor of the Southern Song (which had been forced southwards by the Jin). By mid-year 1130, he was a military commissioner with a concurrent civilian appointment of Prefect in the Lower Yangtze delta. From 1133 on, Yue Fei held the commandership of the mid-Yangtze defence, making him one of the top four military commanders of the Southern Song.

Yue Fei enforced strict discipline, which made his soldiers very dependable; this raised his popularity enormously, as his troops came to be known as the 'Yue family army'.

Portrait of General Yue Fei (in green) from a Song dynasty scroll.

Born and raised in the Yellow River valley, Yue Fei was a patriot who dreamed of recovering the lost Song territory. He led a number of northern expeditions against the Jin and its puppet buffer Qi regime, notably in 1134, 1136 and 1140, reaching as far as the ancient Chinese capital Luoyang. All gains proved temporary. He was, however, so highly regarded at court that when his mother died in 1136, he was ordered to 'relinquish his filial feelings', forgoing the long mourning period dictated by Confucian rules. His mother, a patriot like her son, was said to have tattooed the four characters meaning 'ultimate loyalty to the country' on his back.

In the spring of 1138, Qin Hui, a former prisoner of the Jin who had escaped to the south under very suspicious circumstances, was appointed concurrently Chancellor and Military Affairs Commissioner. With Emperor Gaozong's full trust, Qin Hui immediately started peace negotiations with the Jurchen, which led to humiliating cessions by the Southern Song. Yue Fei openly expressed his disapproval of the peace treaty and was relieved of his command in the spring of 1141. He was subsequently accused of treason and executed on 28 January 1142. When Qin Hui was asked whether Yue Fei was guilty, he said, 'probably'. Qin's response has become the standard idiomatic expression in China for trumped-up charges.

Yue Fei was exonerated in 1162 by a new Song emperor, and has remained a national hero. The temple in Hangzhou dedicated to him remains a popular tourist attraction, at which tourists venerate Yue Fei and spit on the effigy of Qin Hui.

56. ZHANG ZEDUAN (EARLY 12TH CENTURY)
Painter of the Song dynasty

L ittle is known of the life of the painter Zhang Zeduan, except that he was born in Shandong province and left behind one painting of enormous significance: *Qingming shang he tu* ('Painting of the Qingming Festival on the River'), which depicts the Song capital of Kaifeng in the early 12th century. This survives mainly in copies, most probably made in the Ming dynasty. The style of the painting is unusual: it is a very accurate, detailed depiction, quite unlike the more common allusive style of monochrome landscape painting. It is also distinct from the highly coloured court paintings of birds and flowers.

Kaifeng was abandoned by the Song in 1126 when it was invaded by the Jurchen Jin, and the Song court moved south to Hangzhou. This approaching disaster is nowhere apparent in Zhang Zeduan's monochrome scroll, which takes the viewer along the river from the suburbs, past the great main gate of the city, and into the

Two sections from Zhang Zeduan's famous 'Painting of the Qingming Festival on the River'.

A scene from 'Painting of the Qingming Festival on the River'.

bustling streets of the city proper. The streets are lined with shops, stalls and restaurants, and are packed with shoppers, travellers, porters and drovers.

The flourishing mercantile activity depicted by Zhang Zeduan is characteristic of the economic progress made during the Song. Agricultural productivity increased in the 11th century, especially with the introduction of new, early-ripening and disease-resistant strains of rice from Indochina, freeing some of the population from agricultural work to develop the handicraft industries, especially textiles, ceramics and book production.

The form of cities changed during the Song also: while the Tang capital at Chang'an (modern Xi'an) had been divided into separate, walled quarters, facilitating a nightly curfew and carefully controlled markets, the major Song cities had no interior walls or curfews – and the markets thereby flourished. The mercantile Song economy made the most of the extensive navigable waterways, shipping goods along rivers and canals across the country and supplying the growing urban populations with luxury goods of all sorts, domestic and imported. Such was the growth in the internal markets that the Song saw the first appearance of paper money and other negotiable forms such as cheques, promissory notes and bills of exchange.

Zhang Zeduan's painting shows the variety of shops and stalls lining the streets of Kaifeng, from three-storey restaurants to smaller, open-fronted establishments with tables and chairs for diners, and little roadside stalls, shaded by matting, with plates of food set on trestle tables. Another mat-shaded stall has a sheet laid on the road with scissors and knives laid out for inspection. Porters haul sacks from boats moored on the river, a flock of pigs is driven through the suburban streets, single mules are laden with large sacks, and carts are pulled by pairs of mules yoked together. There are huge carts drawn by oxen and haughty camels, loaded with bundles, which plod through the great city gates. Men carry baskets of produce on shoulder poles, a trader shoulders a long pole from which hang dozens of hats for sale and Chinese wheelbarrows (with the load placed over the central wheel) are steered by two men through the crowds. There are closed sedan chairs carried by two men on shoulder poles, and a single official in flowing robes with a black, wide-brimmed, stovepipe hat rides a horse through the throng.

One focal point of the scroll is the intense activity around a major bridge on the river, whose structure is very clearly depicted, as is the variety of boats. Passers-by lean over the parapet as a large boat swirls towards the bridge. Men are trying to haul the mast down so the ship can pass safely under the bridge, as others at the prow row furiously against the current, while more crew members push the boat away from the sides of the bridge with poles. Behind them, men on a boat moored on the shore scramble for safety as the boat threatens to hit them.

Zhang Zeduan's painting is a triumph of activity, but also of serenity, depicting tea-drinkers, unaware of the frenzied activity on the nearby bridge, continuing to sip and chat. This astonishing painting epitomizes the urban growth and mercantile expansion of the Song.

57. ZHU XI (1130–1200)
Neo-Confucian philosopher

The ancestors of the neo-Confucian philosopher Zhu Xi were said to be from the border areas of Jiangxi and Anhui. Zhu Xi himself was born in 1130, farther south in coastal Fujian. His father, a mid-level government official, was a Song nationalist during the ongoing struggle between the Southern Song and the Jurchen Jin dynasty.

Zhu Xi was born with a sharp, inquisitive mind. At the age of three, when his father taught him that above his head was 'heaven', Xi asked immediately, 'Then what is there above heaven?' His father died when the boy was thirteen, after instructing him to study with three disciples of the renowned brothers Cheng Hao and Cheng Yi, the two early Song neo-Confucian thinkers. The three teachers were also open-minded towards Daoism and Buddhism.

In 1148, at the age of eighteen, Zhu Xi passed the highest civil service examination to become a Presented Scholar. He did not show great enthusiasm for a bureaucratic career, however, but concentrated on pursuing his studies, exchanging ideas with other scholars, and developing his own neo-Confucian theories and doctrines. In the half century between achieving his degree and his death, Zhu Xi worked as a government official for less than ten years and was attached to the court for only forty-six days.

Instead, Zhu Xi, a firm believer in education, taught for many years. In 1179, he rebuilt and expanded the White Deer Cave Academy on Lushan Mountain and established the Academy's motto, rules and principles. It remained one of the most influential academies in China for eight centuries.

From the Confucian canon, Zhu Xi chose 'The Great Learning', 'The Doctrine of the Mean', the 'Analects' and 'The Mencius' as the core, and these were henceforth known as the Four Books. Using simple, near-vernacular language, Zhu Xi composed commentaries on these classics. In the post-Song era, the Four Books and Zhu Xi's commentary became the basis for the civil service examinations and remained so up until the eve of the Republican era. No doubt partly inspired by their master's own style, and modelling themselves on the highly colloquial recorded sayings (*yulu*) of the Zen (Chan) Buddhist monks of the time, Zhu Xi's disciples also collected his dialogues and commentaries.

Zhu Xi's philosophy stressed the omnipresent 'heavenly principle' (or 'natural law') in all things. While he acknowledged innate human goodness as part of his heavenly principle, he considered selfish human desire a fundamental source of evil and immorality. Zhu Xi's prescription for solving societal ills was to 'illuminate heavenly principle, eliminate human desire'. An advocate of moral resolution, he was not overly concerned with forgiveness and compassion. His actions in 1194 demonstrated his approach when, that summer, the Song emperor Guangzong abdicated in favour of his son. As soon as Zhu Xi heard the news, he executed eighteen criminals on death row before their punishment could be commuted in the general amnesty customarily proclaimed when a new emperor was enthroned.

Similarly, in the summer of 1182, Zhu Xi worked as an investigative censor in eastern Zhejiang province and tried repeatedly to impeach a local magistrate. He accused the magistrate of having an illicit relationship with a courtesan and had her arrested and tortured. Even the emperor was said to have described the quarrel as 'a pointless feud between two pedants'. Meanwhile, the tortured, defenceless prostitute languished in prison for months, until Zhu Xi's successor released her after reading her poem:

> It's not that I love the wind and the dust.
> Rather, it seems that I was fated by a previous life;
> Blossoms fall or open at the appointed time –
> It all depends upon the Lord of the East.
> In the end, we all must depart.

No matter how much we may wish to stay;

If I could have some mountain flowers to decorate my hair.

You needn't ask this slave where she wants to return.

Zhu Xi held prominent official positions, and his fame gradually rose among the Song intelligentsia, but his teachings and theories were not highly regarded by the Song emperors and the most powerful figures of his day. His philosophy was labelled a 'fake theory', and in 1196 a court censor impeached him with a ten-item indictment that included a number of vicious attacks on his personal morality. He was accused of taking two Buddhist nuns as concubines. For reasons that are unclear, he accepted the charges in a humble memorial of acknowledgment. Ominously, many of his disciples in the government received punishment during this persecution, but Zhu Xi continued to lecture his students as usual. He died on 23 April 1200, and was not exonerated until nine years later. His neo-Confucian teachings became the orthodoxy not only in China, but also in Korea and Japan until the modern era.

58. MA YUAN (FL. C. 1190–1225)
Court painter

Born during the Southern Song dynasty in Qiantang (modern Hangzhou, Zhejiang province), Ma Yuan (also called Qinshan) is one of the best-known exponents of traditional Chinese painting. Ma belonged to a family of court painters that spanned five generations, beginning with his great-grandfather, Ma Fen, and ending with his son, Ma Lin, all of whom served the Song emperors as court painters. Ma Yuan himself served under three emperors, rising to become 'Painter-in-Attendance'. Ultimately he received the highest accolade that a painter could hope for, the Golden Belt.

The original family seat was in Hezhong (near modern Yongji, in the province of Shanxi), but the occupation of north China by the Jurchens forced the family to flee to the south, along with the Song government. The founding of the Jin dynasty in 1115 by the Jurchens in the north resulted in the establishment of the Southern Song in the south. Consequently, Ma Yuan spent his life in the culturally sophisticated environment of Hangzhou, which had an undeniable impact upon his art. Beyond these few facts, however, little is known about Ma Yuan's quotidian existence.

'Dancing and Singing Peasants Returning from Work' by Ma Yuan.

Despite the paucity of information about his life, it is clear that Yuan found favour at court, especially under Emperor Ningzong, who wrote poems for some of his paintings, and whose empress, Yang Meizi, is known to have inscribed a number of his works. Yuan had the odd cognomen 'One-corner Ma' because he was given to placing his main figures in one corner of a painting, often leaving the opposite corner empty, and depicting secondary objects in other parts of the painting with fainter ink. These techniques convey a remarkable sense of asymmetric perspective and depth, giving rise to an influential trend in Chinese painting.

Another distinguishing feature of Yuan's painting is its precision. It was said that his work had 'exact severity'. Moreover, Yuan employed the so-called axe-hewn brushstroke, which was made by slanting the tip of the brush, and which he used to depict the facets of rocks in his compositions. All of these techniques together constituted the spare style for which Yuan is celebrated.

Yet many of these features had first been developed by Li Tang (died after 1130), whose transitional style linked the intricate, monumental art of Northern Song to the more intimate, romantic disposition of Southern Song painting. Li Tang was the senior landscape artist in the Imperial Academy during the last years of the Northern Song period. Yuan was not immune to painting flowers and figures, but it was in landscapes that he excelled. He produced several large screens depicting landscapes, but none have survived. Yuan also painted tall hanging scrolls showing steep mountains with plunging waterfalls, burbling streams and soaring pine trees. Ma Yuan's mostly monochromatic landscapes reflect a philosophical approach to nature characterized by identification with an idealized universe.

Yuan is perennially linked with another Academy painter, Xia Gui, in the Ma-Xia school of landscape painting. The intimate landscapes of Ma Yuan and his contemporary inspired an identifiable style characterized by asymmetrical composition and angular brushstrokes. The Ma-Xia school was sometimes belittled by later critics as consisting of 'remnant mountains and toppled trees', an assessment that was due in large part to the weakness of the Song polity, which ultimately lost the whole of China to the Mongols. With the restoration of the Chinese empire during the Ming period, however, the school regained its influence, which extended even to the great Japanese ink painters of the 15th and 16th centuries.

Two of Yuan's most famous works are 'Bare Willows and Distant Mountains' and 'Walking on a Mountain Path in Spring'. The former is painted on a fan mounted as an album leaf. (Round fans, often painted on one side, with a verse on the other, were much favoured by Southern Song Academy painters.) Although the scene consists of numerous elements, they are mostly vague and amorphous, save for the two starkly sketched willow trees and a quaint bridge over a body of water to their left. The other painting displays unabashed pleasure in nature. In the bottom left ('one corner'), a scholar pauses to enjoy the flight and song of a pair of orioles. He is followed by his servant boy, who is carrying the scholar's lute and is so tiny as to be barely noticed. There is only the slightest suggestion of mountains on the left side of the painting, and the entire right side of the composition is virtually empty, save for a couplet describing the scene.

59. QIU CHUJI (CHANGCHUN; C. 1157–1227)
Daoist leader

Qiu Chuji, a Daoist monk, was born into a peasant family in coastal Shandong. Orphaned in childhood, he received little education until he was taken on as a pupil by Master Chongyang in 1167, when he was given the formal name Chuji and the Daoist name Changchun ('eternal spring').

Despite its renaissance during the Northern Song, especially under Emperor Huizong (Biography 53), Daoism faced many challenges, not the least in Jurchen-occupied northern China, stimulating efforts at reform within the movement. The most prominent denomination that emerged in consequence was the Quanzhen ('completing the true [human nature]') school, founded by the eccentric Wang Chongyang. Qiu Chuji was the fourth disciple of Master Chongyang.

The Quanzhen sect represented a syncretism of the 'Three Teachings' in pre-modern China, namely Confucianism, Buddhism and Daoism. It imported many notions from Hindu-Buddhist thought, such as reincarnation and retribution. In addition to appropriating the Heart Sutra, it took seriously the Buddhist and Jain tradition of religious asceticism. The Quanzhen priests were required not only to renounce all worldly belongings, but also to maintain strict celibacy, in contrast to the old Daoist tradition that regarded sexual relations as an important means to cultivate 'vital energy'. In this respect, Changchun could be described as practising Quanzhen teachings to an extreme, for he is said to have undergone self-castration to better concentrate on his religious duties and shun carnal pleasures.

At the time its founder died, in 1170, the Quanzhen sect had spread primarily among the lower classes in northern China. Chongyang's seven disciples not only continued missionary work among the populace, but also started to promote the new denomination to the upper echelons of society. After years of solitary study and ascetic meditation, Changchun played a major role in the latter process, gaining at least two audiences with the Jin Emperor Shizong in 1188, and thereby greatly enhancing the sect's influence.

Changchun assumed the abbotship of the Quanzhen founding monastery in 1186 and became the patriarch of the denomination in 1203, working tirelessly for the church's expansion through social welfare efforts and political associations with people in power.

Moreover, Changchun possessed an extraordinary political vision. Although he had had no direct contact with the Mongols, he nonetheless saw them clearly as the up-and-coming power. From 1216 on, he repeatedly turned down the Jin monarchs' invitations for an audience. With the Jurchen dynasty crumbling,

Posthumous portrait of Qiu Chuji.

counties and districts in Changchun's home province of Shandong started to pledge allegiance to the Song dynasty in the south, but Changchun refused the invitation of the Song envoy.

An envoy arrived from Central Asia at the end of 1219 with Genghis Khan's personal invitation to an audience, which Changchun accepted. On 23 February 1220, Changchun left Shandong with eighteen disciples and headed north, arriving in the suburbs of Beijing a month later. Realizing that Genghis was in the process of attacking faraway Samarkand, Changchun sent a letter requesting the postponement of the audience until the khan's return from the campaign. The Great Khan urged him to travel on.

Despite the protection and assistance afforded by Genghis, it was an arduous journey to cross the vast Asian continent. One of Changchun's young disciples died on the way. After crossing the Mongolian plateau and the Gobi Desert, Changchun's entourage finally arrived in Samarkand in November.

Changchun had three audiences with Genghis in 1222. The khan was interested in finding the elixir of life and, informed by a courtier that Changchun was 300 years old, respectfully addressed Changchun as 'transcendant'. Changchun replied honestly that longevity has to derive from healthy ways of living, rather than a magic elixir; he preached the sect's semi-Buddhist doctrines of pacifism and respect for life. He also described the riches of China, essentially inviting the Mongols to replace the Jurchen Jin regime.

The next year, Changchun accompanied the Mongol army on its return to the east. He then parted with the Great Khan, crossing the Tianshan Mountains back into China and finally arriving in Beijing in spring 1224.

Changchun turned down all worldly gifts from Genghis, but obtained a decree declaring him the supreme Daoist patriarch under the Mongols. Though the 'transcendant' himself died in Beijing in the summer of 1227, the unmatched political advantage he had gained through his meetings with Genghis would make the Quanzhen sect the most prominent and powerful Daoist denomination throughout the Mongol Yuan dynasty.

In the following Ming dynasty (1368–1644), Changchun was beatified by Chinese eunuchs, many of them self-castrated, as their 'patron saint'.

60. YUAN HAOWEN (1190–1257)
Poet and historian, defender of the Jurchen legacy

Yuan Haowen was born in 1190 into a literati family in Xinzhou, in the modern province of Shanxi (near the city of Taiyuan, the home town of the great Tang poet Bai Juyi, Biography 42), then under the rule of the Jurchen Jin dynasty. Yuan Haowen was a descendant of the royal clan of the Tuoba, a formerly nomadic group that ruled northern China from the late 4th century to the mid-6th century, and he grew up a loyal subject of the Jin.

The Jurchen suffered several disastrous defeats, and Mongol soldiers sacked the prefectural seat of Yuan Haowen's birthplace in early 1214, massacring all residents including his elder brother. The Jurchen court was forced to move south from Beijing to Kaifeng, the old Song capital, in the summer of that year, forgoing its link to Manchuria and the sources of manpower there. Meanwhile, the Southern Song had grown prosperous and militarily strong enough to fend off Jin encroachment.

While a strong sense of nationalism developed in the Southern Song, enabling it to resist Mongol conquest for decades, the political loyalty of the population of northern China is an intriguing subject. These northerners, Chinese and others, had lived under 'barbarian' rule for more than a century, or in the case of the region around Beijing, for several centuries. While ethnic strife was no doubt deeply rooted, the 'Northerners' showed scant identification with the Southern Song court. The literati among them, including Yuan Haowen, considered themselves the embodiment of the Chinese legitimacy of the 'Central Plains' and accepted Jurchen rule with little reservation.

This attitude, and clear awareness of his nomadic ancestry, made Yuan Haowen an unwavering Jin loyalist. He passed the Jin civil service examination in 1221, and served the Jin court in the besieged Southern Capital of Kaifeng until its betrayal to the Mongols in 1232. Yuan's only 'blemish' was that, to save his own skin, he participated in the drafting of an inscription in praise of the Jin general who surrendered Kaifeng to the Mongols (an act that in fact saved the starving city population from a near-certain massacre had the city been conquered militarily).

Yuan Haowen lived out his life as a civilian under Mongol rule until his death in 1257 at the age of sixty-seven. His growing literary fame seems to have afforded a relatively comfortable and peaceful living, in contrast to the incessant warfare of the period. Yuan communicated with the famous sinicized Khitan noble Yelü Chucai, who was serving as Chief Minister at the Mongol court. In 1252 he even obtained an audience with Khubilai, (Biography 61) then the powerful younger brother of the reigning Great Khan Möngke, with the object of promoting Confucianism.

Given Yuan's family background, he probably would have been willing to serve the Mongol court. He was of little value to the ruling Mongols at the time, however, because they had shifted their target of conquest to the Southern Song. Yuan instead spent the rest of his life working strenuously to preserve the legacy of the Jin dynasty. His detailed private treatise, of more than a million characters, *Renchen zabian* ('Miscellaneous Edited Materials of the *renchen* Year [1232–33]') was widely credited as the principal source of the official history of the Jin compiled by the Yuan court much later. His *Zhongzhou Ji* ('Anthology of the Central Plains') preserved a large body of writings by Jin authors who would otherwise have been eclipsed by Southern Song authors. The most striking record is his unique witness to the large-scale, genocidal massacres of the Jurchen population by Han peasants in northern China during the chaos of the Mongol onslaughts, an important episode that would have fallen entirely into oblivion without the loyalty of a sinified descendant of 'barbarians'.

61. KHUBILAI KHAN (1215–94)
Nomadic ruler who became emperor of China

The first Mongol emperor of China, Khubilai was born on 23 September 1215, barely a hundred days after Genghis Khan sacked the Jurchen Jin dynasty's Middle Capital, Beijing. Khubilai's father, Genghis Khan's fourth son Tolui, was almost constantly away on military campaigns, and Khubilai was primarily influenced by his mother, a Nestorian Christian, who made sure that all her four sons received a solid education. Khubilai never became a Christian, however, nor did he learn to read Chinese.

Khubilai's elder brother Möngke was elected and confirmed as the Great Khan at two *khuriltai*s (tribal assemblies of leaders of the Mongol confederation) in 1250 and 1251, and he appointed his two younger brothers Khubilai and Hülegü khans of northern China and West Asia, respectively. Because he had grown up at his original feudal property in northern China, Khubilai was the Mongol prince best versed in the Chinese culture and political system, and he employed an able group of Han advisors and staff members.

Facing fierce resistance from the Southern Song, Möngke ordered Khubilai to lead a flanking expedition to conquer China's southwest in 1252. Khubilai completed his first major military campaign triumphantly, marching thousands of miles in the harsh borderland between the Song territory and Tibet, and conquered the independent state of Dali (in modern Yunnan) in 1254. Despite the stubborn resistance of the king of Dali, Khubilai refrained from the customary Mongol massacre. On this campaign, Khubilai met and befriended the erudite Tibetan monk 'Phags-pa (Biography 63). While maintaining the Mongols' traditional religious tolerance of all faiths, Khubilai was drawn to Tibetan Buddhism.

Möngke died attacking Sichuan in 1259, probably from a battlefield wound. After each was proclaimed Great Khan at separate *khuriltai*s, Khubilai and his younger brother Arigh Böke fought a three-year civil war over the khanship, and the former eventually prevailed.

Khubilai saw his future in East Asia, rather than the grand Mongol empire: he declared a Chinese reign title in 1260. In 1266, he ordered the construction of his *Dadu* ('Great Capital') in Beijing, the old Khitan and Jurchen capital. In 1271, Khubilai proclaimed the new Chinese dynasty of Yuan; he finally completed the military conquest of southern China in 1279.

Despite assuming an increasingly obvious façade as a Confucian Chinese emperor, Khubilai developed a deep suspicion of the loyalty of the overwhelmingly Han population, perhaps influenced by the rebellion of a northern Han warlord, Li Tan, in 1262. Though Khubilai suppressed the rebellion, he put in place a racially based social class structure through discriminatory laws and rules that greatly favoured the so-called *Semu* people (literally 'coloured-eyed', but generally understood as signifying 'classified, categorized'), mostly of Central and West Asian origins, at the expense of native Han and sinicized groups. This offered extensive opportunities to former outsiders, and many of these 'assistant conquerors' flocked to China. Among them (it is claimed) was the family of the Venetian merchant

Khubilai Khan and his retinue on a hunting trip.

and traveller Marco Polo, who later published an account of his journey. The Pax Mongolica (Mongol rule across Central Asia) permitted cross-continental trade and exchange that far exceeded anything seen since the Sui and Tang dynasties. Although the mostly Muslim new immigrants met Khubilai's need for sedentary talent and administrative experience, at the same time they aroused resentment among the Han population. Moreover, they began to change China's fundamental ethnic and religious demographics.

Southern China proved the final limit of the once invincible Mongol horsemen in East Asia. Khubilai's further military conquests resulted in nominal submissions and unmitigated disasters. His two invasions of Japan were both foiled by violent storms in the Sea of Japan, especially the typhoon of August 1281. When the Japanese navy named their suicide pilots in the Pacific War *kamikaze* ('divine wind'), they were resurrecting the term that had been applied to the providential winds that wrecked the Mongol armada.

In reunified China, Khubilai brought peace and economic recovery. He also reintroduced paper money, which, despite some initial success, caused widespread bitterness that contributed to the eventual fall of the Yuan. Khubilai's long reign was largely tranquil, although he mourned the death of his influential and favourite wife Chabi in 1281, and that of their son, Crown Prince Chingkim, in 1285. Khubilai died in Beijing in 1294.

62. GUAN HANQING (FL. C. 1240–1300)
Founder of Chinese drama

The playwright Guan Hanqing, thought to have been born in the 1220s, lived most of his life in the Yuan capital, Beijing, until after 1300, taking occasional trips to the south.

During the Yuan dynasty, access and advancement in government careers was largely determined by ethnic and hereditary status. The civil service examinations either did not take place, or were largely meaningless. This left the educated Han intellectuals, traditionally the pillar of pre-modern Chinese society, with few upward opportunities. A popular saying assigned the Confucian literati to the 'number nine' social class, between that of prostitutes and beggars. This political reality necessitated the pursuit of non-traditional career choices by Chinese intellectuals, like that of Guan Hanqing in the field of performing arts. He was an extremely talented and prolific playwright, responsible for more than sixty dramas

Yuan dynasty figurine of an actor.

(*zaju*) of which eighteen are extant, plus many lyric pieces (*sanqu*). He also participated in performances himself.

Guan Hanqing's dramas, written mostly in the vernacular and widely popular,
covered a variety of subjects, including historical romances, legal cases, love stories
and family and social incidents. Through his theatrical productions, Guan Hanqing
became such a celebrity among contemporary Han Chinese that his name was a
sobriquet for other successful dramatists. He was considered the founder of Yuan
drama and the supreme exponent of the genre, the first fully fledged drama in
Chinese literary history.

Guan Hanqing's dramas and theatrical activities typified the separate cultural orbit of Chinese intelligentsia under alien rule. The Mongol conquerors and
their Central and Western Asian 'assistant conquerors' lived a separate cultural life,
largely illiterate in the Chinese language almost until the very end.

Guan Hanqing's dramas reflected anti-Mongol sentiments: clever Han courtiers outwitted villains and hinted at the emperor's lack of Chinese language,
and Mongol nobles were shown assaulting the Chinese with impunity. His play
'Injustice to Dou'e' is an indictment of the notoriously corrupt administration.
Guan Hanqing is regarded as a pioneer feminist because of his many sympathetic
accounts of women characters, and an unusual aspect of his dramas is his praise of
the literati members, which went far beyond the Chinese love story stereotype of
'gifted scholars and beautiful ladies' (*caizi jiaren*).

His openly anti-government and Han-nationalist dramas and writings were performed and circulated with little response, much less interdiction, from the Mongol rulers. Unlike succeeding administrations, which were much concerned with the suppression of potentially subversive literature, the Mongols' only and obsessive concern was to prevent the Han (and Koreans and sinicized Khitans and Jurchens) from bearing arms.

63. 'PHAGS-PA (1235–80)
Tibetan Buddhist leader who created the Mongol empire's script

'Phags-pa, whose original name was Blo-gros Rgyas-mtshan, or 'Gro mgon Chos rgyal, was born to the prominent Khon clan of the Sakya tribe near Shigatse in Tibet in 1235.

Sakya (Sa-skya, 'pale terrain' or 'grey earth') is a toponym as well as the name of the Tibetan Buddhist school and monastery that were closely related to the tribe. 'Phags-pa's great-great-grandfather Konchog Gyalpo founded the school in 1073. Orphaned at a young age, 'Phags-pa was brought up by his uncle, Sakya Pandita, the erudite fourth supreme master of the Sakya school. The boy showed extraordinary wisdom and mastery of Buddhist sutras, and he was thus given the epithet 'Phags-pa, 'saint'.

At this time, during the height of the Mongol conquest, the Buddhist Xi Xia state, with which the Sakya church maintained relations, surrendered to Genghis Khan in 1227, shortly before his death. The Tibetan Buddhist churches saw the encroaching Mongols as offering opportunities as well as threats, and the visionary Sakya Pandita became the first prominent abbot to reach out to the steppe conquerors. He set off with 'Phags-pa in late 1244 for Liangzhou (in Gansu province, at modern Wuwei) in the former Tangut state, arriving in summer 1246 and submitting to the Mongol prince Godan (Koden) at the beginning of 1247. The Tibetan region thus became, largely peacefully, integrated into the Mongol empire, while the empire rulers became followers of Tibetan Buddhism.

Continuing his Buddhist studies with his uncle at Liangzhou, 'Phags-pa was exposed to Chinese, Uyghur and Mongol cultures. When Pandita died in late 1251, he passed the Sakya abbotship to 'Phags-pa, who thus became the fifth supreme master of the school at the age of sixteen. The next summer, the young prince Khubilai (Biography 61), on an expedition to attack the independent state of Dali in Yunnan, invited 'Phags-pa into his camp. The learned Tibetan master was appointed High Preceptor, performing the Tibetan Buddhist 'baptism' ceremonies in the prince's household. 'Phags-pa went with Khubilai to northern China. In 1255, on reaching adulthood, 'Phags-pa was formally ordained to monkhood.

Soon after Khubilai ascended to the Great Khanship in 1260, 'Phags-pa was appointed National Preceptor, in charge of all Buddhist-related affairs in the empire. In 1264, Khubilai also gave him the feudal lordship over Tibet. 'Phags-pa went back to Tibet that year, enfeoffed as a prince by the Mongols, to preside over the administration and the construction of the magnificent southern Sakya Monastery, a symbol of the sect's new authority. The Sakya family, intermarrying with Mongol princesses, maintained this lordship until nearly the end of the Yuan.

'Phags-pa returned to Beijing in the winter of 1268–69. He received an unprecedented welcome from both mandarins and common folk, headed by Khubilai's designated son and heir Chingkim, as if 'he were the Buddha reborn'.

At Khubilai's request, the National Preceptor created a new script, not only to replace the Uyghur alphabet that had been imperfectly modified for the Mongolian language, but also as a unified script for all languages in use in the empire. The 'Phags-pa script, based on the Tibetan script but written vertically, was given the supreme status 'National Script'. Although it fell into disuse after the end of the Yuan dynasty, the large number of surviving documents written in this script (in Mongolian and other languages) provides valuable sources for linguistic studies.

It also represented the first attempt at writing Chinese with an alphabet. Moreover, the 15th-century creation of the highly successful Korean Hangul alphabet is generally believed to be at least partly inspired by the 'Phags-pa script.

'Phags-pa was promoted from National Preceptor to Imperial Preceptor in 1270, and he helped prepare for Khubilai Khan's conquest of southern China. In 1271 he left Beijing for Lintao (in Gansu), then journeyed back to his home at Sakya, arriving in 1276, accompanied by Khubilai's Crown Prince Chingkim. 'Phags-pa spent his remaining years building up the vast Buddhist library at Sakya Monastery. In 1278, at the request of Prince Chingkim, 'Phags-pa completed his religious treatise *Shes-bya Rab-tu-Gsal* ('Explanation of the Knowable'), which became an important volume of the Chinese *Tripitaka*.

Gravestone with inscription in 'Phags-pa's script.

There was, however, internal strife within the Sakya sect, and a Mongol expedition was sent around 1279 to eliminate 'Phags-pa's opponents. 'Phags-pa died at Sakya on 22 November 1280. (According to the Fifth Dalai Lama, he may have been murdered.) Khubilai Khan deeply mourned 'Phags-pa's death and decreed the construction of a great stupa in Beijing to house his ashes. Forty years later, the Yuan Emperor Ayurbarwada ordered that temples honouring 'Phags-pa be built all over China, to be annually worshipped 'with a protocol no less than that for Confucius'.

64. TOGHTO (1312–56)
The last capable Prime Minister of the Yuan dynasty

Toghto was from an aristocratic family of the Mongol Merkid tribe. Like many Mongol nobles, he began serving in the Kesig, the prestigious Yuan Imperial Guards, at the age of fourteen. In 1331, at nineteen, Toghto was already a Chief Military Commissioner of the Imperial Guards. Three years later he was promoted to Associate Administrator of the Bureau of Military Affairs, and in 1338, he was given the concurrent post of Censor-in-chief.

Toghto's rapid rise was largely due to the fact that his uncle Bayan was the dictatorial Right Chancellor at the time. The nephew repaid Bayan's favour by playing a major role in deposing him in 1340, when the Right Chancellor was away from Beijing on a hunting trip.

In contrast to Han Chinese tradition, Mongol officialdom placed 'right' above 'left', and the Right Chancellor was thus the Prime Minister of the day. After the very brief tenure of Toghto's father, the post passed to twenty-eight-year-old Toghto in November 1340.

With a southern Han statesman as his trusted teacher-counsellor, Toghto reversed many of his uncle's blatant 'apartheid' policies, by reopening the civil service exams and allowing non-Mongols to raise horses, for instance. He quickly won the acclamation 'worthy chancellor' in the opinion of the Han Chinese public.

In another act that secured Toghto's place in Chinese history, he presided over the compilation of the official history of the three preceding dynasties: the Song, Liao and Jin. This undertaking had long been delayed by the controversy over which of the coexisting dynasties should be declared the legitimate successor state to the Tang. While Chinese scholar-officials supported the Song, the Mongols strongly disagreed, with good reason, not least that the Southern Song had long acknowledged the Jurchen Jin's suzerainty. Toghto broke the impasse by giving all three dynasties equal status.

Toghto wielded power by maintaining close personal rapport with the last Yuan emperor, Toghon Temür, and the latter's Korean empress, so much so that their son Ayushiridara, later Crown Prince, was raised from infancy to age five in the Toghto household and called the Right Chancellor 'godfather'.

Persistent court intrigues forced Toghto to resign the chancellorship in 1344, but he was reinstated in 1349, thanks to his intimacy with the palace. Mongol rule was in serious trouble due to numerous peasant insurgencies driven by poverty and natural disasters, particularly the 1344 flood that resulted in multiple breaches of the Yellow River. The inflation caused by the Yuan's uncontrolled printing of paper money, to cover constant revenue shortfalls, exacerbated the situation. Toghto directed a major hydraulic project in 1351 to dredge the Yellow River and close the breaches, mobilizing a total of 170,000 corvée labourers and soldiers. It was successfully completed, but the hardship imposed may have helped drive more impoverished peasants into banditry.

A capable and incorruptible minister who was remarkably loyal to the Mongol emperor, Toghto endeavoured to prop up the declining dynasty. He experimented with rice cultivation in northern China, for example, with the aim of alleviating grain shortages in the metropolitan region when shipments from the south were greatly reduced by the insurgencies. He apparently suffered, however, from the prevailing Yuan tendency to vengefulness: when the peasant insurgency worsened, Toghto excluded Chinese courtiers from deliberations upon Yuan military affairs.

In 1354, Toghto led a large Yuan force south to engage Zhang Shicheng, the strongest insurgent leader. But, just as he was about to breach the last rebel fortress, his enemies at court persuaded the emperor to dismiss him. Toghto immediately surrendered his commandership, and the Yuan army of perhaps a million soldiers melted away. This is widely considered the turning point of the struggle, and fourteen years later the peasant uprising swept away the Yuan dynasty.

Toghto died in exile on 10 January 1356, poisoned by his court enemies.

THE MING DYNASTY TO THE PEOPLE'S REPUBLIC OF CHINA

1368–PRESENT

RUSSIA

T he Mongol Yuan dynasty lost control of China to a series of peasant uprisings, finally headed by the charismatic first emperor of the Ming, born into a desperately poor peasant family. The Ming was a consciously 'Chinese' dynasty, harking back to the glories of the Tang in a bid to remove all trace of Mongol rule. However, the peoples to the north remained a threat, and the Ming, too, gradually declined, with an emperor lacking interest in the administration and failing to control corruption, culminating in peasant uprisings. The Ming was overthrown by a Chinese peasant rebellion, but this was swept aside by the superior Manchu armies who rode into Beijing in 1644 and established the last imperial dynasty, the Qing.

Though the Qing flourished at first, the 19th century, in particular, saw the familiar cycle of natural disasters and local uprisings, complicated by the encroachment of Westerners with gunboats. At the fall of the Qing, the Republic of China was established, but central rule was non-existent as the country was divided once again between different warlords, and the Kuomintang and the Chinese Communist Party struggled for supremacy as Japan invaded in 1937. In 1949, the Kuomintang retreated to Taiwan and the People's Republic of China was proclaimed in Beijing.

Ming 1368–1644
Qing 1644–1911
Republic of China 1911–
People's Republic of China 1949–

China from the Ming dynasty to the People's Republic.

65. THE HONGWU EMPEROR (1328–98)
First emperor of the Ming

Zhu Yuanzhang was born in 1328 to a poverty-stricken tenant farmer family in Anhui province in the Yangtze valley. As the youngest son, he grew up tending cattle for the family's landlord. In 1344, while northern China was hit by devastating floods, southern China experienced a rare drought. Epidemics spread, and, within a month, Zhu Yuanzhang lost both his parents and his eldest brother to the plague. Unable to afford coffins, he and his surviving brother had to beg for a small plot of ground in which to bury their dead.

In order to survive, Zhu Yuanzhang became a boy monk in a local Buddhist temple. He found that even the monks were starving, and after two months he left to beg alms on his own. The next three lonely and wandering years were probably the hardest in his life. Yet they provided him with first-hand knowledge of a wide area, as well as exposure to the White Lotus faith, a heretical Buddhist sect heavily imbued with Manichaean elements, whose messianic doctrine was winning more and more converts in the suffering population.

The young monk returned to his old temple for four more years, and he made use of the time to attain a decent education. Then anti-Yuan peasant uprisings headed by White Lotus leaders began spreading, and the old temple was burned down in 1353. Zhu Yuanzhang was forced to join the local White Lotus bandits, known as the Red-scarf Army or Red Army because of the colour of its headdresses. The rebels had a declared goal of restoring the Chinese Song dynasty, to replace the 'barbarian' Yuan. Zhu Yuanzhang quickly proved his courage and intelligence, and the rebel leader was so impressed that he married his adopted daughter to him.

After the death of his wife's adoptive father in 1355, Zhu Yuanzhang expanded his base along the Lower Yangtze valley, conquering the city of Nanjing in 1356. With the major Yuan forces bogged down in northern China, the south became a battleground contested by various rebel leaders. In 1357, a Confucian advised Zhu Yuanzhang 'to heighten city walls and accumulate supplies, but hold off declaration of kingship', visionary advice that greatly benefited Zhu Yuanzhang and was borrowed six centuries later by Mao Zedong (Biography 95) in his struggle against the two superpowers.

The charismatic Zhu Yuanzhang stood out among the rebel leaders and attracted soldiers from the lower classes and strategists from the Confucian gentry. He managed to form a highly motivated and disciplined military force, though luck played a part in his rise – one of his fiercest rivals was killed by a stray arrow during a naval battle in 1363.

In 1364, Zhu Yuanzhang proclaimed himself King of Wu (the traditional name for the Yangtze delta) and set up a court. Nevertheless, he continued to recognize the nominal 'Song emperor', now a virtual prisoner, to tap into the strong anti-Mongol nationalist feelings in the former Southern Song territories.

After eliminating more rivals and disposing of the puppet Song emperor, Zhu Yuanzhang finally despatched an expeditionary force north in late 1367. With the northern expedition meeting little resistance, Zhu Yuanzhang proclaimed himself the first emperor of the new dynasty called Ming ('bright', a term that had special meaning in relation to the Manichaean doctrine of 'light') in early 1368 in Nanjing. In October, the last Yuan emperor fled Beijing, ending Mongol rule.

Zhu Yuanzhang, known as the Hongwu emperor, spent the rest of his life con-solidating the new dynasty. As the first ever southern-origin national regime in China, the Ming showed a much lower tolerance of 'foreign' cultures and matters than all previous dynasties, which is not unexpected given that the Ming largely resulted from an anti-'barbarian' nationalist revolution.

The Hongwu emperor sought to remove all 'barbarian' elements, including language, clothing, personal names, marriage customs and burial practices. The official use of vernacular Chinese was soon discontinued, marrying one's widowed stepmother was made punishable by death, and multisyllabic surnames and given names were dropped. Cremation, a funerary form popular since the introduction of Buddhism, disappeared altogether. Even the right-over-left Mongol custom in the ranks of officialdom was reversed. Where the Mongols favoured the right side as higher than the left in the placement of officials in relation to the emperor at court, the Chinese favoured the left over the right.

The former alien masters and privileged bore the brunt of this 'Chinese restora-tion'. The Ming legal codes even forbade aliens from marrying each other, though the ban may not have been strictly enforced. These measures, plus the adoption of a Confucian anti-mercantile philosophy, reversed the fortunes of the Muslim population, booming during the Yuan, resulting in the de-Islamization of southeast China. More positively, in order to encourage the landless to return to the land and promote agricultural production, for several years no taxes were demanded and free schools were established throughout the country to encourage poor boys to enter the administration.

Sensitive about his lowly family origin, the Hongwu emperor seems to have developed an anti-elitist inferiority complex, and after the death of his wife he became paranoid and despotic. He initiated repeated purges and killings of Confucian intellectuals and even his former comrades-in-arms. Almost all his top revolutionary lieutenants met a violent death.

Portrait of Zhu Yuanzhang, the Hongwu emperor.

Seeking to monopolize power, the Hongwu emperor abolished the millennia-old institution of the Chief Ministership, replacing it with a rubber-stamp imperial Secretariat. He also established secret service and police agencies with extralegal powers to spy on officials and the general population. He was, however, undeniably hard-working, reading and processing hundreds of memorials and documents daily, and punishing corruption. The Ming dynasty he founded would last nearly three centuries.

66. ZHENG HE (1371–1433)
Admiral who sailed to east Africa

Zheng He (original surname 'Ma'), the eunuch admiral who led massive maritime expeditions throughout Southeast Asia and as far as Africa, was born in Yunnan province in southwest China to a Muslim family. He is said to have been a descendant of the Prophet, and his father and grandfather both made the pilgrimage to Mecca. On the other hand, in his official biography in the Ming history, his given name is recorded as Sanbao, 'three treasures', the Chinese translation of the Sanskrit term referring to the Buddha, the Dharma and the *sangha* (the monastic community), and he declared, as a pious Buddhist, that his voyages were protected by the 'three treasures'.

Yunnan was the last stronghold of Mongol power in China proper, finally conquered in 1382 after a bloody campaign by the Ming. A huge number of Yuan loyalists, including Zheng He's father, died defending Mongol power. The eleven-year-old boy became a prisoner of war and was castrated, a standard Chinese punishment for non-adult male offspring of families convicted of treason.

Little is known about the boy until he emerged as a trusted eunuch of the Yongle emperor, the Ming founder's second son, who had seized the throne from his young nephew. Zheng He seems to have played an important role in the usurper's open rebellion in 1399 and in the resulting civil war, which ended in 1402 with the sack of the first Ming capital, Nanjing.

Zheng He's fame is due to his leadership of naval expeditions from 1405 to 1433. The Yongle emperor's motivation for these great voyages is not known, though some surmise the expeditions may have involved a paranoid search for his deposed nephew, thought to have escaped to Southeast Asia, or they may have been intended to overawe Timur, the Muslim ruler of Central Asia and India.

Whatever the emperor's rationale, Zheng He took charge of the greatest naval enterprise China had ever undertaken. He oversaw the construction and maintenance of a huge fleet of several hundred ships that carried nearly 30,000 men, and commanded a total of seven expeditions.

On the first three voyages, Zheng He visited Southeast Asia, India and today's Sri Lanka. In the fourth expedition, the fleet sailed to the Persian Gulf. In later voyages Zheng He not only landed on the Arabian Peninsula, but also reached the East African coast. However, the theory that his ships may have reached the Americas is pure fantasy.

On all his trips, Zheng He dispensed silk, porcelain and other Chinese gifts and goods. He received spices, jewels and other exotic items in return. The most

A giraffe, brought to China from Africa.

interesting objects he brought back were perhaps the giraffes from Africa, which created a sensation in the Ming capital.

Zheng He's expeditions were generally peaceful and diplomatic. However, the large army he brought on the ships did engage in several battles and numerous skirmishes. In 1411 he captured and deposed a local king in Sri Lanka, shipping him back to China. He also brought envoys from many other states, large and small, to China to pay their respects to the Ming emperor.

Zheng He's Muslim background may have helped in his dealings with these communities. He erected a monument in Sri Lanka honouring the Buddha, Allah and the Hindu god Vishnu, and he appears to have been a practising Buddhist who also worshipped the popular deity Tianfei ('Celestial Consort'), the goddess-protector of Chinese seamen. Although he travelled to the Arabian Peninsula and even allegedly to Mecca, Zheng He never undertook the formal pilgrimage.

However grandiose, Zheng He's expeditions suffered from a lack of long-term vision and clear objectives. The Ming court was seeking neither foreign colonies nor trade benefits, but seems to have been making a show of force. After the death of the Yongle emperor in 1424, the costly endeavour was heavily curtailed. During the reign of the Xuande emperor (1426–35), Zheng He undertook his seventh and final voyage. He died on this trip in the spring of 1433, somewhere on the Indian Ocean near Calcutta, and was buried at sea. Many of the records of his voyages disappeared, some say to discourage future rulers from such extravagant and costly enterprises that brought no benefit to the ordinary people.

67. WANG YANGMING (1472–1529)
Neo-Confucian philosopher

Wang Yangming was born in 1472 to a highly intellectual family in Zhejiang province. Nine years after his birth, his father Wang Hua achieved first place in the nation's highest civil service examination. Wang Hua was also known for having found a bag of gold when he was a child and returned it to its drunken owner. Wang Yangming lived in Beijing with his father and showed a precocious interest in military affairs. He also enjoyed riding out beyond the Ming Great Wall, wandering in frontier territory for days.

Wang Yangming obtained the Presented Scholar degree in 1499 and started his government career. In 1505, driven by Confucian moral courage, he confronted the powerful eunuch Liu Jin and was severely punished. After surviving a nearly fatal court flogging, he was exiled to a remote post station in the southwest province of Guizhou, where the hard life prompted a personal revelation. He began to form and teach his philosophy of unifying knowledge and action.

This philosophy was largely a reaction to the duplicitous tendencies of the neo-Confucian orthodoxy expounded by Zhu Xi (Biography 57), which had reached a point such that the popular term for neo-Confucianism, *daoxue*, was becoming a synonym for hypocrisy.

After the fall of Liu Jin, Wang Yangming was appointed Grand Coordinator for southern Jiangxi in 1517 and continued his rise to important provincial and court posts. His prominence in politics came largely from his superb military leadership. For a civilian official and the product of civil service exams, Wang Yangming was unusual in commanding three major and highly successful military campaigns. In 1517, he pacified a peasant insurgency in southern Jiangxi. Two years later, an ambitious Ming royal prince attempted to usurp the throne, but his revolt was put down by Wang Yangming in little more than a month. In 1527–28, shortly before his death, Yangming suppressed ethnic uprisings in Guangxi by a combination of magnanimous pardons and surprise raids. For these military exploits, he was given the rank of earl.

Wang Yangming's fame derives from the new neo-Confucian philosophy and thought he developed and tirelessly preached. As the principal proponent of the School of Mind, he believed that it is not the world that shapes the mind, but the mind that gives reason to and influences the world. Physical objects do not exist apart from the human mind. This view not only echoes Buddhist ontology, but has close parallels with the principle of modern physics that declares that physical phenomena and their observer are intrinsically related.

Wang Yangming borrowed heavily from the Zen (Chinese: Chan) school of Buddhism and proposed a form of meditation for cleansing the human mind of selfish desires, which led his opponents to accuse him of being a crypto-Buddhist. However, Wang Yangming advocated proactive involvement in worldly affairs based on his moral principles, opposing earlier neo-Confucian thinking that valued knowledge over action. Wang Yangming sought sanction in the ancient sage Mencius to support his view that knowledge and action must go hand in hand. He also proposed that all human beings from the time of their birth were capable of distinguishing good from evil.

Like his neo-Confucian predecessor Zhu Xi, Wang Yangming spent a great deal of time teaching. His philosophy, like that of Zhu Xi, eventually spread beyond national boundaries, particularly into pre-modern Japan.

Wang Yangming provoked the enmity of the staunch followers of the old school. One such once chose Wang Yangming's theory as the subject for a national civil service examination, with the intention of embarrassing the upstart philosopher. The action backfired and only increased Wang Yangming's prestige.

His military achievements also led to jealousy. A court eunuch challenged Wang Yangming's military credentials by asking the philosopher for an archery demonstration in front of the troops. Yangming calmly scored three hits in three shots, to the cheers of the watching soldiers.

Such antagonism prompted Yangming to retire from government service and devote himself to teaching in his home province. The court recalled him, though he was already in poor health, when there was trouble in the south. After loyally executing his duties, Yangming died on 9 January 1529, in a government boat in Jiangxi midway to his home. His final words in response to a disciple about his will were, 'My heart is open as the day. Nothing else needs to be said'.

68. HAI RUI (1514–87)
Incorruptible official

Hai Rui was born on Hainan Island, China's southernmost landmass after the secession of Vietnam. The family name came from a forefather named Haida'er, the common transcription of the popular Muslim name Haydar. Haydar ('lion') was an epithet of Alī ibn Abī-Tālib, the cousin and son-in-law of the Prophet, and the name was popular among the Shi'a, so the Hai clan may well have descended from that denomination of Islam.

Due to the extensive de-Islamization of southeast China after the founding of the Ming dynasty in 1368 (see Zhu Yuanzhang, Biography 65), by the time Hai Rui was born, there was little indication of Islamic faith left in the clan, which had become a traditional Confucian family. Unfortunately, when Hai Rui was small, his father, a stipendiary student at a government school, died, leaving him to grow up in poverty with his widowed mother, who instilled a strong sense of Confucian morality in her son.

In 1549, at the relatively late age of thirty-five, Hai Rui passed the provincial examination, but failed the metropolitan examination in Beijing the following year. He decided to enter government service without the Metropolitan Graduate degree. This lower entry point led to his first appointment as the principal of a state Confucian school in Fujian in 1553.

In 1558, Hai Rui was promoted to District Magistrate in a poor mountainous district in Zhejiang province. It was here that Hai Rui first made his name as an incorruptible and uncompromising official, first by arresting the playboy son of a prominent Governor-general passing through his district, and then by providing an excessively parsimonious reception to an extravagant and all-powerful Censor-in-chief on a supervising tour of eight southern provinces, causing shock in a social system where unctuous flattery of one's superiors was the norm.

In 1564, Hai Rui became an auditor-secretary in the Ministry of Revenue in the capital Beijing. The Jiajing emperor, like several other mid- to late-Ming monarchs, showed little interest in day-to-day governing, failing to hold court for over twenty years. There was a general decline of the welfare of the empire, marked by an increasing tax burden on the populace and rampant corruption in the government. Hai Rui decided to submit a memorial criticizing the emperor for a long list of shortcomings.

Anticipating the emperor's likely reaction, Hai Rui entrusted his elderly mother to friends, dismissed his servants and bought a coffin for himself. The enraged emperor ordered his arrest, but somehow never signed the execution warrant. Hai

Painting of Hai Rui, from his tomb in Haikou.

Rui was released from prison after the emperor's death in January 1567. He became a national hero for his uprightness.

However, Hai Rui's uncompromising comportment made him unpopular with fellow bureaucrats. After serving as Assistant Censor-in-chief in the rich southern province of Jiangsu, he was forced into retirement in 1571. He was recalled in 1585, at the advanced age of seventy-one, to high but largely ceremonial posts in Nanjing. He died two years later, leaving no sons and little money. His funeral had to be paid for by donations, but it was said to have been attended and observed by more than a million common people, extending several hundred *li* (roughly 100 miles or 160 km) along the Yangtze.

Hai Rui's national fame as an upright official who dared to criticize the emperor was to be resurrected four centuries later. In 1961, Wu Han (1909–69), the leading historian of the Ming, also Deputy Mayor of Beijing, published a play called 'Hai Rui Dismissed from Office'. In November 1965, Yao Wenyuan, a close associate of Mao's wife Jiang Qing, published a ferocious attack on Wu Han's play. This was the opening shot of the Great Proletarian Cultural Revolution that would throw China into chaos for the next ten years. As Yao Wenyuan intimated, the drama, published during the aftermath of the Great Leap Forward, which saw more than 30 million Chinese peasants starve to death, was perceived as a veiled criticism of the modern 'emperor' (Mao Zedong) for the catastrophe. Unlike Hai Rui, whose life was spared by the Ming emperor, Wu Han, though a loyal Communist, perished during the Cultural Revolution, together with his wife and adopted teenage daughter.

69. LI SHIZHEN (1518–93)
Physician and naturalist

Li Shizhen was born in 1518 into a physician's family at Qizhou, in modern Hubei province. Both his grandfather and father practised medicine. Doctors in pre-modern China were educated intellectuals and commanded moral respect, but they did not enjoy high socio-political status, which was monopolized by government officials who had passed imperial examinations. Li Shizhen's father tried to climb the social ladder via the examination route, but only succeeded in passing the lowest of the three levels to become a Cultivated Talent. He then pinned his hopes on his intelligent young son. After easily gaining the title of Cultivated Talent at age thirteen, Li Shizhen failed three times in trying to pass the second-level examination.

Much intellectual energy and creativity was spent on the fossilized imperial examinations in pre-modern China. After his third examination failure, Li Shizhen decided to take up a medical career like that of his father, and he underwent many years of hard study and practice. Shizhen became a well-known physician, treating all sorts of patients, from poor peasants to rich aristocrats. This led to an official appointment with a Ming prince in the province, followed by a recommendation, around 1558, to serve in the Imperial Medical Institute in Beijing, where Shizhen was exposed to the large collection of medical books in the Institute library and many rare medicines.

In traditional Chinese medicine, the most important references consisted of various treatises and compendia of medicines and prescriptions. The volumes in which these treatises were written, over the course of more than a millennium, contained many errors, contradictions and other deficiencies. For instance, two different herbs would appear under the same name, or two different names could refer to the same species. None of the volumes provided a complete list of all the medicines that were prescribed. After years of practising medicine, increasingly troubled by these deficiencies, Shizhen felt a calling to compile a complete, accurate and up-to-date encyclopaedia of all therapeutic materials and their application in Chinese medicine, for the benefit of patients and doctors. He called this epic work *Bencao gangmu*, or 'Compendium of Materia Medica'.

The writing started around 1552. It took twenty-seven years and three major revisions to complete the first draft. Shizhen consulted a total of 993 references, including forty-one previous compendia and 361 other medical books. The compendium described in detail a total of 1,892 Chinese medicines (1,094 plants, plus animals, minerals and other items) and 11,096 prescriptions. Hundreds of these

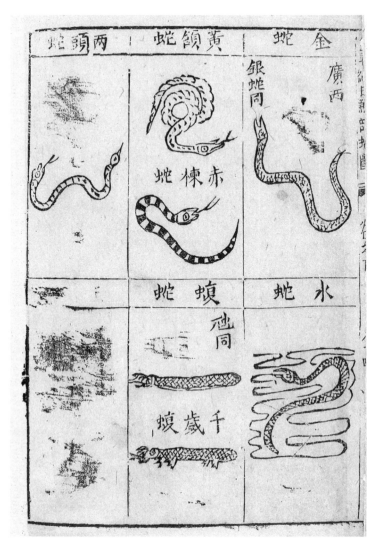

A section of Li Shizhen's *Bencao gangmu*, a vast compendium of traditional medicines and their use.

medicines were documented for the first time. Shizhen developed a well-structured taxonomy to classify the medicines into various categories and sub-categories. The compendium contained 1,109 illustrations and nearly 2 million Chinese characters.

More important than his compiling of previous books, the great majority of listings were based on Shizhen's own explorations, samplings and collections, for which he spent years roaming mountains and forests as well as listening to other people. Such field data and his own practice led Shizhen to challenge and correct many long-existing errors and misunderstandings. Though his work is not free from unfounded theories as judged by modern science, Shizhen did dispel many superstitious and supernatural claims in old medical books.

For years after Shizhen had finally compiled the tremendous work, assisted by his sons, grandsons and students, the huge book did not find a publisher. After a famous scholar-official wrote an enthusiastic preface in 1590, the manuscript was finally accepted by a publisher in Nanjing. Regrettably, the great physician and naturalist died in 1593 before seeing his magnum opus in print.

70. ZHANG JUZHENG (1525–82)
Ming Grand Secretary and economic reformer

Zhang Juzheng, born in 1525, was one of the most successful Chief Ministers in Chinese history. His official title was Grand Secretary, because in 1380 the Ming founding emperor, Hongwu (Biography 65), had abolished the millennia-old Chief Ministership, thereby concentrating and monopolizing imperial power in his own hands. Before long, however, the Grand Secretariat initially set up to assist the emperor became a *de facto* cabinet. The Grand Secretaries, numbering from two to six, assumed the function of Chief Ministers of earlier dynasties.

Though of lowly family origin, Zhang Juzheng was recognized as a child prodigy. He succeeded at the provincial and metropolitan examinations at the ages of fifteen and twenty-two respectively, and started his government career with the prestigious appointment of Hanlin Bachelor, a post widely regarded as 'Chief-Minister-in-waiting'. He rose steadily, especially after serving as the tutor of a prince who would, in 1566, succeed as the Muzong emperor, upon which Zhang was immediately sworn in as a Junior Grand Secretary.

After the Muzong emperor died in 1572, Zhang took advantage of his rapport with a powerful eunuch to gain the position of 'Prime Imperial Aide' leading the Grand Secretariat, a post he filled until his death ten years later. He became tutor and mentor to the nine-year-old boy emperor Wanli, and during this period implemented many reforms to rejuvenate the decadent, two-centuries-old Ming empire. He introduced rigorous, result-based performance reviews of bureaucrats and bureaucratic procedures and conducted a land audit that revealed a large amount of farmland that had been hidden by powerful landlords from the national taxation inventory. His third economic reform was to clean up government taxation by introducing a new tax code (the famous 'single whip' policy) that converted corvée labour to land tax. At the same time, he held down government expenditure and waste. These measures improved the fiscal health of the Ming, and the national treasury was said to be overflowing by the time of his death.

Zhang also strengthened the military by promoting competent generals, building upon a peaceful accommodation with the Mongolian ruler Altan Khan. In 1578, Sonam Gyatso, the first officially recognized (nominally the third) Dalai Lama and the actual founder of Gelugpa Lamaism, arrived at the Ming garrison town of Ganzhou (in modern Gansu province) and sent a letter with gifts to Zhang Juzheng. Recognizing the political significance of good relations with the Dalai Lama vis-à-vis the Mongols, Zhang Juzheng granted the Dalai Lama a title of honour and promised help in building Buddhist temples.

Zhang Juzheng's power naturally created many enemies, who grasped their long-awaited opportunity when his father died in 1577. He should have returned home for the mandatory three-year (actually twenty-seven-month) mourning period, but at Zhang Juzheng's insistence, the boy emperor issued repeated edicts ordering him to 'forgo filial feelings' so that he could remain at his post. A tidal wave of memoranda attacked this blatant breach of the Confucian ethical code. Though Zhang Juzheng survived this grave threat to his power, he lost the moral high ground and much political capital.

The *de facto* regent died in 1582, just before the maturing emperor started to assert sovereign authority. Two years later, Zhang Juzheng was posthumously accused by his opponents of various major offences, and the emperor concurred. Zhang Juzheng's family paid a heavy price: almost all their assets were confiscated, and his eldest son committed suicide to avoid further punishment. Most of Zhang Juzheng's reforms were reversed, and the Ming went into sharp decline.

71. NURHACI (1559–1626)
Founder of the Manchu state

The Ming dynasty was acutely conscious of the explosive power of the northern 'barbarians' – traditional invaders such as the Tanguts, Jurchens, Khitans and Mongols – in preceding centuries. Keeping a close watch on intertribal balances, the Ming adopted a 'divide and rule' frontier policy, using money and force to keep the border tribes at odds with one another. For two centuries, Manchuria had seemed easy to control, for the Manchurian Jurchens were divided into four disconnected branches, and their old Jin dynasty, destroyed by the Mongols

Portrait of the founder of the Manchu state, Nurhaci.

centuries earlier, had left them with no dominant group. Hundreds of Jurchen chieftains accepted Ming titles and fought against each other.

This was to change with Nurhaci, who was born in 1559 to an inconspicuous Jurchen chieftain family that had held Ming appointments for generations.

After the violent death in 1582 of both his grandfather and father in a Ming military campaign against the then-strongest Manchu tribe leader, Atai, Nurhaci went to Li Chengliang, the Ming commanding general (of Korean descent), to demand indemnity. He obtained the right to inherit the tribal chieftainship and the clan's 'thirteen sets of armour'. Nurhaci cultivated a rapport with Li Chengliang, whose prestige at the Ming court helped provide Nurhaci during his early rise with the cover of being a loyal Ming subject. Educated in Chinese, an enthusiast for the 'Romance of the Three Kingdoms', Nurhaci went to Beijing as a tributary chieftain in 1583, 1590 and 1598. Such deep knowledge of China set him apart from rival Manchu chieftains.

Taking advantage of the Ming's deteriorating domestic situation and worsening partisan politics, together with its exhausting expedition to help Korea repel the Japanese invasion launched by Hideyoshi, Nurhaci began expanding his power over other Jurchen clans and tribes, through both matrimony and violence. Because his first target was the tribe that had caused his father's and grandfather's deaths, and because Nurhaci was careful to maintain the image of an obedient Ming subject, the Ming rewarded him with prominent appointments.

After unifying his own Jianzhou Jurchens, Nurhaci expanded his reach to other Jurchen branches, starting with the 'Jurchens from West of the Sea', and finally the 'Untamed Jurchens' whose territories stretched as far away as Kuye (Sakhalin) Island. He also ended the Jurchens' centuries-old blood feud with the Mongols, thus absorbing a large number of Mongol tribes into his fast-growing polity. He ordered the creation of a new Jurchen script in 1599, adapted from the old, Sogdian-based Mongol script.

The Mongols conferred upon Nurhaci the title of khan in 1606 but, in order not to arouse Ming suspicion, he waited until 1616 to declare himself the khan of a new Later Jin dynasty. Two years later, Nurhaci announced his 'Seven Principal Grievances' against the Ming, the first of which was the killing of his father and grandfather, and he led an expedition of 10,000 soldiers to attack them. His magnanimous behaviour towards those who surrendered to him turned the local Han population into his greatest non-military resource.

The growing internal disarray of the Ming, with a weak emperor enthroned in 1620 and control in the hands of a corrupt eunuch (Wei Zhongxian, Biography 73), gave Nurhaci time to expand his conquest, consolidate his innovative and efficient 'eight-banner' system of combined military-civil organization, and to establish his new capital at Mukden (Shenyang). The 'banner' system organized men into fighting units of 300, each distinguished by its coloured banner. Not only did the men belong to a banner, but so did their families, so that men and women who worked as farmers or craftspeople in times of peace, ruled by a hereditary captain, became efficient military companies in times of war.

Nurhaci had four younger brothers, augmented by sixteen sons by his numerous wives and concubines. While many of these proved critically useful in establishing the Jurchen revival and subsequent Manchu insurgence, the northern tradition of familial competition led to instances of fratricide and filicide, notably the execution in 1611 of Shurhaci, a brother of Nurhaci born to the same mother.

In 1626, Nurhaci, attacking the Ming fortress city of Ningyuan in southern Manchuria, was defeated, for the first time, by the Ming commander Yuan Chonghuan, who employed the new European-style cannons introduced by the Jesuits. Nurhaci is said to have been injured by a cannon ball. He died seven months later without having named a successor; his son Huangtaiji (Abahai) succeeded him and, changing the name of his people from 'Jurchen' to 'Manchu', continued the unstoppable onslaught on the Ming, proclaiming himself emperor of the Qing (changed from Later Jin). His son succeeded him as the Shunzhi emperor and saw the conquest of Beijing and the full establishment of the Qing dynasty in 1644.

72. XU XIAKE (1587–1641)
Traveller and geographer

This extraordinary traveller's original name was Xu Hongzu. Xiake, literally 'cloud's guest', was an apt epithet, bestowed by a friend, for his nearly nonstop voyages across the vast Chinese territories all his adult life.

Xu Xiake was born in 1587 in Jiangyin, a toponym meaning 'on the south bank of the Yangtze', not far from Shanghai. The Lower Yangtze delta at the time was economically and culturally the most advanced region in Ming China (see Feng Menglong, Biography 74).

Several favourable factors coincided to give Xu the opportunity to undertake his explorations. First, he came from a rich landlord family that had expanded into the lucrative textile business, operating several weaving mills. Second, though the family was very well educated, it did not take the career path that many intellectuals followed, and neither Xu Xiake nor his father pursued civil service examinations.

(This was because a forefather in the mid-Ming era had been arrested and died in an official examination cheating scandal.) Most important was the strong encouragement of his mother, née Wang, which cleared the obstacle of Confucian filial obligations, because the 'Analects' prominently quotes the ancient sage: 'One should not travel far during the lifetime of one's parents'.

Three years after the death of his father in 1604, Xiake started his journeys to the far-flung places of the Ming empire. He wore a 'distant-voyage hat' hand-made by his mother. He began with the neighbouring provinces, then roamed farther and farther afield, coming home to check on his mother for a short time before the next journey. Xiake's main interest was in natural wonders like big rivers and high mountains, instead of cities and towns. He was accompanied by a family servant.

In more than thirty years, Xiake covered, mostly on foot, nearly all the provinces of Ming China. He was most attracted to remote places difficult of access and rarely visited by his contemporaries. This was often a dangerous undertaking for a private person in pre-modern China. In addition to robbers and gangsters, Xiake had to negotiate deep gorges and steep cliffs with primitive means. He recalled that many times he could easily have lost his life, had he slipped or simply stepped in the wrong direction.

In the wilderness, Xiake often had to walk for days with little food, or go more than a week without a cooked meal. He slept in all possible places, from pigpens to simply under the stars. He became accustomed to being robbed, then turning to his network of friends and Buddhist abbots for rescue. What secured his great achievement for posterity was his steadfast habit of keeping a daily journal. Even in the remotest forest, Xiake would jot down the day's itinerary and observations by a campfire. His journals showed such objectivity, detail and accuracy that Joseph Needham, the modern British authority on ancient Chinese sciences, likened them to the records made by a 20th-century field surveyor rather than those of an early 17th-century traveller.

In his years of exploration, Xiake made many discoveries in geography and the natural sciences. He found, for instance, that the Mekong and Salween are separate rivers. He was also the first in the world systematically to observe and record the geologic formation of karst topography. His detailed records of the climate, minerals, flora and fauna of the places he visited are of great scientific value.

After the death of his dear mother in 1625, Xiake significantly expanded the sphere and duration of his explorations. He travelled to Guangdong province, the most southern in China, in 1628, then visited Beijing, in the north, the following year. In 1636, he embarked on his last and longest journey, to ethnically diverse regions in southwest Yunnan province as far as the Burmese border. He planned

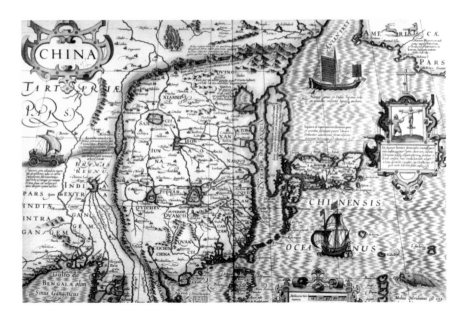

Seventeenth-century map of China.

to visit Tibet and the 'Western Regions' (today's Xinjiang), an ambitious and terrifying prospect that finally prompted the betrayal of his long-time servant. Xiake fell sick while in Yunnan and made his way home with the help of friends, both Han and and of other ethnic groups, that he made there. He died on 8 March 1641.

Three years later, Xiake's home region put up a fierce resistance against the conquering Manchu army. Many of Xiake's friends and his eldest son were killed, and Xiake's unedited travel journals were dispersed. It was through his younger son's painstaking efforts that a great majority of these precious records were re-collected and published for posterity.

73. WEI ZHONGXIAN (1568–1627)
Court eunuch

Court eunuchs occupied a unique position in pre-modern China. They were despised by the Confucian scholar-officials who wrote the official histories, hence their universally bad reputation. Yet eunuchs were indispensable to the imperial household, and they were often the people closest to the emperor, apart from royal consorts and chambermaids. As such, they often amassed enormous power and influence. Even within this privileged group, however, Wei Zhongxian stood out as exceptional.

During the Ming dynasty, the guaranteed livelihood afforded court eunuchs, and the possibility of gaining political power in addition, induced a large number of impoverished households to castrate their young sons as candidates for the profession; repeated court orders banning unauthorized 'self-castration' were ignored because of worsening poverty in many parts of China, and the growing demand for eunuchs, who numbered as many as 100,000 at one time.

Wei Zhongxian, from a poor peasant family in northern China, grew up an illiterate ruffian and compulsive gambler. He married and had a daughter; but, in 1589, possibly to dodge his creditors for gambling losses, he castrated himself (a risky operation for an adult), went to Beijing, and succeeded in entering the imperial palace as a eunuch. After more than a dozen years at the lowest level, he entered the service of the household of the Crown Prince, and befriended the wet nurse of the prince's eldest son.

The Crown Prince had never been the emperor's favourite. The prince's own eldest son was also neglected, and, instead of receiving a formal education, took up carpentry. After losing his mother while a child, this 'carpenter-prince' became strongly attached to his wet nurse. The hapless Crown Prince died barely a month after finally succeeding his father in 1620, and the long-neglected and barely literate young carpenter was enthroned as the fifteenth emperor of the Ming, during a period of factional and partisan infighting among the courtiers. Despite his castration, Wei Zhongxian managed to become the trusted 'husband' of the imperial wet nurse.

With incessant partisan strife among the literati officials, and a young emperor utterly uninterested in governing and under the spell of his wet nurse, Wei Zhongxian took advantage of the institutional weaknesses of the Ming, especially the abolition of the formal chancellorship, and the two secret police agencies staffed and controlled by court eunuchs.

The two secret police agencies outside the normal legal system were ruthless in eliminating Confucian opposition. Their most famous victims were the 'Six Gentlemen' in 1625 and the 'Seven Gentlemen' in 1626, all murdered in prison, except for one who committed suicide. The 1626 event also caused a large-scale popular revolt in the southern city of Suzhou.

Wei Zhongxian's rise continued. He enjoyed, for instance, the sycophantic title 'Nine-Thousand Years (of life to you)', short of 'Ten-Thousand Years' (*wansui*, *banzai* in Japanese) that only the emperor could command. Every piece of (mostly manufactured) good news in the empire was due to Wei Zhongxian's 'wise' leadership, so much so that all court memoranda first had to sing his praises.

The sycophantic governor of Zhejiang built temples in which Wei Zhongxian was worshipped as a living deity and saviour of China, and hundreds of similar temples were built all over the country. Just when the construction of these 'living temples' reached a height in late 1627, the carpenter-emperor died. The new emperor brought his own food into the palace lest he be poisoned.

While initially careful to show the respect due to the entrenched 'Nine-Thousand Years' despot, the new 'Ten-Thousand Years' monarch gradually moved against Wei Zhongxian. Within three months, he was sent into exile and hanged himself to escape further punishment.

Within a few years, while Wei Zhongxian's home county tried to eliminate every trace of him in the local gazetteer, hundreds of plays, dramas and novels about him were published and staged, securing his perpetual opprobrium.

74. FENG MENGLONG (1574–1646)
Popular writer

Feng Menglong, a prolific popular author, was a native of Suzhou, a prosperous city in the Lower Yangtze region with a highly developed cultural life. Feng Menglong's family was rich and intellectual. He, his elder brother, a painter, and his younger brother, a poet, were known in literary circles as 'the three Fengs from Suzhou'.

Feng Menglong performed poorly in the civil service examinations and never passed beyond the lowest level of Cultivated Talent (*xiucai*), despite the commercial success of several books he wrote on how to prepare for the exams. He spent a great part of his life and intellectual energy on the growing industry of popular vernacular literature and has been described as 'the personification of popular Chinese literature'.

It was during the preceding Mongol Yuan dynasty that popular vernacular literature first won intellectual respectability, as Yuan intellectuals were downgraded to a social status somewhere between prostitutes and beggars (see Guan Hanqing, Biography 62). The economic prosperity of the Lower Yangtze region during the Ming period further stimulated the growth of vernacular literature by yielding a relatively high literacy rate (evidenced in part by a significant number of female authors and poets) and an increasingly sophisticated urban cultural life.

Feng Menglong's success derived in part from his own experience with the milieu in which such popular literature was created. In his early adult life, he had fallen deeply in love with a beautiful and well-educated prostitute named Hou Huiqing. Their romance, filled with literary exchanges and discussions, ended with Huiqing's marriage to another man. This lost love was said to have ended Feng Menglong's visits to the 'red-light district' for good, but his fiction was filled with moving stories about good-hearted and faithful prostitutes, with both happy and tragic endings.

Feng Menglong's work covered almost the entire spectrum of popular literature. Besides the civil service exam guides, he wrote and edited short stories, historical romances, folksong collections, popular anecdotal sketches, song lyrics and opera-dramas, jokes and humorous stories, and rule books for popular card games. His most influential works, by far, were the three enormously successful anthologies of some 120 short stories, collectively known as *Sanyan* ('The Three Words'). A large number of these stories originated in the Song and Yuan dynasties, but he greatly improved and expanded them. There were also original tales, including at least one based on contemporary Ming politics.

Feng Menglong's readers were primarily ordinary urban residents, and many of his writings were runaway bestsellers. In meeting this popular demand, his works were often shocking, with plentiful sexual content. His works were so widely read that he was often accused of corrupting young minds.

While his short stories and historical romances preached moral lessons, particularly the retribution of Buddhist cause-and-effect, Feng Menglong's collections of local folksongs, almost exclusively of the love-song genre, were utterly untouched by Confucian and neo-Confucian morality.

With combed hair shining as a lacquer bowl,
A girl openly teases a boy in a crowd with her feet –
It used to be that boys seduced girls;
In this brand-new world, it is now girls who seduce boys.

Don't be so nervous about our illicit affair.
If caught, I shall assume all the fault.
In front of the judge I'll kneel down and confess
Obstinately and resolutely: it was me, a girl, who seduced you, the boy.

Some verses were more erotic:

Such enticing white breasts a young girl is born with
Let her lover stroke them, so long as he stops just at that –
A horse running on a stone bridge leaves no hoofprint,
And a knife cutting the water produces no damage.

In 1630, at the age of fifty-six, Feng Menglong finally settled for the lowest grade in the civil service examinations and was appointed a District Magistrate in a remote county in Fujian in 1634. His most memorable act there was to try to eliminate the local practice of female infanticide.

Feng Menglong returned to Suzhou shortly before peasant uprisings and the Manchu conquest toppled the Ming. Despite the unrepentantly non-Confucian content of his popular writings, he proved himself a Confucian and nationalist by participating in short-lived Southern Ming courts set up against the Qing. He died (perhaps was killed) a heartbroken Ming loyalist in 1646, two years after the formal proclamation of the Qing dynasty.

75. ZHANG XIANZHONG (1606–46)
Bandit and rebel leader

Zhang Xianzhong, infamous for his cruelty to the inhabitants of Sichuan province, was born in 1606 to a well-to-do family in Yan'an, Shaanxi province. He was briefly educated, then conscripted into the Ming army. Court-martialled for an unknown offence, he was sentenced to the death penalty but pardoned, and he subsequently absconded.

In 1630, when Shaanxi suffered a serious famine caused by unusually severe drought, Zhang Xianzhong became the leader of an insurgent band, one of many such groups of peasant armies in northern China. Nicknamed Yellow Tiger for his complexion, Xianzhong quickly rose to prominence among the bandits thanks to his military experience.

In 1635, the Ming government moved several thousand crack troops from southern Manchuria to suppress the peasant insurgency. The battle-hardened frontier troops defeated nearly all the insurgent armies, forcing their leaders, including Zhang Xianzhong, to surrender in 1638. However, when the Ming moved these top units back to Manchuria to confront the rising Manchu threat (see Nurhaci,

Biography 71), Zhang Xianzhong and others rebelled again. Zhang Xianzhong's bandit army became the first insurgent group to capture and kill a Ming imperial prince, in Hubei in 1641.

Zhang Xianzhong also became the sworn enemy of Li Zicheng (see Wu Sangui, Biography 76), a more charismatic insurgent leader whose following grew much stronger. Pressured by Li Zicheng, Zhang Xianzhong led his troops westward into Sichuan in the spring of 1644, as Li Zicheng's army marched to sack the Ming capital at Beijing. During the next few months, Zhang Xianzhong defeated the Ming forces in Sichuan and occupied the province.

In December 1644, the Manchus continued their conquest of northern China after taking Beijing from Li Zicheng's peasant army. Zhang Xianzhong declared himself the 'King of the Country of the Great West' in Sichuan's capital, Chengdu. His regime, propped up by roaming bandits from outside the province, had little local support. Worse still, in contrast to Li Zicheng's better disciplined army, Zhang Xianzhong's troops were notoriously cruel, and the Great West kingdom was maintained by terror and brutality.

Almost immediately, Zhang Xianzhong started a campaign of mass killing as a collective punishment for local opposition. First an entire family, then a whole street, and finally a large community, were massacred for the opposition or disloyalty of a single member. For instance, a whole city quarter was eliminated because one resident, sent by Zhang Xianzhong as a messenger to Shaanxi, did not return to live under his rule of terror.

Zhang Xianzhong's enemies included both Ming loyalists and supporters of Li Zicheng. When a student in Chengdu was discovered to be secretly communicating with Li Zicheng, Zhang Xianzhong organized a fake civil service examination. All participants, reportedly numbering around 20,000, were murdered, and their examination papers piled into a small hill.

Zhang Xianzhong often ordered his victims to be skinned alive. If the victim expired during the process, the executioner himself would be killed. After three years, fewer than twenty of Zhang Xianzhong's six hundred appointed officials in Chengdu survived his repeated bloody purges. In 1645, he killed 140,000 locally conscripted soldiers for failing to take the town of Nanzheng in Shaanxi near the provincial border with Sichuan.

When his favourite executioner died of illness, Xianzhong killed the physician who had treated him. He then killed another hundred doctors as a sacrifice to the dead executioner. He did not spare women and children, and was even reported to enjoy killing a pregnant mother to verify the gender of the foetus. Women were usually savagely raped before being killed. After recovering from malaria, Zhang

Coins from the rule of Zhang Xianzhong.

Xianzhong ordered the killing of many women, including a concubine of his own, by chopping off their bound feet, as a thank offering.

In 1646, marching to Shaanxi to meet a Qing force led by Prince Haoge, Zhang Xianzhong was finally either killed by an arrow or captured and immediately executed by the Qing soldiers. In the words of the Italian Jesuit Martino Martini, who lived through the Manchu conquest in China, he turned 'that populous Province of Suchuen into a vast wilderness'. It is estimated that fewer than 10 per cent of the roughly 5 million Sichuan residents in the late Ming survived. The early Qing administration had to mobilize large-scale immigrations to Sichuan from the southern provinces, primarily Hunan, Hubei and Guangdong (Canton), a process popularly known as 'filling Sichuan from Hu and Guang provinces', attested by the archaic Cantonese dialect still spoken in isolated communities in Sichuan.

It was said of Zhang Xianzhong's massacres that stray dogs left bodies untouched as there were so many of them on the streets. Two Jesuit missionaries, the Italian Ludovicus Buglio and the Portuguese Gabriel Megallaens, narrowly escaped Zhang Xianzhong's massacres. Their first-hand reports were included by Martino Martini in *Bellum Tartaricum*, a book published in 1654 in Antwerp and London a decade after the bloody events, and in other Catholic sources.

As a monument to Xianzhong's atrocities, there still exists in the town of Guanghan, outside Chengdu, the notorious 'Seven Kill Stele'. Whether from Xianzhong's own hand or not, the faded inscription upon it reads simply and starkly, '*Sha! Sha! Sha! Sha! Sha! Sha! Sha!* (Kill! Kill! Kill! Kill! Kill! Kill! Kill!)'.

76. WU SANGUI (1612–78)
General who changed sides

Wu Sangui was born in 1612 in southern Manchuria to a Ming military family. His father was appointed Regional Commander by 1631, and Vice-Commissioner-in-chief two years later.

Wu Sangui's posthumous reputation lies in his initial support for the Manchu invasion of China and his subsequent betrayal of his former masters, ostensibly because of the loss of his favourite concubine. The resulting Chinese cliché, 'his cap flew upward with anger for the sake of a beautiful girl', refers to this impulsive trigger for the eventual Manchu conquest of China.

Wu Sangui's father's military appointments took place during the rapid rise of Manchu power under Nurhaci (Biography 71) and his sons. The Ming military colonies in southern Manchuria were the primary targets of the Manchu army, while the Ming were also fighting peasant rebellions fuelled by drought within China. In 1630, during an encirclement by thousands of Manchu troops, Wu Sangui led some twenty Wu family bodyguards to the rescue of his father, and, in 1638, he became the youngest Chief Regional Commander in the northeast. Despite a disastrous defeat and ignominious retreat in 1641, Wu Sangui remained loyal to the Ming.

In 1643, in Beijing for a court audience, General Wu Sangui fell in love with Chen Yuanyuan, a beautiful courtesan from southern China. He took her as a concubine after paying a substantial amount to her previous master. In the following year, the last Ming emperor called Wu Sangui to the defence of the capital against an approaching peasant army led by Li Zicheng. But before Wu Sangui's troops had arrived, the peasant army overcame Beijing on 24 April, and the last Ming emperor hanged himself from an old tree on Coal Hill behind the imperial palace.

Wu Sangui initially decided to surrender to the new regime. The peasant leaders in Beijing tortured many Ming officials to extort money, including Wu Sangui's own father, who had retired to Beijing, and one of Li Zicheng's top lieutenants snatched Wu Sangui's concubine.

This humiliation was too much. 'If a man cannot even protect one of his women, how could he face the world?' asked Wu Sangui, who then called upon the Manchus for assistance. Prince Dorgon, the Qing regent since the sudden death of the Manchu ruler Huangtaiji, saw the opportunity to take over the Chinese empire and redirected his army to the easternmost end of the Great Wall, occupied by Wu Sangui's troops.

In early June 1644, the combined force of Wu Sangui and Dorgon soundly defeated Li Zicheng's peasant army. For nearly thirty years, Wu Sangui was part of the Qing military as it conquered the entire country. He was also reunited with his concubine Chen Yuanyuan.

Wu Sangui led the march to pacify west and southwest China, culminating in the capture and execution of the last monarch of the Southern Ming regime, who had sought refuge in Burma. Wu Sangui was rewarded with the rank of imperial prince and appointed viceroy of two southwest provinces, Yunnan and Guizhou, with both civil and military control. His son married a Manchu imperial princess.

Wu Sangui's power grew to such an extent that the Kangxi emperor (Biography 80) decided to abolish his feudal estate and two other similar fiefdoms in southern China in 1673. Having amassed a great fortune and a large military force, Wu switched his loyalty once again and rebelled. He adopted a new dynastic name, Zhou, and named himself 'Grand Generalissimo of All-Under-Heaven'.

Although Wu Sangui's forces scored a number of victories and quickly marched to the Yangtze, the Qing army gradually gained the upper hand. Wu Sangui enthroned himself as emperor of the Zhou in March 1678, but died within half a year. Having underestimated the determination of the Kangxi emperor to regain control of the south, yet also failing to gain support among the Chinese intelligentsia because of his betrayal, Wu Sangui's regime quickly collapsed. All his Wu clansmen were exterminated by the Qing. The final fate of Chen Yuanyuan remains a mystery to this day.

77. GU YANWU (1613–82)
Ming loyalist, scholar and social thinker

Gu Yanwu came from a prominent landlord-gentry family in Kunshan, just north of Shanghai. By the time he was born, on 15 July 1613, however, the family was in decline and had no civil service graduate serving the government.

His grand-uncle's only son had died before marriage. The son's fiancée, prompted by neo-Confucian moral codes for women, willingly became a virgin 'widow'. Because Gu Yanwu's birth parents already had a son, Gu Yanwu was adopted by his grand-uncle's family, with the virgin widow as his adopted mother. He caught smallpox at the age of two and lost the sight of one eye.

He became an active member of the Restoration Society, the largest organization of Ming political activist writers. He repeatedly failed the civil service examinations, never obtaining the second-level Provincial Graduate degree, but,

Portrait of Gu Yanwu.

using declining family assets, he purchased the rank of a student in the Imperial Academy in 1643.

When the Ming fell in 1644, the Lower Yangtze valley put up the fiercest resistance to Manchu conquest, in which the entire Gu clan participated: Gu Yanwu's birth mother was killed, and one of his brothers died fighting in 1645. Gu Yanwu himself joined the resistance, accepted an appointment at a rump Ming court in Nanjing, and barely escaped the Manchu massacres. His adoptive mother starved herself to death. Her last words were to forbid him ever to serve the conquerors.

During the next few years, Gu Yanwu lived as a hermit but maintained close contacts with other Ming loyalists in the area. The family's land holdings were coveted by a powerful local collaborator of the Qing regime. The collaborator compelled a servant of the Gu family to accuse Gu Yanwu of association with Zheng Chenggong (Koxinga, 1624–62), a Ming loyalist general. In order to avoid the serious accusation, Gu Yanwu had the treacherous servant killed in 1655 and managed to escape execution for murder.

In 1657, after paying homage at the mausoleum of the founding emperor of the Ming dynasty in Nanjing and bidding goodbye to his home town, Gu Yanwu set off for the north, where he lived for the rest of his life. He travelled extensively and made many friends among Ming loyalists who refused to serve the new dynasty. He spent much of his time researching Chinese history and geography, and writing. To support himself, Gu Yanwu engaged in farming and business, but continued to travel. In 1668, he was falsely accused of compiling an anti-Qing anthology. After being imprisoned in Shandong, he was finally acquitted.

With the publication of his works, Gu Yanwu's fame as a scholar spread nationwide. Meanwhile, three of his nephews became the top winners at the Qing civil service exams and rose to prominent positions in Qing government. They and the Qing court made repeated overtures to Gu Yanwu but, abiding by his adopted mother's last wish, he refused to serve the government in any official capacity.

Having experienced first-hand the collapse of the Ming, Gu Yanwu became a stern critic of neo-Confucianism for creating an intelligentsia that either had little practical ability to deal with national crises, or was too eager to surrender to and serve a new master. Instead of Confucian morals and abstract ideas, Gu Yanwu promoted practical knowledge such as economics and geography, for 'a gentleman studies to enlighten himself and save society'.

His 'Five Studies of Phonology' is recognized as a breakthrough in the study of ancient Chinese phonology, and he is considered to have begun the Qing school of evidential studies. He believed that a deterioration of language ineluctably led to a degradation of morals. To improve the latter, it was necessary to rationalize and rectify the language people spoke. For Gu Yanwu, the most important part of intellectual inquiry was its practical implications.

In early 1682, he was snowed in for days on a trip to Shanxi province. Eager to return home, he took a bad fall while mounting a horse in the snow and died the next day, 15 February.

78. ZHU DA (c. 1626–c. 1705)
Eccentric painter of birds and fish

Zhu Da, often known by his studio name of Badashanren ('man of the eight great mountains'), was one of China's foremost 'eccentric' painters, famous for his brooding birds and wild-eyed fish. Born in Nanchang, he was descended from the sixteenth son of the Hongwu emperor (Biography 65), the founder of the Ming dynasty. At the time that he was preparing for the official examinations, in 1645, the Qing swept into Nanchang. Since he was known to be a descendant of the Ming founder, he had to flee the invading Manchus and take refuge in a Buddhist monastery in the mountains. This was mainly in order to save his own life by going into hiding, but it also had the advantage of permitting him to resist the hated Manchu stipulation that all men should assume the Manchu hairstyle of the shaven forehead and long pigtail, since, as a Buddhist monk, his entire head was shaven. In 1680, as a result of an unknown emotional crisis, perhaps a desire to leave

'Two Birds' by Zhu Da.

the celibate life in order to marry, he burned his Buddhist robes. After a period of secular life, in which he is known to have had a son, he entered a Daoist monastery where he lived for the rest of his life. As a Daoist, he could continue to express his anti-Manchu feelings through his hairstyle, for Daoist priests let their hair grow long and wore it in a bun on the top of the head, in the Ming style.

Forced by his ancestry to live on the margins of society, Zhu Da supported himself by producing calligraphy and paintings. His calligraphic style, though he claimed to base it upon the work of Wang Xizhi (Biography 27) and of his son, Wang Xianzhi (344–86), Yan Zhenqing (709–85) and Su Dongpo (Biography 51), was vigorous and unusual, often executed with a very worn brush.

Zhu Da's paintings, monochromatic studies usually depicting birds, animals or fish, are remarkable in their simplicity, with rough brushstrokes and inkblots. The economy of line is startlingly modern, reflecting Zen (Chan) ideas and even approaching 20th-century minimalism. The feathers of his birds were often ruffled, and their anguished eyes seem to express fear or anger. Often a fish floats below a bird perched on a dead branch, and the fish, with upturned eyes, seems to anticipate trouble or danger, from the bird or an unseen fisherman. His paintings were admired in Japan where minimalist, eccentric painters such as Mu Qi (*c.* 1200–70) were popular. In China, his reputation grew towards the end of the Qing, when his anti-Manchu stance found favour as the dynasty declined and nationalist fervour increased.

79. PU SONGLING (1640–1715)
Popular writer of ghost stories

Pu Songling was born in 1640, during a serious famine, to a small landlord-gentry family that also engaged in commerce. He passed the lowest level of the civil service exam at the age of eighteen, and became a Cultivated Talent.

The civil service examinations were becoming more and more formalized and restrictive, with the notoriously rigid 'eight-legged essay' established as the primary testing instrument. Despite persistent attempts year after year until he finally gave up in 1690, Pu Songling never passed the next level.

After his marriage at the age of seventeen and the division of his parents' household among four brothers several years later, Pu Songling faced dire poverty. He was always away from home teaching or preparing for exams, so it was his wife who raised the family.

An illustration from an 1880s edition of 'Strange Tales from Make-do Studio'.
This particular story, 'Dizhen', describes an earthquake that Pu Songling experienced,
and one of the gentlemen seated inside the building may be Pu Songling himself.

After serving as a magistrate for about a year, Pu Songling spent much of his
adult life as a country schoolteacher, working for the wealthy Bi household from
1679 to his retirement in 1709. He became not only the Bi clansmen's close friend,
but also a trusted family counsellor.

During this period he wrote his magnum opus, *Liaozhai zhi yi* ('Strange Tales
from Make-do Studio'), a collection of nearly 500 elegantly constructed stories
about fox spirits, ghosts and other supernatural phenomena, always built around

some human drama. Many of the stories originated in a wide variety of sources. Pu Songling continued to add tales to the collection, perhaps as late as 1707. Although the book was not printed until fifty years after his death, handwritten copies of the stories started circulating even before the completion of the collection.

Pu Songling also wrote colloquial dramas, including one called 'The Wall' that bears a striking resemblance to *King Lear*, written by his near contemporary, William Shakespeare. The plays were not published until the late 20th century, nearly 300 years after his death.

In 1713, his wife, to whom he had been married for fifty-six years, died, and Pu Songling himself died in early 1715.

80. THE KANGXI EMPEROR (1654–1722)
Emperor who brought the Qing dynasty to its height

Emperor Kangxi's given name was Xuanye; Kangxi is his reign title. He was born in 1654, the third son of Emperor Shunzhi, the first Manchu monarch to rule from Beijing. His mother came from a long-sinicized family that was among China's first Catholic converts. When his father lay dying of smallpox in 1661, the choice of Xuanye, who had already survived smallpox, as the imperial

Emperor Kangxi crossing the Yangtze River on one of his tours.

successor was prompted by his grandmother, Empress-dowager Xiaozhuang, sup-ported by the Jesuit priest Johann Adam Schall von Bell, Director of the Imperial Board of Astronomy.

After the death of his mother in 1663, the boy emperor was brought up mainly by his Mongolian grandmother. The empire was ruled by a collective regency domi-nated by the Manchu noble Oboi, until the young emperor assumed the formal control of government affairs in 1667.

Two years later, with the help of his grandmother, the young emperor impris-oned Oboi and destroyed the latter's once powerful faction. Five years later, against the advice of most of his courtiers, he abolished the three semi-independent feu-datories in southern China and faced the rebellion of Wu Sangui (Biography 76). After the successful suppression of this civil war in 1681, the Kangxi emperor ordered the occupation of Taiwan, the last Ming loyalist stronghold.

Meanwhile, he made strenuous efforts to alleviate the strong anti-Manchu feeling among the Han population, particularly in the south, promoting southern talent and personally presiding over examinations in which southern candidates were favoured over those from the north. He was exceptionally open to Westerners and Western science, allowing the Jesuits to cure his malaria with quinine (after testing it on various courtiers). Impressed by the superiority of Western astronomy in calculating calendrical events, he studied Western mathematics, including geom-etry and trigonometry, with Jesuit missionaries at court. He was also interested in Western musical instruments and painting, and he ordered the compilation of an atlas of the world and of China with the help of Jesuit specialists. He prac-tised Chinese calligraphy and published various literary works, including a series of poems on rice cultivation and silk production (*Gengzhi tu*), illustrated by one of his many court artists, Qiao Bingzhen. Works published on his orders that indicate his interest in classical Chinese include the complete Tang poems and a phrase dic-tionary, as well as the Kangxi dictionary (commissioned in 1710, published in 1716), which remains a standard reference work for classical scholars.

Russia had expanded to Siberia and begun to encroach upon the Manchus' ancient homeland in the Heilongjiang (Amur) River valley. After successfully fending off the encroachment in the northeast, Kangxi's representatives, including Jesuits, signed a peace treaty with Russia in 1689.

The peace with Russia was partly prompted by the growing power of the Western Mongols, originally based in the Ili Valley in today's Xinjiang, and the emperor personally led an expedition that resulted in a crushing defeat of the Western Mongols in 1696, winning the loyalty and submission of the Khalka Mongols of Outer Mongolia. He also formally annexed Tibet in 1720.

In addition to the territorial gains he brought to the Chinese empire, Kangxi had a considerable impact on his subjects. He insisted on being informed about weather records and grain prices in all provinces. He toured southern China six times, partially to placate the local intelligentsia, but he also paid particular attention to water conservation projects and facilities there. He made the historic decision in 1712 permanently to freeze the national head tax at the current level regardless of rapid population growth. Throughout his long reign he always personally read court memorials and made his own notes and comments on them, using his left hand when his right hand was injured.

The differences between Chinese and Manchu practices over inheritance led to a succession crisis. Following the Chinese principle, he appointed his chief consort's eldest son (the second of Kangxi's twenty sons) as heir apparent in 1676 when the latter was still a child, but the competitive Manchu tradition led to fratricidal conspiracies between his fifteen eldest sons. The original Crown Prince was deposed, then reinstated, then deposed again; the emperor was eventually succeeded in 1722 by his fourth son, the Yongzheng emperor. Controversies about Kangxi's death and the succession, including allegations of patricide, immediately arose and continue to this day.

81. ZENG JING (1679–1736)
Anti-Manchu intellectual

The Qing court was ultra-sensitive to anti-Manchu sentiments, real and imagined, and Zeng Jing was one of countless victims of literary persecution. Born in the southern province of Hunan in 1679, Zeng Jing repeatedly failed the civil service examinations and, like thousands of similarly unsuccessful intellectuals, made a living by teaching. He had studied a popular examination preparation book and was impressed by its author, a Ming loyalist named Lü Liuliang, a southerner like Zeng himself, who had died in 1683. During the early years of the Yongzheng emperor's reign (1722–35), Zeng Jing sent a student to collect Lü Liuliang's other writings, which were filled with anti-Manchu statements and allusions.

Zeng Jing regarded the Yongzheng emperor as a usurper and, seeking an opportunity to overthrow the Qing, contacted a general named Yue Zhongqi, who held the powerful post of Governor-general of Sichuan and Shaanxi. Zeng's hope was founded on the premise that General Yue was a descendant of Yue Fei (Biography 55), the anti-Jurchen (the Jurchens being the Tungusic ancestors of the Manchu)

The Yongzheng emperor and his court offering sacrifice.

hero of the Southern Song dynasty some six centuries earlier, who might follow his ancestor in toppling an illegitimate regime.

Zeng Jing wrote an anonymous letter to General Yue, who was stationed in Xi'an, in the autumn of 1728. The letter listed the Yongzheng emperor's ten alleged personal vices, including patricide, fratricide and the maltreatment of the emperor's mother. However, the general had not the slightest intention of repeating his forefather's heroism, and informed the emperor.

Arrested and tortured, Zeng Jing quickly broke down and confessed, also naming like-minded friends who were quickly rounded up. Convicted of 'treason by the book', the bodies of the long-dead Lü Liuliang, Lü's dead son, and a dead disciple were exhumed for posthumous beheading. Others implicated were executed, together with their adult male relatives. Women and children were enslaved and exiled. The surviving members of the entire Lü clan were banished from Zhejiang to Manchuria.

Strangely, Zeng Jing was pardoned by the Yongzheng emperor, who combined Jing's 'confessions' and his own edicts in a book entitled 'Awakening from Delusion' and published it in 1730, providing a point-by-point rebuttal of the anti-Manchu opinions revealed by this case.

Zeng Jing was released back to his native province of Hunan, but his good fortune was short-lived. The Yongzheng emperor died five years later and was succeeded by his son, the Qianlong emperor (Biography 83), who felt that 'Awakening from Delusion' was bad publicity and had it recalled and destroyed. Zeng Jing was rearrested and executed in 1736. The Qianlong emperor went on to take literary inquisition and persecution to an unprecedented height.

82. CAO XUEQIN (1715?–63)

China's greatest novelist

Long acknowledged as China's greatest novelist, Cao Xueqin has been compared to Shakespeare and Homer. Extensive research has been carried out on him during the past hundred years, but despite this depth of study, his fame, and the fact that he died barely two and a half centuries ago, little is known about his personal life. Nobody knows his birth year, the identity of his father, or anything about his career, or even where exactly he spent his final years in the suburbs of Beijing.

The Cao clan were originally Ming subjects living in Manchuria. The rising Manchu polity captured the clan members and turned them into hereditary *baoyi*, or bond-servants of the Qing imperial household. As such, though ethnically Han, they became legally and culturally part of the endogamous Qing 'banner' system that consisted mainly of Manchus and Mongols. Foot-binding was not practised among the women, for instance. Cao Xueqin's great-grandmother had served as a nurse of the young Kangxi emperor (Biography 80), thus securing the political fortune of the clan. Beginning with her husband, the family held the lucrative post of Commissioner of Imperial Textiles in the southern metropolis of Nanjing, plus other concurrent posts, for three generations over the course of nearly sixty years.

The Qing was the best-educated imperial house in Chinese history. This emphasis on education extended to the entire ruling elite. There thus emerged a large number of literary talents among the proportionally very small 'banner' population, be they Manchu, Mongol or Han. Xueqin's grandfather Cao Yin (1658–1712) is one example. Yin was known to be an outstanding poet, book collector and publisher, and, not overly burdened with Confucian delicacy, a connoisseur of plays.

An illustration from 'Dream of the Red Chamber' by Cao Xueqin.

During the Kangxi emperor's six southern royal tours, the Caos hosted him in Nanjing four times, in itself a mark of his favour. The benevolent emperor rewarded the family handsomely, sponsoring the marriage of Cao Yin's eldest daughter to a Manchu princely family, so that her son eventually inherited the princedom. The entire Cao family lived in luxury and opulence, into which the baby Xueqin, originally named Zhan, was born around 1715.

The good times came to an end in 1722 with the succession to the throne of Emperor Yongzheng, following a fierce struggle that found the Cao family allied with losing factions. It owed a huge debt to the government, the result of decades of extravagant living and repeated lavish accommodation of the Kangxi emperor. The family quickly fell out of favour and lost its long-held commission and other positions. Finally, in 1728, the Qing court ordered the confiscation of all Cao properties. The entire family, impoverished, was uprooted from Nanjing and moved to Beijing. Despite the 1735 amnesty declared by the new emperor, Qianlong (Biography 83), whereby the debts owed by disgraced officials who were unable to pay them were forgiven, the Cao family never regained its former glory and wealth.

Xueqin quickly gave up trying for a government career, traditionally the only way to rise out of poverty, in part because he admired the naturalness of the Western Jin dynasty, unconstrained as it was by Confucian morals. All banner members, or bannermen, were entitled to receive basic government rations, but Xueqin's circumstances worsened to the point that he went short of food at times. He left the family's urban residence and went to live in a rural village near the Western Hills of Beijing, probably making a living selling his brush paintings.

Around the mid-1750s, Xueqin started writing the novel that would make his name immortal. Eventually titled 'Dream of the Red Chamber', it describes a powerful and rich family gradually drifting into decay and finally ruin. Widely believed to be autobiographical, the novel mirrored the Cao family saga of the previous hundred years and provided a colourful picture of contemporary aristocratic life, including elements of homosexuality, incest and official corruption. The dozens of major characters, ranging from chambermaids to the family matriarch, are depicted with such individuality and vividness that it was thought they must be based on real personalities.

The major storyline, with many parallel plots seamlessly interwoven, is the tragic love between the protagonist Jia Baoyu, generally identified as the young Xueqin himself, and his beautiful yet sickly cousin Lin Daiyu, from their innocent childhood onward. This sad story has endeared the novel to millions of readers over the centuries and made the two lovers of the story household names. Although he was a talented classical poet, Xueqin wrote the novel in a vernacular Chinese based largely on contemporary Beijing dialect.

The novel's allure was enhanced by its tantalizing incompleteness: the author left behind at his death only the first eighty chapters, ending just before the downward spiral of the family. Among the many efforts to finish it, the most popular is the 120-chapter version completed by another bannerman, Gao E (c. 1738–c. 1815). No one knows whether Gao's extension truly reflected Xueqin's intentions. It is even possible that Xueqin wrote chapters that were later lost.

Xueqin reportedly died on Chinese New Year's eve (12 February 1763), destitute, following the death of his infant son a few months earlier.

The Qianlong emperor on horseback.

83. THE QIANLONG EMPEROR (1711–99)
The height of the Qing dynasty

The Qianlong emperor was born in 1711, with the given name Hongli, the fourth son of Prince Yong, who was in turn the fourth son of the Kangxi emperor (Biography 80). Prince Yong's own controversial succession to the throne in 1722 as the Yongzheng emperor remains to this day something of a mystery.

The young boy Hongli was said to be a favourite of his grandfather, and thus he spent much time in the imperial palace. At the age of eleven, he showed extraordinary courage in facing an injured bear in a royal hunting tour with his grandfather. Hunting was an important feature of the Manchu heritage, which stressed horsemanship and hunting skills.

Like all Manchu princes, Hongli received a rigorous education. According to an eyewitness report, the school day started before daybreak and included Chinese, Manchu and Mongol lessons as well as martial arts training. Because Hongli was secretly designated the imperial heir soon after his father's enthronement, his upbringing was even more demanding.

These preparations ensured a smooth succession when his father died suddenly in the summer of 1735. The new emperor reversed many of his father's policies, and his long reign was undoubtedly the height of the Qing dynasty. It was marked by continuous territorial expansion. After years of fierce campaigns, the Qing broke Western Mongol power, forcing its last charismatic leader, Amursana, to seek refuge in Russia, and ethnically cleansed their old base in the Ili Valley region. Suppressing the Turkic Muslim groups, the Qing extended its empire as far as Lake Balkhash and the Ferghana Valley. In the southwest, the emperor not only consolidated control of Tibet, but also despatched an expeditionary army to repel the Gurkhas from Nepal, pushing them all the way to the outskirts of Kathmandu in 1792, when the Nepalese sued for peace. He also sent expeditions to Burma (Myanmar) and Vietnam.

No less impressive were the Qianlong emperor's cultural achievements, the most prominent of which was the compilation of 'The Complete Library in Four Branches of Literature' (*Siku quanshu*), the largest collection of books in Chinese history. The work started in 1773 and ended nine years later. The editorial board, consisting of more than 360 scholars, collected and annotated over 10,000 manuscripts from the imperial collections and other libraries, and selected 3,461 books for inclusion in 'The Complete Library'. The finished collection had 36,381 volumes with more than 79,000 chapters. It had about 2.3 million pages, and approximately

800 million Chinese characters. Nearly 4,000 copyists produced a total of seven copies of 'The Complete Library' that were deposited in different palaces, and two sets still survive.

The emperor's motivation for this ambitious enterprise was not entirely cultural. He was sensitive to the persisting anti-Manchu attitude of the Han intelligentsia. The collection of works for inclusion in 'The Complete Library' provided an opportunity to discover and destroy 'seditious' books, and to edit out anti-Manchu bias in other existing works, however old they were.

The Qianlong emperor was an erudite ruler with excellent literary and artistic taste. In addition to the three languages every young Manchu prince had to study, he also learned to read Tibetan and Turkic (Uyghur). He hired European Jesuit painters and craftsmen to work in the palace and greatly expanded the Yuanming Garden with a small area of 'European' buildings. He built a library, a Buddhist temple and a garden complex for his retirement in the Forbidden City, and enlarged the imperial hunting park at Chengde, northeast of Beijing. He was said to have composed more than 42,000 classic poems, although they may not all have been his. He also painted and enjoyed practising Chinese calligraphy. He greatly enlarged the imperial collections of paintings and works of art.

No matter where he was, the emperor always rose every morning at six and spent the mornings on government business, consulting with ministers and receiving new appointees and other dignitaries. He was devoted to his first wife, who died in 1748. With dozens of other consorts and concubines, the Qianlong emperor had a total of seventeen sons and ten daughters, but only ten sons and five daughters survived to maturity.

Qianlong gradually grew extravagant and self-aggrandizing. His six grand tours of southern China, ostensibly to show himself to the southern population and investigate their concerns, became costly pleasure trips. His earlier strict precautions against dishonesty and corruption were replaced by indulgence in his old age, particularly towards his venal minister Heshen (Biography 84).

In summer 1793 the Qianlong emperor received the British ambassador Lord George Macartney but denied his request to open more trade ports, preferring the self-sufficiency of the 'celestial empire', an attitude that would cost China dearly within half a century.

Claiming not to wish to exceed his grandfather Kangxi's sixty-one-year reign, he formally abdicated in favour of his chosen heir, the Jiaqing emperor, on Chinese New Year of 1795. However, the 'retired emperor' continued to influence affairs. He died on 7 February 1799, ending the longest reign in the entirety of Chinese history.

Portrait of the corrupt official Heshen.

84. HESHEN (1750–99)
Corrupt Qing official

Born in 1750, Heshen was from the Niuhuru clan of the Manchu and belonged to the Main Red banner of the Qing organizational system. Handsome and intelligent, he received a solid education at the court school for Manchu noble children, and married the granddaughter of a powerful Manchu noble and Minister of Justice.

Heshen started his official career in 1772 as a low-ranking Imperial Guard. His opportunity came when the Qianlong emperor (Biography 83), studying a memorial, quoted a passage from the 'Analects'. The other Manchu guards present did not understand what the emperor had said, but Heshen was able to respond with an apt quote from the same Confucian classic. The emperor was pleasantly surprised by the erudition of the lowly officer, and thus began his meteoric rise.

Barely four years later, Heshen was Vice Minister of Revenue, Grand Minister of State, Grand Minister of the Imperial Household, and Commander-General of Metropolitan Infantry. In 1780, Emperor Qianlong betrothed his youngest princess to Heshen's son. In 1782, Heshen became Assistant Grand Secretary, the formal title of the Qing Chief Minister, and Minister of Personnel, with a portfolio covering the Ministry of Personnel, Ministry of Revenue and Court of Colonial Affairs. From this point, he remained China's most powerful Prime Minister until his death in 1799.

Heshen accumulated great wealth through various flagrantly corrupt means. His control of the ministries of revenue and military affairs allowed him to appropriate government funds. His position at the Ministry of Personnel attracted bribes, particularly from provincial governors. It was said that when the governor of Shaanxi province wanted to give Heshen 200,000 taels (in the Qing period, about 6,240 kg or 13,750 lbs) of silver, the governor's envoy had first to bribe Heshen's doorman with 5,000 taels of silver merely for the privilege of depositing the bribe in Heshen's private storerooms.

The emperor's favour meant that Heshen could escape the normal checks on corruption, and he had his own methods for avoiding detection, such as ordering that all vacant imperial censor positions could be filled only by those aged sixty or more, since they would be more interested in securing a comfortable retirement than in digging up corruption cases.

In 1793, on the emperor's behalf, Heshen entertained the first British ambassador to China, Lord George Macartney, at his villa on the outskirts of Beijing (now part of Peking University campus), where Heshen was fitted with a truss by the British embassy's doctor.

The Qianlong emperor maintained actual power after his nominal abdication in 1795, so his successor, the Jiaqing emperor, long aware of Heshen's venality, could do nothing. As soon as the 'retired emperor' died, Heshen was arrested and his personal wealth seized and counted. The total value of his assets came to the astronomical amount of 800,000,000 taels ($14,400,000,000 in current US dollar value) of silver, more than ten times the government's annual national revenue (about 70 million taels). Heshen was ordered to commit suicide on 21 February 1799, fourteen days after the death of the Qianlong emperor.

85. LIN ZEXU (1785–1850)
Official who banned the British opium trade

L in Zexu was born in 1785 to a struggling schoolteacher in Fujian, one of China's smallest and most mountainous provinces, on the southeast coast. At the age of nineteen, he passed the highly competitive provincial examination. Though Lin Zexu twice failed the next, highest examination, the governor of Fujian invited

Western depiction of an opium den, 1842.

him to join his staff. He finally passed the highest examination in 1811 and was appointed to the prestigious Hanlin Academy.

In 1821, Lin Zexu embarked on a brilliant succession of provincial appointments, in which he demonstrated a combination of moral integrity and practical ability. He was regarded by the Daoguang emperor as a reliable problem-solver, and to the general population he was known as 'Lin, the Blue Sky', because he was known to be incorruptible and concerned about the welfare of the common people.

While Lin was on mandatory bereavement leave for his mother's death in 1824, the emperor asked him to make an exception to the Confucian rule of lengthy mourning and oversee the repair of breaches in the embankment containing Lake Hongze that had disrupted the critical grain shipments to Beijing. Repeatedly he was called upon in such emergencies.

Lin Zexu was appointed Governor of Jiangsu in 1832, where he made successful agricultural innovations, and in 1837 he was promoted to Governor-general of Hubei and Hunan. His major challenge now was to confront the opium trade and opium addiction.

Since the 1780s the British East India Company had monopolized the production of opium in India, which was exported to China by private traders. China's huge trading surplus with England (based largely on the sale of tea) turned into an equally large deficit as a result of the British export of opium to China, in addition to which opium addiction became a serious social problem. Tens of millions of ordinary Chinese became addicts, and opium use spread to high society, including court and government officials and the army. By the late 1830s, the British were selling an estimated 1,820 tons of opium to China annually. Already in 1729, the Qing court had issued strict laws banning opium production, trade and consumption, but to little avail. Open opium smuggling led to rampant societal and government corruption.

Lin Zexu submitted a series of memoranda to the emperor requesting urgent and strict measures banning the opium trade, and he was appointed Imperial Commissioner to Guangdong to enforce strict prohibition of the trade. Arriving at the treaty port of Guangzhou (Canton) on 10 March 1839, he immediately imposed a trade embargo on British merchants to force them to surrender their opium stock. Qing officers at the time were lamentably ignorant of the outside world, but Lin Zexu had chapters of a European handbook of international law translated to inform his actions against foreign merchants.

Charles Elliot, British Superintendent of Trade in Guangzhou, submitted to the demand and ordered all British subjects to turn in their opium. However, by promising that the British crown would compensate the merchants, Elliot acknowledged the British government's role in the opium trade and set the stage for British military reprisal against China for the lost property.

Lin Zexu destroyed nearly 20,000 chests of confiscated opium, each chest weighing about 63 kg (140 lbs), on a beach near Guangzhou, by dissolving it with water, salt and lime and dumping it in the ocean. Meanwhile, he also sent an open letter, poorly translated by a Yale graduate working as a missionary in Guangzhou, to Queen Victoria, questioning the moral ground on which the British government perpetuated the trade. No answer was ever received.

Instead, London sent gunboats to the Chinese coast in June 1840. British military superiority was beyond question. Perhaps because Guangzhou was the site of Lin Zexu's destruction of the opium, the British fleet sailed north. After sacking an island in Zhejiang, the British flotilla sailed all the way to the port of Tianjin, seaport of the Qing capital.

The Daoguang emperor quickly caved in, condemning Lin Zexu to exile in Ili, on the northwest border with Russia. Nevertheless, the British took one coastal city after another. When the Royal Navy penetrated deep up the Yangtze, the emperor sued for peace, ceding Hong Kong and paying large indemnities for the destroyed opium and British expeditionary expenses. Thus began the century of China's humiliation by the Western powers.

In 1846, Lin Zexu was recalled from exile to fill a sequence of provincial governorships. Poor health forced him to retire in 1849, but he was recalled the next year to serve as Imperial Commissioner, to pacify an anti-Qing secret society (Tiandi Hui) in Guangxi province. Lin Zexu died on 22 November 1850, in Guangdong, on the way to his new post, amid rumours that he had been poisoned by foreign merchants, thus prolonging the mystery that surrounded one of the most upright and capable officials in Chinese history.

86. WANG DUAN (1793–1839)
Woman poet of the Qing dynasty

Wang Duan was born in 1793 to an intellectually accomplished family in Hangzhou. She was one of many talented and educated women of the Qing, particularly in the south, whose talents went largely unrecognized and unused in the male-dominated society. Wang Duan's grandfather was a Presented Scholar and worked in the Qing Ministry of Justice. Her father, Wang Yu, decided to pursue a quiet scholarly life at home, teaching his two sons and two daughters after the death of their mother.

The special gifts of Wang Duan, the youngest child, were evident very early. At the age of six, she wrote a poem, 'Spring Snow', that was considered comparable to that of a mature poet. Her father hired a private teacher for his 'pearl in her father's palm', as cherished daughters were called. Wang Duan wrote this poem when she was just ten years old:

'A Farmer's Family'

After a night's rainfall on blossoming pear trees,
Rice paddies fill up with fresh water;
A neighbour wishes to feed his sallow calf –
He exits a hedged fence, hoe on his shoulder.
The young wife busily cooks breakfast,
While children hope for clearing skies in the afternoon;
In winds blowing through bamboo bushes,
Cuckoos are again calling for ploughing the fields.

Note The Chinese name *bugu* for 'cuckoo' is a pun for 'to sow'.

Marriages were arranged by the family, of course, and Wang Duan's father tried to find a worthy spouse for his artistic daughter. He went to Suzhou to meet Chen Wenshu, a native of Hangzhou and a noted scholar-official whose son, Chen Beizhi, was a poet. At the age of fourteen, Wang Duan was betrothed to Chen Beizhi. Shortly afterwards, her father and elder brother died, and she went to live with a maternal aunt. The aunt, married to a prominent scholar-official, herself enjoyed considerable literary fame and encouraged her studies. The aunt's husband, who often failed to beat Wang Duan in debates on Chinese history, referred to his erudite niece as 'Tiger Duan'.

In 1810, she married Chen Beizhi. Her father-in-law, Chen Wenshu, was an admirer of the famous Qing poet Yuan Mei (1716–98), who had taught and promoted talented women poets, and he was impressed by his daughter-in-law's wide literary and historical knowledge.

In addition to composing poems, Wang Duan compiled and published a two-volume selected anthology of Ming poetry, interlaced with her own commentaries. Her husband's government career was not a success. Of the couple's two sons, the first died young, and the second was physically and mentally weak. In line with Confucian family custom, Wang Duan asked her husband to take a concubine in order to have more sons, but the young concubine died two years later.

In 1826, Wang Duan's husband died while working in another province. Then Duan's only surviving son developed serious mental problems. Wang Duan became a fervent Daoist, and began to meditate for months without leaving her room.

With the male literary world largely closed to her, Wang Duan could employ her historical knowledge solely in her poems, yet she also wrote 'The Untold History of the Yuan–Ming Transition', a novel of eighty chapters that presented a version of events and personalities quite different from the official histories. When she became absorbed with Daoism, however, she burned the manuscript.

Wang Duan died on 1 February 1839, just short of her forty-sixth birthday, leaving behind more than 1,100 poems. She was not the only woman writer in her extended family. A distant aunt of her husband's, Chen Duansheng, wrote a long poetic drama called 'Fated Reincarnation', a Qing feminist manifesto recounting the story of a talented girl who impersonates a man and rises to the exalted position of Prime Minister. Moreover, Wang Duan's two female cousins were the closest friends of the most famous Manchu woman poet, Gu Chun (1799–1877), who wrote a sequel to the *Honglou Meng* ('Dream of Red Mansions').

Nineteenth-century painting of Sengge Rinchen on campaign.

87. SENGGE RINCHEN (1811–65)

The last great Mongol warrior

Sengge Rinchen (pinyin Senggelinqin) was born in 1811 to the Borjigit tribe in Inner Mongolia. He was said to be a descendant of Khasar, the younger brother of Genghis Khan.

Sengge's family was poor, and he lived by herding animals with his father. Nevertheless, because the clan had been the first among the Mongols to submit to Manchu power, it held a perpetual princedom; the current prince, a brother-in-law of the reigning Qing Emperor Daoguang, died without issue in 1825. Sengge, already known as a *baatar* ('hero') for his exceptional athletic prowess, was chosen to inherit the princedom and go to Beijing to serve in the imperial court.

Sengge rose quickly. By 1834, he was already a Grand Minister in Attendance, one of the four most intimate imperial bodyguards. He commanded a Mongol banner (military and administrative unit) and then a Manchu banner.

At the time of the outbreak of the Christian-inspired Taiping rebellion (see Hong Xiuquan, Biography 88), in 1853, Sengge, as Grand Minister Consultant, was put in charge of the defence of the capital region. He drove back the Taiping army, capturing the two commanding generals in 1855. The Taiping rebels never again posed a threat north of the Yellow River.

In June 1859, Sengge successfully defended the port of Tianjin against a joint Anglo-French naval attack. However, when the reinforced invaders came back the next year, Sengge's valiant Mongol mounted soldiers, no match for troops with advanced European weaponry, were slaughtered. When the Anglo-French forces sacked Beijing, and burned the imperial Yuanming Garden, with its corner of European-style buildings, Sengge was severely reprimanded, demoted and deprived of his princely rank.

In 1851, the Qing court had faced a more immediate threat, the widespread uprising of the northern Nian peasant 'bandits', who at times allied with the Taiping regime in Nanjing, and Sengge was given back his original rank and ordered to suppress the Nian insurgents. For five years Sengge executed this new mission tirelessly and was honoured for it. In the 1861 palace coup after the death of the Xianfeng emperor, Sengge sided with Empress-dowager Cixi (Biography 89). This act further enhanced his standing and prestige, which eventually included two noble titles in addition to his princedom.

Despite losing many able lieutenants in the ensuing battles, Sengge pushed on hard across the northern provinces. Eventually he fell into an ambush set by the insurgents in Shandong in May 1865. Hungry, exhausted, with half of his guards dead, Sengge fought on through the night until he was finally killed in action.

His death shook the court, which subsequently honoured Sengge, one of only two Mongols so treated, by commemorating him in the Qing Imperial Ancestral Temple in the Forbidden City.

88. HONG XIUQUAN (1814–64)
Taiping rebel leader

Hong Xiuquan was born into a Hakka peasant family in Guangdong on 1 January 1814. The Hakka (Kejia or 'Guest Families') are a sub-ethnic group of Han Chinese found mainly in southern China, the descendants of migrants from north and central China who maintained their own language and many cultural traits over the centuries. For instance, Hakka women did not bind their feet. A number of modern Chinese leaders were either Hakka themselves (Sun Yat-sen, Deng Xiaoping, Li Teng-hui), or related to Hakka (Chiang Kai-shek married a Hakka wife, and Mao Zedong's mother may have been Hakka).

Hong Xiuquan studied the Confucian classics and showed scholastic potential, and his clansmen had high hopes that he might become the first ever successful civil service examination graduate of the Hong clan. But between 1827 and 1843, Xiuquan four times failed the prefectural examination in Guangzhou, the second of three exams for obtaining the lowest degree of Cultivated Talent (*xiucai*). Hong Xiuquan fell gravely ill after his failure in 1837 and almost died.

In 1836, Hong Xiuquan had come across a Chinese and a foreigner preaching the Christian gospel together on a Guangzhou street. They gave him a set of nine booklets written by a Chinese Protestant convert titled *Quanshi Liangyan* ('Good Words to Exhort the World'). Seven years later one of his cousins read and recommended them.

Hong Xiuquan was immediately interested. He claimed that when he had fallen ill six years earlier, he had had a dream, or rather a revelation, of going to heaven to be received by God the Father and God's elder son, Jesus. Hong Xiuquan thus conceived of himself as God's younger son (Jesus's younger brother) who had been given the mission of destroying the demons in the world.

Hong Xiuquan started preaching his brand of Christianity, first among his family. The new faith was given the name of 'God-Worshipping Society' (*Bai Shangdi Hui*). Feng Yunshan, a relative and one of the first to be baptized, was a hard-working and charismatic missionary who found success among the Hakka communities in the mountains of the neighbouring Guangxi province, where other ethnic minorities lived and Confucian teachings were sparse. Meanwhile, Xiuquan kept developing his theology by studying with a young American Protestant missionary, Issachar Jacox Roberts, in Guangzhou.

When Hong Xiuquan joined Feng Yunshan in Guangxi in August 1847, the God-Worshipping Society had grown in size to tens of thousands of followers. Feng Yunshan was arrested by the authorities and Hong Xiuquan temporarily left the city.

In the summer of 1850, the Society openly set up its headquarters in the village of Jintian ('Golden Field'), and Hong Xiuquan started wearing a yellow-dragon overcoat, a style that only an emperor was entitled to wear. His followers were organized into militarized units, with all personal property turned over to the shared 'Holy Treasuries'. Men and women were separated into different camps. Late in the year the alarmed Qing government sent a pacifying force, but it was quickly defeated.

On 11 January 1851, at a victory celebration, the establishment of *Taiping Tianguo*, or 'Heavenly Kingdom of Great Peace', was proclaimed. Not long after, Hong Xiuquan himself was enthroned as the Heavenly King.

Under military pressure, Xiuquan moved his troops north. On 12 January 1853, Taiping troops conquered the provincial capital of Hubei and killed the first Qing provincial governor. With its ranks rapidly swollen by the poor and disenfranchised, the peasant army then marched down the Yangtze. On 19 March, the Taiping soldiers entered Nanjing, the old Ming capital. Ten days later, Hong Xiuquan arrived and renamed the city Tianjing, or 'Heavenly Capital' of his Heavenly Kingdom.

德天

Portrait of Hong Xiuquan, the self-styled 'Heavenly King'.

During the next few years, the kingdom consolidated its control of the Middle and Lower Yangtze valley, but its initially successful northern expedition army was defeated by the Mongol prince Sengge Rinchen (Biography 87) in 1855. Meanwhile, serious internal power struggles developed among the top echelons of the Taiping leaders, resulting in a bloody coup and a countercoup in 1856, and the killing of the Heavenly King's two top sub-kings, accompanied by the massacres of tens of thousands of their respective followers, and the departure of another charismatic top lieutenant. In the end, Hong Xiuquan won a pyrrhic victory by replacing a collegiate brotherhood with his dictatorial power, but the Heavenly Kingdom was much weakened.

The man who had failed at imperial examinations now launched his own civil service examinations, but he failed to win the support of the traditional Confucian gentry in southern China. The gentry instead organized efficient armies to fight the Heavenly Kingdom. While quite a few Westerners joined Xiuquan's 'Christian'

The Taiping rebellion.

cause, some Western powers, fearing disruption to trade, allowed and even encouraged their citizens to serve as anti-Taiping mercenaries. Among the most outstanding Western figures to confront the Taipings were an Englishman, Charles George Gordon (later the famed hero at Khartoum), and an American, Frederick Townsend Ward.

As the siege of the Heavenly Capital by the Qing forces tightened, the anti-Confucian 'Christian' Heavenly King continued to issue reassuring edicts made up of 'heavenly words' and 'dream words'. These were messages he claimed to have obtained from his father God and elder brother Jesus, which stated that everything would be all right.

The Heavenly King fell ill and died on 1 June 1864. Seven weeks later, the Qing army finally sacked Nanjing. The cause of the Heavenly Kingdom of Great Peace together with the family of the Heavenly King were completely exterminated, ending a rebellion in which up to a quarter of China's population died.

89. EMPRESS-DOWAGER CIXI (1835–1908)
Manchu ruler who brought down the Qing

Empress-dowager Cixi was born in 1835 to a mid-ranking Manchu family of the old Yehe Nara clan. Despite intermarriage with the family of Nurhaci (Biography 71), the tribal alliance soured into a feud, resulting in a legend that the Qing dynasty would some day be destroyed by the Yehe descendants. Cixi entered the palace as a low-level imperial concubine in 1851 at the age of sixteen. The next year, her father was dismissed from his post in the southern province of Anhui, for abandoning his office to escape the advancing Taiping insurgents (see Hong Xiuquan, Biography 88), and he died soon afterwards.

Her position in history was determined by her giving birth in 1856 to a son of the reigning Xianfeng emperor. By that time, the Manchu imperial house seemed to have lost all its earlier vitality, such that, except for another prince who died in infancy, Cixi's son turned out to be the very last child born to a reigning emperor of a dynasty that would linger on for fifty-five more years.

In the summer of 1861, the Xianfeng emperor died in the imperial hunting park at Rehe (Chengde) after fleeing the invading Anglo-French army during the Second Opium War. With her five-year-old son enthroned as Emperor Tongzhi, Cixi was made junior Empress-dowager, and the dead emperor's chief consort became the senior Empress-dowager.

The two deposed the eight senior courtiers appointed as regents by the late emperor and had three of them executed. It is probable that the more ambitious and ruthless Cixi played a decisive role in this life-and-death plot. The two Empresses-dowager then formed a joint regency, and were said to rule 'from behind screens', sometimes actually sitting hidden behind the throne. Popularly differentiated by the location of their respective residences, the senior lady became the 'Eastern Empress-dowager' and Cixi the 'Western Empress-dowager'. The Eastern Empress-dowager was far less politically inclined than the Western, that is, Cixi, and she allowed Cixi, who had a much better education in Chinese, gradually to assume the dominating role.

Though the regency was formally terminated when the young emperor reached maturity in 1873, Cixi continued to exert political and domestic control. The young emperor was widely reported to be fonder of the less dominating Eastern Empress-dowager and to have followed her advice on the selection of his empress in 1872, thereby incurring Cixi's wrath. It is also alleged that he was a secret frequenter of Beijing's brothels, where he contracted syphilis, although officially he died of small-pox on 12 January 1875.

Cixi then chose her nephew, aged three, as his successor, so the two elder Empresses-dowager could continue their regency. The Tongzhi emperor's widow, rumoured to be pregnant, committed suicide. In 1881, the Eastern Empress-dowager died rather suddenly, removing the last restraint on Cixi.

While China's international status continued to deteriorate during her long regency, the domestic situation showed considerable improvement. The Taiping rebellion was finally defeated, though at great human cost. Several other insurgencies were similarly put down. With the restoration of domestic peace, daily life for much of the population, particularly in areas once devastated by the Taiping, was significantly bettered. The period was regarded, therefore, as the Qing's revival, although some scholars attribute the relative prosperity and peace to the reduction in China's population resulting from the rebellion.

Cixi spent exorbitantly to celebrate her sixtieth (by Chinese reckoning) birthday, including massively renovating the Summer Palace in Beijing's northwestern suburbs. The court had to appropriate the navy budget to finance her birthday party on the eve of the first Sino-Japanese War in 1894, in which the Chinese navy was routed; hence the irony of the marble boat Cixi constructed at the Summer Palace.

When her nephew, the Guangxu emperor, reached maturity in 1889, Cixi 'retired', but she never really let go her control of the court. The young emperor, stunned by China's repeated humiliations and loss of territories to foreign powers, especially the cession of Taiwan after losing the 1894 war with Japan, wanted to enact drastic institutional reforms to revive the moribund Qing dynasty. The conservatives, backed by Cixi, stubbornly resisted.

The reform clique then called upon Yuan Shikai, a rising Han general, asking him to force Cixi's abdication. The scheming General Yuan, however, is said to have quickly betrayed the plot to Ronglu, the Governor-general of the capital province. Cixi launched a countercoup in September 1898, imprisoned her nephew, the Guangxu emperor, executed six leading reformers, and reversed the critical reform measures.

Cixi became increasingly bitter about Western encroachment, to the point of approving the attack on foreign embassies by the Boxers (peasant mobs) and government troops in 1900. In response, a coalition force from eight countries invaded and occupied Beijing to relieve the siege of the foreign legations, forcing Cixi to flee.

The crisis was settled through the tireless negotiations of the able courtier Li Hongzhang, but China paid a huge indemnity totalling 450 million taels of silver, though much of it was later waived or used to educate young Chinese abroad. Cixi returned to Beijing unscathed and became less hostile to the outside world.

大清國當今聖母皇太后萬歲萬歲萬萬歲

光緒癸卯年

Portrait of the Empress-dowager Cixi.

An astute politician, she made the decision to receive foreign ladies at court, and the wives of senior diplomats and missionaries were charmed by this apparently welcoming old lady who invited them to sit on her bed and offered them tea in Worcester porcelain. She carefully arranged the reception rooms to create the desired impression, temporarily removing Buddha figures and substituting Western clocks. She also accepted an American painter, Katherine Carl, into the palace to paint her portrait for public exhibition – a true break with tradition, because most portraiture in China, especially of imperial persons, was used only on ancestral altars, after their deaths.

Belatedly, Cixi allowed many measures for modernizing China, such as the introduction of modern industry, the abolition of civil service exams, and the proscription of foot-binding. However, these actions, significant though they were, came too late, and more and more Chinese intellectuals gave up on a constitutional monarchy and joined the Republican revolutionaries.

On 15 November 1908, Cixi died after ruling China for almost half a century. The Guangxu emperor, a virtual prisoner since 1898, died the day before. Recalling the old Yehe curse, the Qing dynasty crumbled within three years.

90. QIU JIN (c.1875–1907)
Feminist heroine and martyr

Though her family was from Shaoxing, in Zhejiang province, Qiu Jin was born in Fujian, in about 1875. Both her father and grandfather were examination graduates, and her family provided her with an education. Qiu Jin wrote poetry and admired traditional Chinese national heroes. She spent her childhood in Fujian, and it is possible that Western encroachment along the coast encouraged her growing nationalism. At fifteen, Qiu Jin accompanied her parents to their home town, Shaoxing. Though, like most girls, she had bound feet, she, unusually, learned martial arts and horseback riding with her maternal uncle and cousins.

In May 1896, she entered an arranged marriage with a Hunanese man, Wang Zifang, who was four years her junior and less well educated, and who did not share her taste for literature. Her lack of enthusiasm for the marriage is reflected in poems written months after the wedding. Within the next few years Qiu Jin gave birth to a son and a daughter.

In 1899, her husband obtained an entry-level post in Beijing through a large 'donation', and the family moved to the city.

Dissatisfied with her married life, and encouraged by living in the city among young intellectuals who were embracing ideas of reform and modernization, Qiu Jin wanted to study abroad. Her husband opposed the idea and took the jewels that were part of her dowry to prevent her from leaving. She nevertheless managed to set off for Japan in 1904, first attending a language school in Tokyo, then registering in a teacher training programme. She associated with many people who would later play important roles back in China, including revolutionaries such as Huang Xing (Sun Yat-sen's lieutenant) and Song Jiaoren (the first secretary-general of the Kuomintang), and future literary giant Lu Xun (Biography 92).

In early 1905, Qiu Jin went back to China to see her mother and raise funds for further study. She joined a secret revolutionary group called Guangfu Hui ('Restoration Society'). Returning to Japan, she became one of the earliest members of the anti-Manchu Chinese [Revolutionary] Alliance founded by Sun Yat-sen (Biography 91).

Though educated in classical Chinese, she helped publish one of the first vernacular Chinese magazines and revived a women's organization that advocated 'the liberation of two hundred million Chinese sisters'. The most famous image of Qiu Jin is a photograph in which she wears Western male clothing.

On her return to China, Qiu Jin started the magazine 'Chinese Women's Journal' (*Zhongguo Nübao*), to promote women's liberation. She became a leading organizer of anti-Manchu activities in Zhejiang province, mobilizing secret societies, infiltrating the Qing's 'modern armies', and training revolutionary cadres. In February 1907, she took over the principalship of the Datong Normal School (high school) in her parents' home town at Shaoxing, a secret training camp for revolutionaries, and involved herself in organizing a multi-province anti-Qing uprising. The plot was exposed, and Datong School became a government target.

After evacuating many students, hiding weapons and destroying documents, Qiu Jin stayed on, perhaps assuming that, as a woman, she was less at risk, although Lu Xun and others later speculated that she might have had martyrdom in mind.

The Qing troops despatched from the provincial capital at Hangzhou attacked the school on the afternoon of 13 July 1907, and arrested Qiu Jin and others. Told to write a confession, she only wrote repeatedly her surname, Qiu, meaning 'autumn' in Chinese, in a seven-character verse: 'Autumn wind, autumn rain – utterly autumnal melancholy!' Condemned to execution, she asked that she be allowed to write to her family, that she not be undressed for execution as was normally done for male criminals, and that her severed head not be publicly displayed. The last two wishes were granted, and Qiu Jin was beheaded before dawn on 15 July. Her death was a public relations disaster for the Qing government. Newspapers across China,

Photograph of Qiu Jin.

particularly those published in the foreign concession in Shanghai, condemned the execution of an educated woman, and the officials associated with her execution had to request transfers, the presiding magistrate later committing suicide. After the revolution, Qiu Jin was finally buried with great honour beside the West Lake in Hangzhou, alongside the tomb of the national hero Yue Fei (Biography 55). Ironically, half a century later she was labelled a 'bourgeoise revolutionary', and her remains were desecrated on the eve of the Cultural Revolution, removed to a nameless tomb in the suburbs, and nearly lost. It was only in 1981 that the heroine's tomb was rebuilt.

The two figures at front centre are Song Qingling and Sun Yat-sen.

91. SUN YAT-SEN (1866–1925)
Idealistic revolutionary and founder of the Republic of China

Sun Yat-sen was born on 12 November 1866, in a village not far from Guangzhou (Canton). The Sun family is said to have been of Hakka ancestry. As a peasant's son, the young boy received a standard Confucian primary education. At thirteen, he went to Honolulu to join his much older brother, who had become a successful merchant. Sun attended the Iolani School and quickly mastered the English language. As the Hawaiian Islands were in the process of being annexed by the United States, he obtained American citizenship.

When Sun showed interest in Christianity, his conservative elder brother, disapproving, sent him back to China in 1883, but he was baptized in Hong Kong by an American missionary. In May 1884, he entered into an arranged marriage with a village girl, and they had one son and two daughters. In 1892, Sun graduated from the Hong Kong College of Medicine for Chinese and began to practise medicine.

Throughout his years in Western educational establishments, Sun continued to study Chinese language and history. Troubled by the backwardness of Qing China in contrast to what he saw abroad and in Hong Kong, he felt the strong need to improve Chinese society and modernize China. In early 1894, he attempted to present a reform programme to the minister Li Hongzhang (see Empress-dowager

Cixi, Biography 89), but received no response. He returned to Hawaii and organized China's first modern revolutionary society, the Society to Rejuvenate China (*Xing Zhong Hui*), on 24 November 1894, then quickly expanded it to Hong Kong.

Despite meagre funding and few followers, the Society started planning an anti-Qing uprising in Guangzhou in March 1895, tapping into the local network of secret societies, but the plot was discovered by Qing authorities. Sun Yat-sen barely escaped, finally travelling to America, with a government reward of 1,000 dollars on his head. He continued to argue his cause and to raise money, mostly among overseas Chinese. In 1896, Sun Yat-sen arrived in London. Visiting the Chinese legation under a pseudonym, he was recognized and detained. Just when he was about to be secretly shipped back to China, Sun Yat-sen managed to alert a former teacher from his medical school in Hong Kong, now living in London. The resulting public pressure brought about his release. In a matter of weeks he had become internationally known and gained many supporters, to the point that when he went to Japan in 1897, he was hailed as an undisputed leader by the many anti-Qing Chinese there.

He developed a political philosophy known as the Three Principles of the People (nationalism, democracy and the people's livelihood); although he was an indefatigable leader, some felt that he possessed more righteous enthusiasm than practical abilities.

During the Boxer movement and the ensuing foreign military intervention in 1900–1, Sun attempted to persuade Li Hongzhang, then the Qing Governor-general of Guangdong and Guangxi, to set up an independent non-Manchu government in southern China. After another military uprising failed, he toured America and Europe to gain support, then became president of a united anti-Qing revolutionary front called the Chinese [Revolutionary] Alliance in Tokyo.

This was a turning point for the revolutionary movement. Though military uprisings kept failing, the movement's propaganda efforts made great headway among Chinese intellectuals, and its secret society connections began to penetrate the new, modern Qing army units. When the 1911 revolution broke out along the Yangtze, Sun Yat-sen, in the USA, was not directly involved. He rushed back immediately, touching Chinese soil for the first time in more than sixteen years since his first, failed, Guangzhou uprising. His international prominence and long years of revolutionary efforts made him the consensus candidate to be a leader of the new nation, and he was sworn in as the first provisional president of the embryonic Republic of China.

However, the loosely organized and mostly southern revolutionaries proved no match for the entrenched power and control of the former Qing general, Yuan

Shikai, who managed to become the first formal president of the republic. Sun Yat-sen led an unsuccessful 'second revolution' in 1913 against Yuan but was forced into exile in Japan.

There Sun Yat-sen reorganized the Kuomintang, the successor political party to his Society to Rejuvenate China, and married Song Qingling, daughter of an influential Christian family of Hakka descent in Shanghai, who was two years younger than his own son.

As China gradually sank into warlordism, Sun Yat-sen returned; in 1921 he set up a military government in Guangzhou, accepted aid from the Communist International organization (Comintern), and began a policy of active cooperation with the Chinese Communists. He established a military academy, with Chiang Kai-shek (Biography 93) as its commandant, to train military officers for the new revolutionary army, and turned the Kuomintang into a Leninist-style party.

The Kuomintang-Communist united front was in part prompted by the egalitarian, socialist element of Sun Yat-sen's Three Principles of the People, but it led to deep ideological division within the Chinese Nationalist movement, with the result that Sun Yat-sen's son would die as a loyal Nationalist in Taiwan in 1973, whereas his second wife Song Qingling died as 'honorary president' of the People's Republic in Beijing in 1981.

Though convinced that China could be unified only through military means, Sun Yat-sen's idealism led him on a peace mission to northern China, arriving in Beijing on the last day of 1924. He died of liver cancer on 12 March 1925, at the Rockefeller Hospital in Beijing. His last words are said to have been, 'peace, struggle, to save China'.

92. LU XUN (1881–1936)
Greatest Chinese writer of the 20th century

Lu Xun was born in the town of Shaoxing, in Zhejiang province, in September 1881. His real name was Zhou Shuren, Lu Xun being but the best known of his more than a hundred pen-names and aliases.

His grandfather, Zhou Fuqing, was a high official in the capital city Beijing, but he was caught bribing an examination supervisor in 1893. He was sentenced to death, but after nearly seven years in jail, he was finally released in 1900, by which time the Zhou family had nearly exhausted its wealth by paying officials every autumn to delay his execution.

Portrait of Lu Xun.

Lu Xun's father failed to obtain a degree beyond that of 'Cultivated Talent' (*xiucai*). All chance of advancement ending with his own father's crime, he lapsed into drinking and smoking opium, dying in 1897. During his father's long decline, Lu Xun was often sent to a pawnshop, which had a counter taller than himself, to get money to buy him Chinese medicines.

In spring 1898, at the age of seventeen, Lu Xun left for Nanjing to attend newly established modern schools, against his traditionalist mother's wishes. He first studied in the Jiangnan Naval Academy, then the School of Railways and Mines attached to the Jiangnan Infantry Academy. He graduated in 1902 and won a scholarship to study in Sendai, in Japan.

In 1906, despite his more modern views, his mother forced him into an arranged marriage with an illiterate woman two years older than himself, who had bound feet and who lacked any interest in changing herself or society. Lu Xun returned to Tokyo a few days after the wedding ceremony, but he supported his mother and his wife all his life.

Lu Xun stayed in Japan for nearly seven years, first studying medicine, then devoting himself to literature, feeling that he could do more good by changing many minds than by curing individual bodies. In spring 1912, in the first year of the Republic of China (see Sun Yat-sen, Biography 91), Lu Xun took up a position in the Ministry of Education in Nanjing at the invitation of minister Cai Yuanpei.

Soon the Ministry moved to Beijing, which was in chaos, with two warlords vying for power and two attempts to restore the imperial house. There Lu Xun wrote his masterpiece, 'Diary of a Madman' (*Kuangren riji*), in 1918, for the most influential magazine of the New Culture Movement, *Xin Qingnian* ('New Youth'). Written in vernacular Chinese, it describes the psychological terror of a man who gradually discovers the cannibalistic nature of traditional Chinese society.

Often compared to the Russian master Gogol, Lu Xun continued writing short stories in modern vernacular Chinese and experimented with different styles. In 'Medicine' (*Yao*), the main hero, Xia Yu, a revolutionary, never directly appears in the story. Xia Yu (an apparent allusion to the late Qing heroine, Qiu Jin [see Biography 90]) is beheaded and, in an echo of the strange potions prescribed ineffectively for Lu Xun's father, his fresh blood is used as medicine for another youth suffering from tuberculosis. His most famous work of fiction, *A Q zhengzhuan* ('The True Story of Ah Q'), tells of a pathetic peasant, symbolizing the Chinese nation as a whole, whose greatest talent is making excuses for his miserable failures. Other noteworthy short stories by Lu Xun are *Lihun* ('Divorce') and *Zhufu* ('Benediction'), which respectively reveal the horrors of feudalism and superstition. *Feizao* ('Soap') is a clever satire on Confucianism, one of Lu Xun's favourite targets. His 'Old Tales Retold' offers brilliant satirical retellings of Chinese legends.

Lu Xun wrote most of his celebrated short stories while he was in Beijing. In 1919, he bought a big house there with spacious courtyards. His two younger brothers, Zhou Zuoren and Zhou Jianren, as well as their wives and children, lived with him.

Lu Xun taught at Peking University, the Women's Normal College and the Esperanto Institute. He supported the student movement at the Women's Normal College and the demonstrations against the corrupt regime of the warlord Duan Qirui. Upon learning that he had been put on a government blacklist, he left Beijing in September 1926 for Xiamen (Amoy) University, at the invitation of the noted humourist and scholar, Lin Yutang. One of his former students, Xu Guangping, a woman eighteen years his junior, travelled to the south with him and went on to Canton (Guangzhou) to teach at the Canton Girls' Normal School (high school).

Lu Xun went to Canton in January 1927 to teach at Sun Yat-sen University, where Xu Guangping was his teaching assistant. They left Canton for Shanghai in September 1927, where they lived together until Lu Xun died of tuberculosis in October 1936. Their only child, Zhou Haiying, was born in September 1929.

In Shanghai, Lu Xun had a number of friends who were Communist Party members, and many were killed by the Nationalist government. This and the earlier October Revolution in Russia had a profound effect upon him and caused his political views to shift to the left. In 1930 Lu Xun co-founded the League of Left-Wing Writers and helped to edit its periodicals.

It was in Shanghai that Lu Xun wrote most of his *zawen* ('miscellaneous essays') to express his ideas of social justice and humanity, dealing with such issues as corruption, women's liberation and children's welfare. He also maintained a voluminous correspondence with a broad array of intellectual, literary, political and other figures. Among the many objects of his criticism were the censorship and oppressive political 'white terror' of the government of the Kuomintang Nationalists. He also addressed matters of cultural reform such as the promotion of vernacular writing and the creation of a Romanized Chinese script. His many short essays, called 'daggers' (*bishou*) or 'spears' (*touqiang*), led to his being hailed by Mao Zedong as 'the greatest and most accurate thinker, revolutionary, and man of letters', but his works were banned in Taiwan until martial law was lifted in the 1980s.

93. CHIANG KAI-SHEK (1887–1975)
Kuomintang leader

Chiang Kai-shek was born in 1887, in a small town near the port city of Ningbo in Zhejiang province, to a salt merchant family, and received a standard Confucian education. After the death of his father in 1895, the family went through some difficult times. Chiang's mother, a former Buddhist nun, was sufficiently enlightened to allow Chiang to study in Japan for a military career, but also old-fashioned enough to make him marry a local wife four years his senior when he was fourteen. (This wife, née Mao, happened to come from the same clan as Mao Zedong.)

After studying in a junior military school, Chiang enlisted in the Japanese army in 1909. More consequential was his close association with anti-Qing Chinese revolutionaries who had taken refuge in Japan. Chiang joined Sun Yat-sen's (Biography 91) Chinese [Revolutionary] Alliance in 1908 and met Sun the next year.

Chiang played an active role in the 1911 Republican revolution, working with a comrade of Qiu Jin (Biography 90), organizing and participating in 'dare-to-die units' in the revolution. He was appointed a regimental commander in the new Republican army.

However, in 1912, Chiang was involved in the assassination in Shanghai of a revolutionary leader who was a rival of Sun Yat-sen, and he was forced into exile in Japan. As a founding member of the Kuomintang (Nationalist Party), he opposed

Photograph of Chiang Kai-shek.

Yuan Shikai, the first official president of the republic, who posted a reward of 3,000 silver dollars for Chiang's arrest. Back in Shanghai, Chiang received financial and other support from the secret society 'Green Gang' (*Qing bang*), and he became the 'sworn brother' of some unsavoury underworld bosses.

His initial loyalty won him the trust of Sun Yat-sen, especially after Chiang's rescue of Sun during a southern warlord's assassination attempt in June 1923. In his efforts to unite a China fragmented by warlordism, Sun accepted aid from the Soviet Union and sent Chiang to Moscow to study the Communist political and military system. Returning to Guangzhou (Canton), then the Kuomintang strong-hold, Chiang in 1924 was appointed commandant of a new military school known as the Whampoa Military Academy. The academy became Chiang's power base, as its graduates formed the backbone of the Kuomintang's best-organized army, which in turned played a decisive role in the party's northern expedition in 1926 to unify the warlord-ruled China. This also enabled Chiang to eclipse more senior Kuomintang veterans, until he finally emerged as the party's *de facto* leader.

Although he had sent his eldest (and only biological) son, Chiang Ching-kuo (Jiang Jingguo), as a student to the Soviet Union, Chiang openly split with and purged the Chinese Communists in 1927 and declared a new national government in Nanjing. No less importantly, Chiang divorced his first and second wives and dismissed a concubine, converted to Christianity, and married Song Meiling, the American-educated sister-in-law of the recently deceased Sun Yat-sen. Together with his new wife, Chiang founded the highly moralistic and nationalistic New Life Movement in February 1934.

During the next ten years, Chiang's government made efforts to build a modern China. In a practical sense, China's unification at the time was nominal, and Chiang controlled no more than the provinces on the southeast coast and in the Middle to Lower Yangtze valley. Yet, as well as suppressing military rivals and Communist insurgencies, the Nanjing government made progress on many fronts.

Modern education was expanded and the Academia Sinica, the national academy of sciences, was founded. Nanjing made the first official effort to simplify Chinese characters, and even tried to ban 'unscientific', traditional Chinese medicine. Three national athletic games were held, and the sports facilities built would remain the best stadia in Nanjing and Shanghai until the 1970s.

Despite the autocratic tendencies of a regime that maintained strong Leninist characteristics from earlier Soviet influence, and repressive measures including imprisonment and even assassination, China saw an unprecedented cultural revival.

Chiang relied on a succession of German military and economic advisors, the first being Max Bauer, who worked with him from 1927 to 1929, at the beginning of a decade of development that took place under Chiang's rule, followed by Alexander von Faulkenhausen, who played a key role in routing the Chinese Soviet Republic in Jiangxi in 1934.

These achievements were threatened by Japanese aggression against China. After the Japanese occupation of Manchuria in September 1931, Chiang's policy, 'fending off foreign aggression requires first of all domestic stability', came under increasing criticism.

On 12 December 1936, the famous Xi'an Incident took place: Chiang was kidnapped by General Zhang Xueliang, his 'sworn brother' and the husband of Song Meiling's 'sworn sister', when Chiang flew to the city to organize 'the final battle against the Chinese Communists'. As part of the negotiated settlement, Chiang was forced to agree to the integration of the Communists into his government for a 'united front' against Japan.

After the provocation by the Japanese of the Marco Polo Bridge incident on 7 July 1937, Chiang was forced to initiate full-scale hostilities in Shanghai, on 13 August. The long, drawn-out war provided the Communists an opportunity to grow and expand 'behind the enemy lines', with organization and propaganda skills that the Kuomintang could not match. The enormous destruction and impoverishment brought on by the war, and the difficulties suffered by the middle class, weakened the Kuomintang's social base. The eight war years also led to serious corruption within the Kuomintang ranks. Nevertheless, when the Allies finally won World War II, Chiang gained for China the status of one of the five major powers, a permanent seat on the UN Security Council, and the abolition of all unequal treaties and foreign concessions in China except Hong Kong.

Chiang had face-to-face talks with Mao Zedong (Biography 95) in autumn 1945, but the peace agreement was soon broken by both sides. The Communists, grown to a strength of one million armed men during the war with Japan, eventually came out on top in the ensuing civil war. Chiang was forced to move the rump Kuomintang government to Taiwan in 1949.

Maintaining despotic, one-party rule in his remaining years, as president of the Republic of China, Chiang never realized his dream of 'recovering the mainland'. Surrounded by his loyal wife Meiling and numerous grandchildren, Chiang died on 5 April 1975, to be followed in death by Mao a little more than a year later.

94. HU SHI (1891–1962)
Intellectual leader

Hu Shi was born in Shanghai in 1891 to a tea merchant family from the township of Jixi in southern Anhui. His father became a Cultivated Talent, the lowest degree-holder, in 1865, and went into public service in 1882, serving in posts from the northern border in Manchuria to the southernmost Hainan Island, ending up in Taiwan before the island's cessation to Japan in 1895.

Just before the death of his father, Hu Shi and his mother left Taiwan for their ancestral home in Anhui. After a traditional primary education, Hu Shi went with an elder brother to Shanghai to seek a 'modern' education in 1904. After attending several schools, including the one Qiu Jin (Biography 90) had helped set up, Hu Shi won a Boxer Indemnity scholarship examination to study in the US. The scholarship programme was financed by funds collected as reparation for the siege of the foreign legations in Beijing in 1900 (see Empress-dowager Cixi, Biography 89).

In August 1910, Shi arrived at Cornell University to study agriculture, as China was in need of modern science and technology. In a personal revelation not unlike that of Lu Xun (Biography 92), Hu Shi decided after a year that he should switch to philosophy and literature, both for his own sake and that of China. He was active

Hu Shi.

in student politics and, as a delegate to the Eighth International Congress of the Fédération Internationale des Etudiants, went to Washington, DC in 1913 to be received by President Woodrow Wilson.

After obtaining his undergraduate degree and attending some graduate courses at Cornell, Shi transferred to Columbia University. He was strongly influenced by John Dewey's experimentalism and 'instrumentalism', and became a lifelong disciple of Dewey. He defended his doctoral dissertation on 'The Development of the Logical Method in Ancient China' in May 1917, with Professor Dewey sitting as chairman of the examination board (though for reasons that are unclear, the PhD was not officially awarded until 1927).

Hu Shi returned to China to a professorship at Peking University. His name was well known even before his arrival, thanks to a series of essays he had published earlier in the 'New Youth', then China's leading journal among modern intellectuals. In particular, his 'Tentative Proposals for the Improvement of Literature', published in January 1917, is widely regarded as marking the beginning of China's literary revolution, which called for the replacement of the millennia-old domination of the classical written language by a vernacular one closer to spoken Chinese. Hu Shi's intellectual legacy is considerable, and he was a primary leader in the fundamental change, not only of Chinese literature, but also of the national mode of thinking. The literary revolution became the main element of the May Fourth Movement in 1919.

In his private life, however, Hu Shi was a prisoner of the old traditions. His mother arranged his marriage to a local, largely uneducated girl with bound feet, and after years of resistance, Hu Shi finally married her in late 1917. Despite a passionate affair with a relative (a bridesmaid of his wife), Hu Shi was never able to break away from this arranged marriage. His lover, Cao Chengying, later obtained a master's degree in genetics from Cornell University and died in the chaos of the Cultural Revolution. Hu Shi also had a long-term, apparently platonic relationship with an American woman, Edith Clifford Williams.

With degrees from two US Ivy League universities and his professorship at Peking University, Hu Shi became a national celebrity while still in his twenties. Friendly and easy to approach, he met people from all walks of society, including the young library assistant Mao Zedong and the boy ex-emperor Puyi. He remained true to Dewey's experimentalism. In the famous debate of 'problems versus –isms', Hu Shi advocated finding practical solutions to China's manifold problems, instead of appealing to radical ideologies.

Believing in tolerance, Hu Shi maintained amicable relationships with and helped many Communist and left-wing friends, colleagues and students, but he stood firmly in the anti-Marxist camp. The 1920s and 1930s witnessed a Chinese intellectual renaissance. While the Kuomintang government was anti-Communist, it was pro-education. With the rapid expansion of schools and universities and the founding of modern research institutions, the humanities and Chinese literature flourished. Nevertheless, with growing Japanese aggression and the rise of radical nationalism, Hu Shi's status and influence lessened.

He was, however, appointed ambassador to the USA in 1938. He worked to win American government support and public sympathy during the Japanese invasion of China, to the point that a Columbia University historian has blamed him for instigating the Japanese attack on Pearl Harbor. He remained in the USA in various semi-official capacities until appointed president of Peking University in 1946. Hu Shi was elected to the 1948 National Assembly, which was boycotted by the Communists. Radicals ridiculed Hu Shi as 'a man with a Chinese body but an American brain'. In 1948, days before Beijing fell to the Communists, he left the city in a plane despatched on the personal order of Chiang Kai-shek (Biography 93).

In the next decade, Hu Shi lived mostly in New York City as a political refugee. After serving as ambassador to the United Nations in 1957, he finally went to Taiwan in 1958, where he had lived as a child, to assume the presidency of Academia Sinica. He worked to improve the island's scientific education, but died suddenly of a heart attack on 24 February 1962. In his will, he left his personal assets to his wife and two sons, not knowing that his American-educated younger son Sidu, who had chosen to remain in mainland China, had committed suicide in 1957 after being labelled a 'rightist' by the Communist government.

95. MAO ZEDONG (MAO TSE-TUNG; 1893–1976)
Communist revolutionary

The future radical revolutionary was born in 1893, in a rural village in Hunan province, to a peasant family rich enough to provide him with an education that the great majority of farmers could not afford. He graduated from a normal school, the equivalent of high school, in the provincial capital. In 1918, Mao travelled to Beijing with the school's principal, Yang Changji, who had obtained a professorship at the prestigious Peking University.

Professor Yang helped him get a job as an assistant librarian at the university, where Mao was fascinated by the ongoing student movement driven by Western ideas. He sat in on many lectures, including those given by Hu Shi (Biography 94), but was never accepted as a formal student. Despite an existing arranged marriage at home, Mao married Professor Yang's daughter Kaihui. Attracted by Marxism, Mao attended the first session of the National Congress of the Chinese Communist Party in Shanghai in July 1921, thus becoming a founding member of the Party.

Mao made his name in the short-lived first alliance between the Communists and the Kuomintang arranged by the Comintern, rising to be propaganda chief of the Kuomintang. He was made a member of the Peasant Movement Committee and spent much time in the countryside investigating rural conditions. After the bloody partisan split between the Communists and the Kuomintang in 1927, Mao turned to his then radical idea of mobilizing Chinese peasants. Ridiculed by orthodox Communists, who regarded the peasantry as a backward class compared to the urban proletariat, Mao demonstrated his incisive understanding of Chinese history – that new dynasties were often the result of peasant uprisings.

In 1927, Mao organized his first peasant uprising in his home province of Hunan, but the peasant army was quickly defeated. This taught Mao another lesson: to move his insurgency to hard-to-reach remote areas. He therefore established a military camp in the Jinggang Mountains in Jiangxi province and developed it into a 'Soviet Republic of China'. Mao was elected chairman of the Republic and married a local woman in May 1928, more than two years before his second wife, Yang Kaihui, was arrested and executed by the Kuomintang in the autumn of 1930 in Hunan.

Mao's Soviet Republic faced a double threat: from Chiang Kai-shek's military campaigns and also from the central leadership of the Chinese Communist Party. The Party had been forced to move from the comfortable city of Shanghai to Ruijin in southeast Jiangxi province in 1932. Mao was sidelined and his military command taken over by Zhou Enlai. The Kuomintang army under its German advisors finally broke the back of the Soviet Republic in a fifth encirclement in 1934, forcing the Red Army into what was later named the 'Long March', essentially an opportunistic retreat.

Mao had already clashed with the Communist Party leadership, and such clashes continued as the Long March made its way southwest and then north. In early 1935, in remote Guizhou province, Mao launched an intra-party coup, forced an ad hoc Party conference, and assumed for the first time overall Party leadership, terminating the domination of the Comintern faction trained in the Soviet Union. When the Red Army finally arrived in Yan'an in impoverished northern Shaanxi province, it had lost 90 percent of its original strength.

The Sino-Japanese War, as Mao later acknowledged, provided the Communists with the historical opportunity to expand and grow 'behind the enemy lines'. When Japan surrendered in 1945, the one-million-soldier-strong Communist power was indestructible and in 1949 took over the entire country except Taiwan. The victory is generally attributed to Mao's 'people's war' fought by a huge peasant army, but the Communists' success in winning over the Chinese intelligentsia by the appeal of its egalitarian ideology played an equally critical role.

Apart from the execution of over one million landlords and 'counterrevolutionaries', the first few years of Mao's rule of 'new China' were largely successful in terms of economic recovery and political cohesion. Significant technological and scientific assistance was provided by Russian advisors (they would be unceremoniously expelled in the early 1960s when Mao broke with the Soviet Union).

Mao pushed ahead with the collectivization of agriculture over considerable high-level opposition, and in 1957 he launched the 'Hundred Flowers Campaign', in which he invited constructive criticism. This was followed immediately by the Anti-Rightist Movement, when it seems that he was genuinely surprised by the heavy criticism of his rule from intellectuals. Several million 'rightists', almost all highly educated intellectuals, who had answered the call for constructive criticism, as well as their relatives within and outside the Party, were purged.

Mao's Great Leap Forward of 1958 was marked by the creation of large 'people's communes' and 'rapid industrialization' through primitive production of iron and steel in backyard furnaces. The net result was a devastating famine in which 30 million or more people lost their lives. Mao was forced to make his first

Mao Zedong.

Mao Zedong greeting crowds.

and only 'self-criticism', and relinquished day-to-day leadership of Party and state to Liu Shaoqi in 1962.

In 1966, feeling upstaged and sidelined by Liu and other pragmatic leaders in the Communist Party, Mao launched the Great Proletarian Cultural Revolution, promoting 'nonstop class struggle' and 'ongoing revolution'. Liu Shaoqi and his associates were cruelly purged. Mao encouraged all of China's youth to abandon their studies and travel across the country, attacking all in authority and destroying all objects declared 'feudal-bourgeois-revisionist'. A main target of their violence was the educational system: professors and experts were beaten and sent away to perform manual labour.

Mao's Cultural Revolution depended on two primary helpers: Marshal Lin Biao, Mao's new heir apparent, and former movie actress Jiang Qing, Mao's fourth wife, whom he had married against the strong opposition of the Party elders shortly after the Long March. The first part of the alliance soon fell apart. Marshal Lin died in a mysterious plane crash in Mongolia in 1971 after an alleged coup and assassination attempt upon Mao.

Isolated, the aging 'Great Helmsman' refused to halt his 'ongoing revolution' and launched further political campaigns. After the death of Zhou Enlai, widely viewed as a moderate counter to Mao's radicalism, popular discontent was revealed in the first Tiananmen Square Incident in April 1976. In July, an earthquake not far from Beijing that killed nearly a quarter of a million people seemed a sign that the Mandate of Heaven had been withdrawn, and Mao died not long after, on 9 September 1976.

Mao's achievements in uniting China after a century of foreign wars and encroachments and of re-establishing the economy in the early 1950s have been overshadowed by the unprecedented peacetime starvation after the Great Leap Forward and the draconian political campaigns of his later years.

Mao was a considerable poet and calligrapher, and his political writings, their complexity not reflected in the 'Little Red Book' of short quotations compiled prior to the Cultural Revolution (1966–76), demonstrate his interpretation of Marxism-Leninism in the Chinese context. Having irreversibly destroyed many Confucian social traditions, Mao, who was often compared with China's First Emperor (Qin Shihuangdi, Biography 11) by himself and others, fundamentally changed the historical and future path of the Central Kingdom.

96. DENG XIAOPING (1904–97)
Leader who transformed post-Mao China

Deng Xiaoping, Chairman of the Central Military Commission of the Chinese Communist Party, Vice Premier and architect of China's post-Mao economic reform (see Mao Zedong, Biography 95), was born in 1904, to a well-to-do landlord family of Hakka ancestry in rural eastern Sichuan. He had several other names before assuming the given name Xiaoping as an adult. After brief preparatory study, in the summer of 1920 he joined a work-study programme in France.

Deng spent most of his time in France working, including at a Renault factory in the Paris suburbs. He was soon attracted to Marxism and joined the Chinese Communist Youth around 1922, then the European branch of the Chinese Communist Party (CCP) two years later. Together with Zhou Enlai, Deng became a full-time revolutionary. When the French police wanted him for questioning, he left for Moscow in January 1926, retaining a deep impression of his European sojourn and a love of croissants.

After studying at Sun Yat-sen University in Moscow, Deng returned to China in late 1926 and joined the Chinese Communist movement. He served as a political commissar in the Chinese Communist army, from the Long March in 1934 until its final victory. In late 1947, Deng and Liu Bocheng led a bold expedition from the Yellow River to the heart of the Kuomintang realm, posing a grave threat to Chiang Kai-shek (Biography 93). Deng was also the battlefront Party chief in the decisive Huaihai campaign from November 1948 to January 1949 that destroyed the bulk of the remaining Kuomintang army.

After the founding of the People's Republic of China in 1949, Deng was appointed a Vice Premier in 1952, and in 1956 became a standing member of the Politburo and Secretary-general of the CCP. While he loyally served Mao's political front, especially in the Chinese Communists' open split with the Soviets, Deng grew disillusioned with Mao's disastrous economic and social policies. He worked closely with Liu Shaoqi when the latter was asked to deal with the terrible famine caused by Mao's Great Leap Forward in the early 1960s. This was when (in 1961) he uttered his most famous epigram, illustrating his preference for pragmatism over political correctness: 'It doesn't matter whether it's a white cat or a black cat; so long as it catches mice, it's a good cat'.

Like Liu Shaoqi, Deng was persecuted during the Cultural Revolution that started in 1966. He was forced to retire from all his positions and work in a tractor factory far from Beijing. His eldest son was forced to jump or was pushed by Red Guards from the upper story of a building and became a paraplegic.

In 1973, Deng was rehabilitated and rejoined the CCP's central committee. Many people believed Zhou Enlai promoted Deng's return, given their old association in Paris. However, it is likely that it was partly because, after the death of Lin Biao, Deng was the only potential counterbalance to Zhou, who now occupied the precarious number two position in the old CCP establishment. Deng was quickly promoted to Executive Vice Premier. In that capacity, he attended the United Nations Assembly in New York in 1974, his first trip to the USA.

The biggest difference between Zhou Enlai and Deng was the latter's more principled stand on fundamental issues. Deng implemented many policies during his short tenure that negated Mao's Cultural Revolution. These measures not only expanded Deng's following within the CCP, but also won him broad support from a people tired of Mao's political campaigns and economic failures.

The death of Zhou Enlai in January 1976 ended Deng's political usefulness to Mao, and he was purged for the second time. When Mao's death in September was followed by a coup against some of his closest followers in October 1976, Deng Xiaoping's comeback was assured. After assuming *de facto* control of the CCP at the end of 1978, Deng began the drastic economic reforms that in a quarter of a century turned China into one of the world's largest economies.

Deng Xiaoping.

In his international policy, Deng developed Mao's *de facto* alliance with the USA against the Soviet Union. Immediately after his historic 1979 visit to the USA, which established formal and full diplomatic relations between the two countries, China launched a 'punitive' invasion of Vietnam, the Soviet satellite in Southeast Asia. The USA and China then cooperated closely on countering the Soviet invasion of Afghanistan, including setting up extensive American military listening posts on China's western frontier.

Deng's greatest legacy is China's irreversible transition to a market-driven economy, following his push for broad economic liberalization during his 1992 tour of the south. China's current economic system is more in line with that of the USA than with any brand of socialism. Deng was not without authoritarian tendencies, however, as seen in the suppression of the 'democracy wall' movement of 1979 and the crushing of the 1989 democracy movement at Tiananmen Square.

No less importantly, Deng smashed the political caste system built by Mao, in which each citizen's fate was determined more by his or her 'class origin' rather than individual ability. He also single-handedly set up a system of limited tenure and peaceful succession within the CCP. Both have great historical significance for China.

He died on 19 February 1997.

NOTE
ON SPELLING/
TRANSCRIPTION

Readers may be perplexed by the plethora of spellings for the same Chinese name or term (Tao/Dao, Peking/Beijing). These differences may be due to a variety of reasons, including historical, dialectal and individual preferences. The Chinese characters for these terms remain the same; it is only the transcriptions that change. One of the main reasons for the discrepancies in the spelling of Chinese names and terms is the diverse Romanization systems that have been used at different times and places. For example, there are separate transcriptions for French, German, Italian, and so forth. The standard system for English for around a century was one called Wade-Giles after the names of its two devisers. Since the founding of the People's Republic of China, the prevailing system has gradually come to be *pinyin* (which simply means 'spelling'). Pinyin has been designated the official Romanization for Mandarin by the International Standards Organization and by the United Nations.

PRONUNCIATION GUIDE

In pinyin, most letters are pronounced approximately the same as in standard English, but not all. The important differences are listed below.

A = A as in f*a*ther (H*a*n dynasty)

AI = AI as *ai*sle (B*ai* Juyi)

C = TS as in i*ts* (*C*ao *C*ao)

E = U as in s*u*n (Shi L*e*, Sh*e*n Gua, D*e*ng Xiaoping

I = I as in mach*i*ne (Cix*i*), but I as in d*i*vide after c, s, z (C*i*xi), and IR as in s*ir* after ch, r, sh, zh (Q*i*n Sh*i*huangdi)

IA = YA as in y*a*rd (X*ia*ng Yu)

IAN or YAN = YEN (Sima Q*ian*)

IU = YO as in y*o*yo (Q*iu* Jin)

O = O as in m*o*re (Su Dongp*o*), except before n or ng, when it is pronounced OO as in s*oo*n (S*o*ng)

OU = O as in j*o*ke (Zh*ou* dynasty)

Q = CH as in *ch*in (*Q*in Shihuangdi)

U = U as in pr*u*ne (D*u* F*u*), but U as in the French t*u* after j, q, x, y (Bai J*u*yi)

UI = WAY (S*ui* dynasty)

X = SH as in *sh*e (*X*iang Yu)

Z = DS as in bu*ds* (Mao Ze*d*ong)

ZH = J as in *j*ump (*Zh*uang Zi)

FURTHER READING

GENERAL

de Bary, W. Theodore, Irene Bloom, eds. 1999. *Sources of Chinese Tradition: From Earliest Times to 1600*. Vol. 1, 2nd edn. Introduction to Asian Civilizations. New York: Columbia University Press

de Bary, W. Theodore, Richard J. Lufrano, eds. 2001. *Sources of Chinese Tradition: From 1600 through the Twentieth Century*. Vol. 2, 2nd edn. Introduction to Asian Civilizations. New York: Columbia University Press

Dillon, Michael. 1979. *Dictionary of Chinese History*. London: Frank Cass

Ebrey, Patricia Buckley. 2010. *The Cambridge Illustrated History of China*. 2nd edn. Cambridge and New York: Cambridge University Press

Fenby, Jonathan. 2009. *The Penguin History of Modern China: The Fall and Rise of a Great Power 1850–2009*. London and New York: Allen Lane

Hook, Brian, Denis C. Twitchett, eds. 1991. *The Cambridge Encyclopedia of China*. Cambridge and New York: Cambridge University Press

Hucker, Charles O. 1985. *A Dictionary of Official Titles in Imperial China*. Stanford: Stanford University Press

Mair, Victor H., Nancy Steinhardt, Paul Goldin, eds. 2005. *The Hawai'i Reader in Traditional Chinese Culture*. Honolulu: University of Hawai'i Press

Theobald, Ulrich. *Chinaknowledge – a universal guide for China studies*. http://www.chinaknowledge.de/index.html

Wilkinson, Endymion. 2012. *Chinese History: A New Manual*. Cambridge, Massachusetts: Harvard University Asia Center

ANTHROPOLOGY, ETHNOLOGY AND SOCIOLOGY

Abramson, Marc S. 2008. *Ethnic Identity in Tang China*. Philadelphia: University of Pennsylvania Press

Chen, Sanping. 2012. *Multicultural China in the Early Middle Ages*. Philadelphia: University of Pennsylvania Press

Wyatt, Don J. 2009. *The Blacks of Premodern China*. Philadelphia: University of Pennsylvania Press

ART AND ARCHAEOLOGY

Barnhart, Richard, Xiaoneng Yang, eds. 1999. *Chinese Art and Archaeology.* New Haven, Connecticut: Yale University Press

Barnhart, Richard *et al.*, eds. 1997. *Three Thousand Years of Chinese Painting.* New Haven, Connecticut and London: Yale University Press

Clunas, Craig. 1997. *Art in China.* Oxford and New York: Oxford University Press

Fu Xinian *et al.* 2002. *Chinese Architecture.* Trans. Nancy S. Steinhardt. New Haven, Connecticut and London: Yale University Press

Sullivan, Michael. 2009. *The Arts of China.* 5th edn, rev. and enlarged. Berkeley and Los Angeles: University of California Press

Yang, Xiaoneng, ed. 2004. *New Perspectives on China's Past: Chinese Archaeology in the Twentieth Century.* New Haven, Connecticut and London: Yale University Press

BIOGRAPHY

Boorman, Howard L., ed. 1967–79. *Biographical Dictionary of Republican China.* 5 vols. New York and London: Columbia University Press

Franke, Herbert. 1976–. *Sung Biographies.* 2 vols. Wiesbaden: Steiner

Giles, Herbert A. 1898. *A Chinese Biographical Dictionary.* London: Bernard Quaritch; Shanghai: Kelly & Walsh; numerous reprints; available online

Goodrich, L. Carrington, Chaoying Fang. 1976. *Dictionary of Ming Biography, 1368–1644.* 2 vols. New York and London: Columbia University Press

Hummel, Arthur W., ed. 1943–44. *Eminent Chinese of the Ch'ing Period (1644–1912).* Washington, DC: US Government Printing Office; various reprints

Rothschild, N. Harry. 2007. *Wu Zhao: China's Only Female Emperor.* Harlow: Longman; New York: Pearson Longman

Wood, Frances. 2007. *The First Emperor of China.* New York: St Martin's Press; London: Profile.

FOOD

Anderson, E[ugene] N. 1988. *The Food of China.* New Haven, Connecticut: Yale University Press

Chang, K. C., ed. 1977. *Food in Chinese Culture: Anthropological and Historical Perspectives.* New Haven, Connecticut and London: Yale University Press

HISTORY

Adshead, S. A. M. 2000. *China in World History.* New York: St Martin's Press

Adshead, S. A. M. 2004. *T'ang China: The Rise of the East in World History*. New York and Basingstoke: Palgrave Macmillan

Brook, Timothy, ed. 2009–12. *History of Imperial China*. 6 vols. Individual vols by Mark Edward Lewis (3), Dieter Kuhn, Timothy Brook and William T. Rowe. Cambridge, Massachusetts: Harvard University Press (Belknap)

Di Cosmo, Nicola. 2002. *Ancient China and Its Enemies: The Rise of Nomadic Power in East Asian History*. Cambridge and New York: Cambridge University Press

Dreyer, Edward L. 2006. *Zheng He: China and the Oceans in the Early Ming Dynasty, 1405–1433*. New York: Pearson Longman

Elman, Benjamin A. *Classical Historiography for Chinese History*. http://www.princeton.edu/~classbib/

Fairbank, John K. 1968. *The Chinese World Order: Traditional China's Foreign Relations*. Cambridge, Massachusetts: Harvard University Press

Golden, Peter B. 2011. *Central Asia in World History*. Oxford and New York: Oxford University Press

Hansen, Valerie. 2000. *The Open Empire: A History of China to 1600*. New York and London: W. W. Norton

Jenner, W. J. F. [William John Francis]. 1992. *The Tyranny of History: The Roots of China's Crisis*. London: Allen Lane; New York: Penguin Books

Loewe, Michael, Edward L. Shaughnessy, eds. 2002. *The Cambridge History of Ancient China*. Cambridge and New York: Cambridge University Press

Mair, Victor H. 2005. 'The North(west)ern Peoples and the Recurrent Origins of the "Chinese" State'. In *The Teleology of the Modern Nation-State: Japan and China*, ed. Joshua A. Fogel. Philadelphia: University of Pennsylvania Press, pp. 46–86

Nienhauser, William H., Jr, ed. 1994–. *The Grand Scribe's Records*. Multiple vols. Bloomington, Indiana: University of Indiana Press

Sen, Tansen, Victor H. Mair. 2012. *Traditional China in Asian and World History*. Key Issues in Asian Studies. Ann Arbor, Michigan: Association for Asian Studies

Shin, Leo K. *Guide to Ming Studies*. http://www.history.ubc.ca/faculty/lshin/research/ming/index.htm

Twitchett, Denis C., John K. Fairbank, eds. 1978–. *The Cambridge History of China*. 15 vols. Cambridge: Cambridge University Press

Waldron, Arthur. 1992. *The Great Wall of China: From History to Myth*. Cambridge and New York: Cambridge University Press

Waley-Cohen, Joanna. 1999. *The Sextants of Beijing: Global Currents in Chinese History*. New York and London: W. W. Norton

Watson, Burton, trans. 1993. *Records of the Grand Historian of China*. 3 vols, rev. edn. Hong Kong and New York: The Research Centre for Translation of The Chinese University of Hong Kong and Columbia University Press; originally published 1961 by Columbia University Press

Wood, Frances. 2003. *The Silk Road: Two Thousand Years in the Heart of Asia.* Berkeley: University of California Press; London: British Library

LANGUAGE

DeFrancis, John. 1984. *The Chinese Language: Fact and Fantasy.* Honolulu: University of Hawai'i Press

Norman, Jerry. 1988. *Chinese.* Cambridge and New York: Cambridge University Press

Ramsey, S. Robert. 1987. *The Languages of China.* Princeton: Princeton University Press

LITERATURE

Chang, Kang-I Sung, Haun Saussy, Charles Y. Kwong, eds. 1999. *Women Writers of Traditional China: An Anthology of Poetry and Criticism.* Stanford: Stanford University Press

Lau, Joseph S. M., Howard Goldblatt, eds. 1995; 2007. *The Columbia Anthology of Modern Chinese Literature.* New York: Columbia University Press

Mair, Victor H., ed. 1995. *The Columbia Anthology of Traditional Chinese Literature.* Translations from the Asian Classics. New York and Chichester: Columbia University Press

Mair, Victor H., ed. 2000. *The Shorter Columbia Anthology of Traditional Chinese Literature.* Translations from the Asian Classics. New York: Columbia University Press

Mair, Victor H., ed. 2001. *The Columbia History of Chinese Literature.* New York and Chichester: Columbia University Press

Mair, Victor H., Mark Bender, eds. 2011. *The Columbia Anthology of Chinese Folk and Popular Literature.* New York: Columbia University Press

Nienhauser, William H., Jr, ed. 1985; 1998. *The Indiana Companion to Traditional Chinese Literature.* 2 vols. Bloomington: Indiana University Press

Owen, Stephen. 1997. *Anthology of Chinese Literature: Beginnings to 1911.* New York and London: W. W. Norton

MUSIC

Lee, Yuan-Yuan, Sinyan Shen. 1999. *Chinese Musical Instruments.* Chinese Music Monograph Series. Naperville, Illinois: Chinese Music Society of North America

Shen, Sinyan. 2001. *Chinese Music in the 20th Century.* Chinese Music Monograph Series. Naperville, Illinois: Chinese Music Society of North America

Buswell, Robert E. Jr, ed. 2004. *Encyclopedia of Buddhism*. 2 vols. New York: Macmillan Reference USA/Thomson-Gale

Ch'en, Kenneth. 1964. *Buddhism in China: A Historical Survey*. Princeton: Princeton University Press

Kieschnick, John. 2002. *The Impact of Buddhism on Chinese Material Culture*. Princeton and Oxford: Princeton University Press

Kirkland, Russell. 2004. *Taoism: The Enduring Tradition*. London and New York: Routledge

Kohn, Livia, ed. 2000. *Daoism Handbook*. Leiden and Boston: Brill

Pregadio, Fabrizio, ed. 2008. *The Encyclopedia of Taoism*. 2 vols. London: Curzon

Robinet, Isabelle. 1997. *Taoism: Growth of a Religion*. Translated by Phyllis Brooks. Stanford: Stanford University Press

Schipper, Kristofer. 1993. *The Taoist Body*. Trans. Karen C. Duval. Berkeley, Los Angeles and London: University of California Press

Sen, Tansen. 2003. *Buddhism, Diplomacy, and Trade: The Realignment of Sino-Indian Relations, 600–1400*. Honolulu: University of Hawai'i Press

SCIENCE AND TECHNOLOGY

Needham, Joseph. 1954–. *Science and Civilisation in China*. Multiple vols. Cambridge and New York: Cambridge University Press

Temple, Robert. 1998. *The Genius of China: 3,000 Years of Science, Discovery and Invention*. Abridgment of Needham 1954–. London: Prion

THOUGHT

Goldin, Paul R. 2005. *After Confucianism: Studies in Early Chinese Philosophy*. Honolulu: University of Hawai'i Press

Graham, A. C. 1989. *Disputers of the Tao: Philosophical Argument in Ancient China*. La Salle, Illinois: Open Court

Mair, Victor H., trans. and intro. 1990. *Tao Te Ching: The Classic Book of Integrity and the Way*. New York: Bantam

Mair, Victor H., trans. and intro. 1994. *Wandering on the Way: Early Taoist Tales and Parables of Chuang Tzu*. New York: Bantam

Mair, Victor H., trans. and intro. 2007. *The Art of War: Sun Zi's Military Methods*. New York and Chichester: Columbia University Press

Van Norden, Bryan W. 2009. *Virtue, Ethics and Consequentialism in Early Chinese Philosophy*. Cambridge and New York: Cambridge University Press

ACKNOWLEDGMENTS

We are indebted to Paula Roberts for help with the preparation of the manuscript, and to the Thames & Hudson team: Alice Reid for constant help and support, Carolyn Jones for editing, Louise Thomas for picture research and documentation, Avni Patel for her design, Rachel Heley for production and Colin Ridler for suggesting the project to us in the first place and for sage advice from beginning to end.

Sanping Chen is grateful to his son Brian and wife Ruying for their patience and understanding during the prolonged gestation of this book. Victor Mair thanks the Swedish Collegium for Advanced Studies in Uppsala, the Nalanda-Sriwijaya Centre of the Institute for Southeast Asian Studies in Singapore, the Tsinghua Academy of Chinese Learning in Beijing and the International Academy for Chinese Studies at Peking University for providing him the time and collegial atmosphere in which to work on these biographies.

SOURCES
OF QUOTATIONS

All quotations from Chinese sources were translated by Victor Mair and Sanping Chen, except the following, which are all reproduced from *The Columbia Anthology of Traditional Chinese Literature*, ed. Victor Mair, 1995, by courtesy of Columbia University Press:

Page 69, Biography 29: 'I built my hut beside a travelled road ...' translated by James Robert Hightower

Page 88, Biographies 39 & 40: 'To Send to Du Fu as a Joke' by Li Bai (Li Po), translated by Elling Eide

Page 112, Biography 51: 'Tune: "Immortal by the River"' by Su Dongpo, translated by James Robert Hightower

Page 118, Biography 54: 'Tune: "Spring at Wu Ling": Spring Ends' by Li Qingzhao, translated by Jiaosheng Wang

Pages 118–19, Biography 54: 'I have a power for memory ...' translated by Lin Yutang

The quotations on pages 30 ('Once upon a time, Zhuang Zi ...'), 89 ('A Guest Arrives'), 92 ('Iranian Whirling Girls') and 106–7 ('Bald Mountain') were translated by Victor Mair and were also previously published in *The Columbia Anthology of Traditional Chinese Literature*, ed. Victor Mair, 1995. They are reproduced here by courtesy of Columbia University Press.

SOURCES
OF ILLUSTRATIONS

Maps by ML Design.

2 Seikado Bunko Art Museum, Tokyo **11** Bibliothèque Nationale, Paris/Archives Charmet/ Bridgeman Art Library **14** Private Collection/Chambers Gallery, London/Bridgeman Art Library **19** National Gallery of Art, Washington, DC **23** Palace Museum, Beijing **27** Qianlong Garden, Beijing **28** Shandong Provincial Museum, Jinan **31** Private Collection/ Christie's Images/Bridgeman Art Library **32** Royal Ontario Museum/Corbis **35** Museum of Qin Shi Huang's Tomb, Xi'an **38** National Palace Museum, Taipei **42** Wang Miao/ Redlink/Corbis **44** from Sima Qian, *Shiji: Records of the Grand Historian*, 1525–1527 **46** Private Collection **47** from *Wan hsiao tang-Chu chuang-Hua chuan*, 1921 **49** Hebei Provincial Museum, Shijiazhuang **51** from Ren Xiong, *Liquor License of the Immortals*, 1923 **55** National Palace Museum, Taipei **58** Private Collection/Archives Charmet/Bridgeman Art Library **62** Private Collection/Bridgeman Art Library **66** Metropolitan Museum of Art, New York **67** Kizil Thousand-Buddha Caves, Aksu **68** Honolulu Academy of Arts **71** Suzanne Held/akg-images **75** Museum of Fine Arts, Boston **78** Palace Museum, Beijing **79** British Museum, London **82** Shaanxi History Museum, Xi'an **83** Robert Harding Picture Library/Alamy **85** Freer Gallery of Art, Smithsonian Institution, Washington, DC **86** VISIOARS/Alamy **90** Freer Gallery of Art, Smithsonian Institution, Washington, DC **91** British Library, London/ akg-images **93** Craig Lovell/Eagle Visions Photography/Alamy **95** Bibliothèque Nationale, Paris/The Art Archive **101, 103, 104** National Palace Museum, Taipei **108** Beijing Ancient Observatory **111** Keren Su/China Span/Getty Images **113** from Fang La, *Water Margin*, *c.*15th century **116** Museum of Fine Arts, Boston **120** National Palace Museum, Taipei **121, 122** National Palace Museum, Taipei/The Art Archive **126** Palace Museum, Beijing **129** Shanghai Museum **133** National Palace Museum, Taipei **135** Erich Lessing/akg-images **137** Gravestone of Liu Yigong, Quanzhou **144** National Palace Museum, Taipei **146** Philadelphia Museum of Art **150** Tomb of Hai Rui, Haikou City **152** Wellcome Library, London/Wellcome Images **155** Palace Museum, Beijing **159** Superstock/The Art Archive **165** Private Collection **168** National Palace Museum, Taipei **170** K. Sumitomo Collection, Oiso **172** from Pu Songling, *Strange Tales from a Chinese Studio*, 1668 **173** National Palace Museum, Taipei **176–177** Palace Museum, Beijing **178** from Cao Xueqin, *Dream of the Red Chamber*, 1889 **180, 183** Palace Museum, Beijing **185** Thomas Allon, *Chinese Opium Smokers*, 1842 **189** Private Collection **192** akg-images **193** Eileen Tweedy/School of Oriental and African Studies, London/The Art Archive **196** Bibliothèque des Arts Décoratifs, Paris/Archives Charmet/Bridgeman Art Library **199** Xia Gongran/Xinhua Press/Corbis **200** Hulton Archive/Getty Images **203** Bettmann/Corbis **206** Corbis **209** British Library, London **213** Swim Ink/Corbis **214** British Museum, London **217** Ullstein Bild/akg-images.

INDEX